C000160592

THE LAUREL AND HARDY MOVIE SCRIPTS

Annotated By
Randy Skretvedt

*With love and thanks to Spencer, Zelda, Rob and Jay-Jay,
and to Laurel and Hardy fans everywhere.*

THE LAUREL & HARDY MOVIE SCRIPTS
20 Original Short Subject Screenplays (1926 – 1934)

Published by
Bonaventure Press
Post Office Box 51961
Irvine, CA 92619-1961
USA
www.bonaventurepress.com

All rights reserved. No part of this book may be reproduced or transmitted in any form
or by any means, electronic or mechanical, including photocopying, recording or by
any information storage and retrieval system without written permission from the
author, except for the inclusion of brief quotations in a review.

Copyright © 2018 by Randy Skretvedt

Designed by David Koenig

Manufactured in the United States of America

Library of Congress Cataloging-in-Publication Data
Library of Congress control number: 2018946326

Skretvedt, Randy

     The Laurel & Hardy Movie Scripts: 20 Original Short Subject Screenplays
(1926 – 1934) / by Randy Skretvedt;
       p. cm.

     1. Laurel, Stan. 2. Hardy, Oliver, 1892-1957. 3. Comedy films—United
States—
History and criticism. I. Skretvedt, Randy, 1958 -

ISBN-10: 1937878074
ISBN: 978-1-937878-07-8

CONTENTS

Prologue   4

Untitled S-14   11

Duck Soup   29

Slipping Wives   60

Love 'em and Weep   86

With Love and Hisses   103

Sugar Daddies   122

The Second 100 Years   132

Their Purple Moment   144

Early to Bed   155

Perfect Day   165

The Hoose-Gow   173

Our Wife   185

One Good Turn   196

"Scram!"   215

Twice Two   228

Me and My Pal   240

Dirty Work   252

The Live Ghost   266

Tit for Tat   276

Epilogue   285

PROLOGUE

In the summer of 1980, I was privileged to attend the second convention of the Sons of the Desert, the international Laurel and Hardy appreciation society. This was held at the Los Angeles Hilton hotel. Grand Sheik Bob Satterfield and a great team including Lori Jones-McCaffery and Earl Kress had done an astonishing job of bringing together most of Laurel and Hardy's surviving co-workers and family members; it was a wonderful few days filled with hilarious and informative stories from dozens of people who had helped to make the films which we all loved so much.

Although I was dazzled by all of these wonderful anecdotes, some new surprises awaited me in the dealers' room, where all sorts of L&H memorabilia was on sale. A man named Douglas Hart, who ran a small store in Hollywood called Backlot Books, had a table filled to overflowing with original 8x10 Hal Roach stills, lobby cards and posters – and in the corner was a stack of original scripts from Laurel and Hardy shorts.

Scripts?!! In 1980, we weren't even sure that Laurel and Hardy had used scripts for their short films. A couple of the feature-film scripts had surfaced, but after so many of the boys' co-workers had spoken of their talent for improvising while the cameras were rolling, a lot of us doubted that anything for the shorts had ever been written down. And yet, looking at the first script I saw, which identified itself merely as "L-9," I could instantly recognize the opening scene for *"Scram!,"* one of my favorites. Mr. Hart was charging $35.00 for each script, a reasonable price indeed, but still one that was daunting to me, as I was then a 21-year-old college student with highly limited finances.

A number of my friends were huddled near me, and shared my astonishment when I alerted them to this treasure trove. We agreed that we would each buy one script, and then make photocopies for each other. Done and done. Within a few days, we each had copies of six or seven of these rare documents. However, I already had it firmly in mind to write a book about the creative process by which Laurel and Hardy made their movies, and the rest of the scripts would provide essential information that was unavailable anywhere else. I asked Doug Hart if, after the convention was over, I could come to his store and go through the scripts for research purposes. He was very understanding and accommodating. He explained that he didn't want me to make photocopies, which was entirely understandable. When I asked if I could bring a cassette tape recorder and dictate the scripts, he agreed.

Backlot Books was a small shed on Sunset Boulevard near Poinsettia Place, and Doug Hart was open for business only on Saturdays. So, for four or five consecutive Saturdays in the late summer of 1980, I drove from my home in Buena Park to

Hollywood – about 30 miles, and never a happy drive thanks to the congested Los Angeles freeways. I would sit outside his building on a couple of plastic milk crates, sweating in the hot sun and dictating the scripts as fast as I could, to maximize each precious day and get as much of this unique material as possible.

Since time was of the essence, and there were many scripts, eventually I began dictating only the portions of the scripts which deviated from the finished films. However, some scripts had so many changes that it was necessary to read them in their entirety. Ultimately, I got through all of the L&H scripts that Doug Hart had, about 30 or so, and at home I began the long and tedious process of typing up what I'd read into my tape recorder.

Not long after I began that next phase, I got a phone call from Don and John Cannon, who ran a wonderful store, Aladdin Books, in Fullerton. They had a friend, an antiquarian bookseller named John McLaughlin, who was the proprietor of The Book Sail in the nearby city of Orange. He had just purchased another collection of Laurel and Hardy scripts; Don and John had told him of my project, and he generously asked them to put me in touch with him. When I called Mr. McLaughlin, he invited me to come to his store and likewise dictate his collection for my research purposes.

God smiled upon me when I arrived at the store, because John McLaughlin's script collection was a perfect complement to Douglas Hart's. John had the scripts that Doug did not. Furthermore, these appeared to be Stan Laurel's personal copies, and occasionally there would be notations in the margins. This became especially apparent in the scripts for the 20th Century-Fox features, written by other hands who had no idea how to create Laurel and Hardy material. Whenever a scripted sequence appeared which was entirely unsuitable for the long-established Stan and Ollie characters, Stan had taken a red pen and made large, unmissable squiggles in the margins, as if to inform the director or producer that under no circumstances would he and Babe perform these egregious betrayals of their screen personalities.

Ultimately, I was able to read almost all of the Laurel and Hardy scripts. Other 20th Century-Fox films were represented at USC, and the ever-wonderful Ned Comstock facilitated my research there, as he has done for hundreds of dedicated film scholars. My friend and fellow lifelong Laurel and Hardy admirer Jordan R. Young discovered a cache of papers donated by Roach studio alumnus Fred L. Guiol to the library of California State University, Fullerton, our alma mater. Several of the scripts for the earliest L&H movies, which Guiol had directed, were among the treasures. A script for *Babes in Toyland* turned up at the Margaret Herrick Library of the Academy of Motion Picture Arts and Sciences.

There are still a few scripts which I have never seen – ironically, among these are *Two Tars*, *Big Business* and *The Music Box*, three of the team's finest short films. Anybody with information about locating these is more than welcome to contact me.

The scripts for the Laurel and Hardy shorts, as well as the other two-reelers produced by Hal Roach, were on legal-sized, 11x14 paper, with a thick sheet of brown paper in back that was folded over the top and stapled to keep the pages together. There was no set number of pages; today, one page of a TV or movie script is supposed to equal one minute of screen time, but there was no such restriction on the

Hal Roach screenplays. The silent films tend to have longer scripts, running between 16 and 21 pages, while the talkies were generally four or five pages long, and sometimes barely two.

At the big movie factories, the written documentation for any film would progress from a single-page story idea to a longer treatment, then to a full script which indicated the dialogue and camera angles, and usually a couple of revised final drafts. The final – not to mention only – draft for a Laurel and Hardy short would be the treatment anywhere else. Action is described, and once in a while a close-up or long shot is specified. Dialogue is spelled out only when it's essential; it's rare to see a complete dialogue routine, although it does occasionally occur. The action is written in short paragraphs, separated by a line of space. (Those have been omitted for this book.) Depending on the writer, sometimes the paragraphs are numbered.

The scripts are written in plain and sometimes blunt English, full of terms endemic to a studio specializing in slapstick. "Get over" means to convey in pantomime. "Does a brodie" means that someone takes an elaborate fall, which might be a "108," a fall in which the participant does a mid-air somersault before landing. A "takem" is a heightened reaction, usually a widening of the eyes and a look of surprise, fear, anger or whatever emotion would be prompted by the preceding event. A "double take" is a reaction in which someone looks at something, looks away, and then as realization dawns, quickly looks back in surprise. James Finlayson took particular pride in what he called his "double take and fade away," an exaggerated reaction followed by a squint of his right eye and a raising of his left eyebrow.

References to specific film techniques are rare in the scripts. An "eyemo shot" is a section of film photographed with a small hand-held camera, ideal for extreme close-ups or traveling shots where the camera follows along with a line of action.

There was never any onscreen credit assigned for the screenplay of a Laurel and Hardy short. (For the features, Jeanie Macpherson, a frequent collaborator with Cecil B. DeMille, received credit for adapting Auber's 1830 opera *Fra Diavolo* into L&H's *The Devil's Brother*, and later in 1933 Byron Morgan and Frank Craven were acknowledged for the story and screenplay of *Sons of the Desert*.) In the silent era, most of the shorts bore the credit "Titles by H.M. Walker," and with the coming of the talkies this evolved into "Dialogue by H.M. Walker."

Harley Marquis Walker was born in West Middlebury, Ohio on June 27, 1878. He wrote a sports column, "The Wisdom of Blinkey Ben," for the *Los Angeles Examiner* before joining the Roach studio as a part-time story and title writer for Harold Lloyd in 1917. He became the full-time had of the editorial department for Roach in 1920, and proved to be a skilled writer of witty and concise titles. Walker was credited for more than 350 comedies produced by Hal Roach.

In 1930 and '31, he would write a separate, dialogue-only script for the L&H shorts, which was used, or was supposed to be used, in tandem with the "action" script. Walker's witty and urbane style resulted in dialogue that was a bit too ornate and high-toned for Stan and Ollie, and since nobody on the set was paying much attention to what he'd written anyway, it probably didn't come as a surprise when Henry Ginsberg, a relentless cost-cutting executive installed by Roach's creditors at the Bank of America,

HAL ROACH
(1892 - 1992)

STAN LAUREL
(1890 - 1965)

CHARLIE ROGERS
(1887 - 1956)

LEO McCAREY
(1896 - 1969)

H.M. WALKER
(1878 - 1937)

JAMES PARROTT
(1897 - 1939)

terminated him on July 25, 1932. After that, Walker worked on scripts at Paramount and Universal; he died at 58 of a heart attack on June 23, 1937, in the Chicago home of his friend Leroy Shield, who had written musical scores for the Roach shorts.

Although Walker got the only onscreen credit remotely connected to the writing of stories, there was a small army of idea men who contributed plot suggestions and gag ideas in meetings with Hal Roach and Stan Laurel. Roach himself often suggested the initial ideas, and one short was usually being written as another was being filmed. After the Laurel and Hardy series really got going, Stan would function as the story editor, taking ideas he liked and embellishing them with his own gag and plot ideas. Laurel recalled, "I had some very fine boys who worked with me. We'd all have ideas. No one thought one was any better than the other. We'd just work out a script and get to shooting it as quick as we could."

Marvin Hatley, who often worked as a gag man in addition to being the studio's musical director, said of the writers' meetings, "Stan had three or four guys hanging around, you know, but he was the main one who did everything. He always had these other people to offer suggestions, and he'd twist them around. Then they'd get up in the projection room and they'd act out their ideas. If somebody had a gag where a character was choking, he'd demonstrate it; he'd put his hands to his neck and say, 'He's choking!' They wanted to show the other guys what they meant."

Writing meetings often took place after hours at Stan's home, and his daughter Lois remembered that there were pads of yellow legal paper and pencils in most rooms of the house, to be readily available whenever inspiration struck.

Despite the time spent in crafting a script, the finished result was never thought of as the be-all and end-all which had to be filmed exactly as written. In 1959, Stan told film journalist Boyd Verb, "We did have a script, but it didn't consist of the routines and gags. It outlined the basic story idea and just a plan for us to follow. But when it came to each scene, we and the gagmen would work out ideas. Oh, a few gags were mentioned here and there in the script, but they were always worked out on the set. We'd rehearse them a few times and then shoot them."

For the record, actor Henry Brandon and actresses Anita Garvin and Dorothy Granger all recalled Stan's method of filming the first run-through of a scene, which usually resulted in the one and only finished take. Brandon, a 21-year-old actor making his film debut as the villain Barnaby in *Babes in Toyland*, recalled his first day on the set: "I had never worked with comedians before. My first day I was pretty scared; we had a very long scene to do, about eight pages. They all sat down, and there was quite an entourage — mostly Stan's. Babe had no entourage at all, but Stannie had a lot of friends, a lot of co-workers and seconds and gofers, and they sat around and told jokes for about half an hour. Then they said, 'All right, let's look at the script.' So they got out the script, which was very well written — and they said, 'Well, let's throw that out, let's throw this out.'

"Then, Stan turned to Babe and the other actors and said, 'Now you say that, and Henry you say that, and then I'll do that, and Babe'll do that, and you'll do that...' That went on for about 10 minutes, and then Stannie got up and said, 'All right, let's shoot it!'

"Then," recalled Brandon, "I made the mistake that I will never make again in my life. I said, 'Aren't we going to rehearse?' And Stannie turned to me and said, 'Do you want to spoil it?'

"The only things they rehearsed were physical stunts. They never rehearsed the dialogue. They would sort of say what they were going to do, but they wouldn't get up and do it physically until the camera was rolling; they wanted to capture the magic of the first time."

Leo McCarey, as the supervisor of all Roach films from early 1927 through late 1928, was the man who suggested that Hal Roach should build a series around Laurel and Hardy, so posterity owes him a tremendous debt of thanks. McCarey directed three L&H silents and no doubt contributed many a gag to the others. He left the Roach lot just as *Big Business* was being filmed in late December 1928, and went on to direct classic features such as *Ruggles of Red Gap*, *The Awful Truth* and *Going My Way*.

The other gag men came and went over the years – Hal Roach was always looking for new creative talent. The studio payroll ledgers, now at USC, assign payments specifically for writing the L&H shorts to Hal Yates and Mauri Grashin in 1928 and '29. Yates directed most of L&H's 1929 short *That's My Wife* without credit, and later became a

HAL YATES
(1899 - 1969)

MAURI GRASHIN
(1901 - 1991)

FRED GUIOL
(1898 - 1964)

LEWIS R. FOSTER
(1898 - 1974)

LLOYD FRENCH
(1900 - 1950)

FRANK BUTLER
(1891 - 1967)

prolific director of comedy shorts for RKO and TV sitcoms for Hal Roach. Grashin continued to write shorts and features for Roach and other studios through the late 1940s.

Carl Harbaugh collaborated with Stan on several scripts for various Roach series in 1925 and '26, and returned to add material to L&H features in the mid-'30s. Frank Butler had starred in Roach's early '20s series *The Spat Family*, came back as a gag man, and in the mid-1930s was head of the story department. James Parrott, Lewis R. Foster and Lloyd French were frequent gag contributors who became directors for Laurel and Hardy and other comedians.

The first seven scripts here come from the papers of director Fred Guiol (pronounced "gill"), who had a charming habit of making diagonal lines in pencil across each section after he'd filmed it. Guiol was born in San Francisco on February 17, 1898 and was a prolific director for Roach from 1923 through 1930. After that, he made shorts for Pathé and features for RKO, notably several Wheeler and Woolsey comedies. He came back to the Roach lot in the early '40s as an associate producer, writer and director. A close friend of Roach cinematographer and director George Stevens, Guiol worked in various capacities on Stevens' feature films of the 1950s, including *A Place in the Sun, Shane* and *Giant.* Guiol's younger sister Clara appeared in many L&H comedies (she's a cigarette girl in *Their Purple Moment*). Known to all on the Roach lot as "Chili Guiol," Fred died in Bishop, California at 66 on May 23, 1964.

Just how many copies were printed and distributed of each script isn't exactly known, although certainly the main actors, director, cameraman, film editor and head of the prop department each got one. Copies originally assigned to "Mr. Currier" – Richard Currier, head of the film editing department – and "Mr. Sanders" – Bob Sanders, chief prop man – have shown up in auction catalogs.

Hal Roach had a pet theory which he continued to espouse long past his days as an active film producer: "Fifty percent of the script will not play." In other words, what seems to be very funny on paper may not prove to be so funny once it is acted out in front of the cameras. In reading the scripts, I found that Mr. Roach's estimate was correct. Usually, about half of the script corresponded to the film, and the other half – whether it was spotted throughout the script or was a separate section – did not. For this reason, gag men, Charlie Rogers chief among them, were always present on the set during the filming, to suggest ideas better than those in the written outline. There was no caste system at the Roach lot, and if one of the crew members had an idea, he was welcome to contribute it.

Most of the scripts contained in this book are included because they differ significantly from the films, and thus offer a wealth of comedy ideas that don't exist anywhere else. Even when the scripts recount scenes that we remember, it's fun and interesting to see how the writers conveyed in print comedy routines that were exclusively visual.

The scripts have a fair share of misspellings and occasional strike-overs, which have been omitted here, but some period spellings, such as "foney" for "phony," have been retained. Allusions to obscure events, performers or products of the era are explained in the introductory notes to the individual scripts. There are a few references to minorities which employ slang words of the era; bear in mind that the scripts are relics of their time and occasionally exemplify attitudes which would not be acceptable today.

Oliver Hardy was beloved by everyone at the Roach studio, and it's no surprise that the scripts refer to him as Babe, his nickname. The only variation here is in H.M. Walker's dialogue script for *One Good Turn*, which assigns lines to "Hardy" – an indication of Walker's rather formal personality. (He gave film editor Richard Currier a Webster's dictionary with an inscription reading, "Richard – having listened for years to your astonishing and, at times, highly-charged vocabulary, I hasten to add to your voltage.") Babe gets much more of the dialogue in the scripts than Stan, who is often left to his own devices to provide something funny on the set. In fact, the script writers depended upon Stan and Babe to improvise many a scene with phrases like "we go for several gags here," "play this for what it is worth" and "we go for a wow finish."

The original screenplays collected here represent a good cross section of Laurel and Hardy's short subjects, ranging from *Duck Soup*, the first rudimentary appearance of Stan and Ollie (despite its being planned for Stan and Sid), through early talkie classics like *Perfect Day* and *The Hoose-Gow*, to late gems such as *Tit for Tat*.

Reading these scripts was a delightful experience for me when I first encountered them many years ago, and I hope they will bring great pleasure to you as well.

UNTITLED S-14

Production history: Proposed script for Production S-14. Written from early to mid-August 1926.
Proposed cast: Stan Laurel (A young sailor), Oliver Hardy (Petty Officer Leggit), Sojin Kamiyama (The money lender), Anna May Wong (Delamar).

This elaborate script, which seems at some points more like an action-adventure film than a comedy, might have been the first teaming of Laurel and Hardy at the Roach studio. Its nautical setting at first made it seem as though it was a blueprint for *Why Girls Love Sailors*. However, new access to the scripts reveals that this never-filmed story was slated to be production S-14, and *Why Girls Love Sailors* was written five months later as production S-20. (The eventual S-14 was *On the Front Page*, which featured Stan in its cast but not Babe.)

We will leave it to the script and its opening synopsis to reveal the rather complicated plot. It's likely that the exotic settings, the many extras, and the length of the story combined to put this story on the shelf. However, reading this script provides the pleasure of imagining an entirely new Laurel and Hardy film.

Sojin Kamiyama, usually billed in films simply as "Sojin," was born on January 30, 1884 in Sendai, Miyagi, Japan. He made his film debut in the 1917 Pathé serial *Patria*, which starred Irene (Mrs. Vernon) Castle and Milton Sills. Swedish-born Warner Oland played the Japanese Baron Huroki in that picture and would later play Charlie Chan in a series of films for Fox, but Sojin played Chan first, in the 1927 Universal feature *The Chinese Parrot*.

Sojin's film career began in earnest with his portrayal of the Mongol Prince in Douglas Fairbanks' 1924 feature *The Thief of Bagdad*. Through the mid-1920s, he was featured, usually as a villain, in several prominent feature films, among them *East of Suez* (Paramount, 1925, starring Pola Negri), *The Sea Beast* (1926, Warner Bros., starring John Barrymore), *Eve's Leaves* (DeMille Productions, 1926, starring Leatrice Joy), and *The Road to Mandalay* (MGM, 1926, starring Lon Chaney).

He appeared in a few talkies, but his difficulty with English prompted his return to Japan in 1931; he appeared in another 30 features there through 1954, one of the last being Kurosawa's *Seven Samurai*. He died on July 28, 1954 at 70 in Tokyo.

Although this proposed S-14 script went unfilmed, Sojin and Anna May Wong did manage to appear in one Hal Roach comedy, *The Honorable Mr. Buggs*, which also had Oliver Hardy in its cast – along with Priscilla Dean (who would appear in *Slipping Wives*) and Laura La Varnie (also in the cast of *Duck Soup*).

Had this script been filmed, Stan might have worn garb like his gob in *Why Girls Love Sailors*.

Babe, too, might have been costumed similarly.

Anna May Wong appeared in Hal Roach's short *The Honorable Mr. Buggs...*

...as did Sojin Kamiyama, cast as the villain in this script.

One can see why Eric Mayne was suggested to play an Admiral.

Anna May Wong, a Los Angeles native, was born on January 3, 1905 and had a busy career in films, radio, the stage and television despite the obstacles of racism. She auditioned for many Asian roles that were ultimately given to Caucasian actresses; producers often complained that she was "too Chinese to play a Chinese" despite the fact that she was born in downtown Los Angeles and grew up on Figueroa Street.

Entranced by the movies from childhood, she began appearing in them at age 14. In 1922, she was given the leading role in the first all-Technicolor feature, *The Toll of the Sea*, and like Sojin, she had a featured part in Douglas Fairbanks' 1924 *The Thief of Bagdad*. At the time the unfilmed Laurel and Hardy script was written, she had essayed roles in *Peter Pan* (1924) with Betty Bronson, *Mr. Wu* (1927) starring Lon Chaney, and *Old San Francisco* (1927) featuring Dolores Costello.

She continued in films, many of them made in Europe, through the '30s and '40s and was active in television beginning in 1951. Her last role, in an episode of TV's *The Barbara Stanwyck Show*, aired three days before her death at 56 on February 2, 1961. A documentary about her, *Anna May Wong, Frosted Yellow Willows*, was released in 2007.

S-14

Cast:

> The Hero – Stan Laurel
> His Companion, a Petty Officer – Babe Hardy
> The Money Lender – Sojin
> The Girl – Anna May Wong
> Her Father – Chinese character

The story concerns a young gob on board a United States battleship lying at anchor off the coast of China. The time is around the Fourth of July. Living in this seaport town is a young girl known as Delamar, meaning "of the sea." Her father, a fisherman, finds himself greatly in debt, his notes being held by Sojin, who is the richest man on the coast and the big power in that district. Sojin is madly in love with Delamar and has sought by all sorts of schemes to get the girl's father in his power so that he in turn will force the father to turn the daughter over to him to become his wife. While Delamar is swimming around the battleship, a flirtation starts between her and our hero. The hero makes a promise to the girl to come over and see her at her home. The girl swims back to the island and there learns from her father that he has promised her hand in marriage to Sojin, and the date is set for the wedding.

Our hero, along with his companion, who is a comedian but holds the important position of Petty Officer, go ashore and arrive there on the day the wedding is arranged. Our hero meets the girl on her way to the wedding and they vow their love for each other. Sojin in the meantime becomes aware that the girl is infatuated with this young gob, and dispatches his henchmen to inveigle him into his home and there to hold him prisoner until after the marriage has been performed.

Fade in on a battleship lying at anchor off the coast of China. Dissolve to the side of the boat, two sailors painting. They are on two different scaffolds that are let down on ropes over the side of the battleship. Introduce our hero, Stan laurel, with closeup and title to the effect that he is a new gob, as dumb as he looks.

Title introducing Petty Officer Leggit; he thinks he is a man of great importance. He is smoking a cigar and admiring himself in a mirror. Get over that this is the captain's cabin and that Leggit is there to perform some duty. As he is admiring himself in the mirror, his eyes fall on the captain's cap and he tries it on. It is a lousy fit but he still admires himself, hoping that some day he will be a captain.

While he is admiring himself, the captain comes out of an adjoining door, presumably the bathroom, getting over that he has just finished dressing. He doesn't see hardy, but goes right over to the table and picks up Hardy's cap, thinking it is his own, puts it on and it goes down over his ears. He does a double takem, pulling the cap off quickly, bewildered, looks around and sees Hardy with his cap standing at the mirror admiring himself and practicing salutes. Hardy suddenly turns with much gusto, not realizing that the captain is there. When his eye falls on the captain he comes to a sudden halt and becomes very much embarrassed. (Would suggest gag here of Hardy's cap going up in the air and back on his head.) The captain just looks at him as if he could eat him up. Hardy, very much embarrassed, comes over and puts the captain's cap on the table, picks up his own cap, and still trying to hide the cigar from his superior officer, keeps it at his back, sneaking back near the porthole, with the captain still eyeing him. The captain shakes his head with an expression of superior disgust and sits down at his desk and starts working with some papers, Babe still standing near the porthole all embarrassed.

Cut to the outside and show Stan having finished rolling a cigarette. He asks the other gob, an incidental character, for a light. The bog pays no attention to him, but from out the porthole we see Hardy's arm with the cigar in the act of trying to hide it from the captain in the room. Stan, without looking, reaches and gets the cigar out of Hardy's hand. He lights his cigarette off of it and without turning reaches out and says "Here." The other gob, thinking Stan is giving him a cigar, takes it and thanks him, and starts smoking it.

Cut to the interior, showing Babe pulling his empty hand in and looking at it, getting over the idea that somebody has taken his cigar. He looks out through the porthole.

Set camera in the cabin shooting out the porthole, showing that he sees the gob smoking his cigar, getting over that the gob is enjoying the smoke very much. Then cut to a shot of Hardy taking it big. Then outside the boat, set the camera to get a shot of the porthole and the gob smoking. Hardy's fist comes out, takes the cigar and gives the gob a punch on the nose and pulls his arm in quickly.

Cut to a shot of the two gobs. The one who was hit on the nose thinks that Stan hit him. His mental attitude now is to get back at Stan, so he takes a firm hold on his scaffold rope and reaches out and clunks Stan on the jaw, nearly knocking him from the scaffold. Stan can't understand why he has been struck. They start a fight on the two scaffolds, swinging and kicking at each other. Finally they clinch and the two scaffolds become entangled. Work this fight up for all it is worth.

When the fight is at its height, we see a beautiful girl in a one-piece bathing suit, with her hair down and a wreath entwined around her hair. Would suggest a wreath made of seaweeds or kelp or anything that would look picturesque. This girl is introduced as Delamar, meaning "of the sea." She "hoo-hoos" and immediately the two gobs stop quarreling and are greatly surprised to see this beautiful girl swimming beneath them. She seems to direct her conversation to Stan, and speaks title, "I thought you were coming over to the Island to see me." (This title is used to get over the idea that they have met before.) He says in reply, "We get shore leave as soon as we give this ship a Duco finish."

During the conversation, an officer on the top deck looks over and pantomimes, "You boys get back to your work!" They all look up and the girl takes a dive and swims away very gracefully, waving her hand back at the gob, and disappears. Make this shot so as to get over the girl's figure as she exits from the scene.

Stan goes on painting and we can see by his moon-eyed expression that his mind is in a trance, but he continues painting.

Cut back to the captain's cabin; Babe is still standing near the porthole. The captain looks up at him, giving him a dirty look. Hardy feels very sheepish and turns away bashfully, and his face comes up to the porthole.

Cut to the outside, with Hardy's face at the porthole, and show Stan painting. He gives a long, dreamy swipe with the brush and it goes right across Babe's face and the porthole, Stan being unaware of what he has done.

Cut to the inside; Hardy with his hand over his mouth taking it big, spits a little of the paint out on the captain's desk. (Be careful not to make this sloppy.) The captain looks up and says, "What the hell is going on?" Hardy covers his face with his hand and points to the porthole, getting over that what has happened, happened out there. The captain, being inquisitive, sticks his face out of the porthole just in time to receive the contents of a big brushful of paint delivered by Stan, who immediately stops, gives a big lovelorn sigh and glances out to sea, so that we can connect up that he is still thinking about the girl.

Cut back to the cabin, where Babe is picking the paint out of his eyes, and the captain has a big takem, spitting the paint out of his mouth. He looks out the porthole and sees the other gob still painting, and says "Report to me immediately!"

Cut outside, semi-close scene of Stan taking it, then cut to the two of them where Stan is kidding the other gob about getting in trouble. The gob gets mad at Stan, takes a swing at him, knocking Stan off the scaffold and into the water, and starts to pull himself up to the deck, leaving Stan floundering around in the water calling for help.

Sailors on the deck rush to the side of the ship and an officer yells down at Stan, "Can you swim?" Stan says, "Not a stroke." The officer yells down, "Take off your pants until I can get a life preserver to you."

Go to underwater shot getting in Stan from his shoulders down. Show him unbutton his pants and the pants leave his form and go straight down out of sight as if weighted down, leaving him in sweatshirt and drawers. (The drawers are to be long and slim.)

Back to the deck, where the sailor enters with life preserver and tosses it to the sinking Stan, who immediately puts it around his head. Show close shot of Stan in the water inside the life preserver. The men on deck start to pull it in and they get him half way up the side of the boat.

Cut to the other side of the boat and the Admiral's launch nears the battleship. Introduce the Admiral, a type like Eric Mayne, with a closeup.

Cut to a bugler blowing the inspection call.

Cut to the gang who are pulling up on the life preserver. Stan is just up to the top of the rail, and when they hear the bugle they drop the rope and dash off, all falling in line and standing at attention. Stan lands in the water in the center of the life preserver and paddles out of the set.

Back to the sailors on deck, all standing at attention and saluting, everybody excited, the officers giving orders and being sure that their men are in first class condition. Up the little steps on the side of the boat comes Stan, wringing wet, the long sweatshirt hanging down very leaky. He starts wringing out his shirt, not realizing that he is standing in front of all the sailors.

The Admiral comes up the steps with his staff. Stan realizes the big official, looks and sees the men all attention, then he immediately comes to attention with his hand to his forehead for a salute. The Admiral comes to attention and doesn't notice Stan there, then sees him and calls to the captain and bawls him out. The captain calls Petty Officer Hardy and bawls him out and says, "Get that guy off here!" Hardy gets Stan and takes him off. They get into the adjoining set and Hardy starts to bawl out Stan. They pass a window where there is some pants. Hardy gets the pants and hands them to Stan. Stan is putting on the pants, trying to keep step with Hardy (walking insert).

Hardy gives Stan a can of polish when they reach the turret and tells him to polish up the cannon, and leaves him.

The goat, a mascot on the ship, is in the set. He looks at Stan and says "B-a-a-a." Stan takes it and says "I've taken orders from everybody, but I'll be damned if I am going to be ba-a-'d by you." He bawls the goat out, turns away and starts to go to the cannon to polish it. He is bending over with his fanny exposed to the goat. The goat looks at him, and the mental attitude of the goat is "I'm going to get this guy!" He butts Stan, who leaves that set and goes sliding on his stomach through the set where the Admiral is standing at attention with all the sailors holding their salute. Everybody in the set takes it big.

Hardy leaves the admiral's set and rushes after Stan, who gets up off the deck, sees Hardy coming after him. Stan has the can of polish and rags, and jumps up on a big cannon which extends over the rail of the boat. Hardy is bawling him out, telling him that he will clean every cannon in the pace. Hardy then leaves the set, leaving Stan polishing the cannon.

Cut to a closer shot of Stan on the cannon, which is ten or fifteen feet out over the side of the boat. He takes the top off the polish can and puts the can in the mouth of the cannon and starts polishing. Then he reaches his hand into the mouth of the cannon to get more polish, and accidentally the can tips and rolls back into the cannon. He peeks in the mouth of the cannon and tries to reach the can, but without success, so he starts crawling in the cannon after the can and goes right out of sight.

A gunner and a swabber enter the turret, getting ready to fire a salute for the admiral's departure. They open up the breech and the fellow starts to swab out the gun. (This swab is a long pole about fifteen feet long, with a big brush on the end.) He takes a couple of pokes with the swab and realizes that the gun is clogged.

Cut to the inside of the cannon where Stan is getting the swab jabbed in his face.

Back to the gob, who calls a couple of sailors over to give him a hand. They use great force. One more cut inside of Stan getting it in the face, then back to the sailors working the swab. They give a big heave.

Cut to the mouth of the cannon and half of Stan's body comes out and is jerked back in quickly. Repeat this action two or three times, and then cut back to the sailors working the swab, heaving much harder. Back to the mouth of the cannon; Stan comes out full figure, hanging to the end of the swab. He is immediately pulled back in. He comes out gain hanging onto the brush. They start to pull it back and his head gets caught. It comes out again, and this time the swab is jerked away and Stan hangs onto the mouth of the cannon.

Cut to the breech of the cannon and they make ready to put a big shell in.

Cut back to Stan hanging with his hands in the cannon and his face right in the mouth of the cannon. He looks in.

Cut to a shot shooting through the barrel of the cannon from the breech and show Stan's face at the other end taking it big. Reverse the angle to the mouth of the cannon shooting down through it and show the big shell being lifted into place and the breech is closed.

Cut outside to the mouth of the cannon showing Stan taking it big. He gets over that the shot is about to be fired. He lets go and the minute his fingers leave the cannon the shot is fired, a large puff of smoke coming from the mouth of the cannon.

Cut to Stan down below. He looks up at the cannon, saying to himself, "What a narrow escape that was!"

He swims around the side of the boat just as the Admiral's launch is pulling away. Stan stands at attention and goes down under the water and comes up again at attention, three or four times. As the Admiral's boat pulls out, Stan comes up at attention for the last time, and we show a boat hook enter the scene from above. It goes under the water, getting Stan by the seat of the pants, and starts pulling him up, Stan all the while saluting. Stan leaves the scene saluting, with the boat hook in his fanny, as we fade out.

Fade in on the home of Delamar. The home is a typical fisherman's cabin situated on the seashore, with the ocean in the background, fishing nets, cars, etc., to give it the atmosphere of a fishing village. The girl is discovered seated on the edge of a boat with a fishing net across her lap, mending the net. Under the net we see that she is still dressed in her bathing suit and the wreath on her hair.

The girl's father enters carrying a basket of fish, showing that he has just come in from his fishing trip. There is a little scene with the girl and her father; she gets over the idea that the father is worried about something and tries to comfort him. He tells her that Sojin, the money lender, is coming today to collect a note that is due. The girl tries to laugh the father out of his worries, but the old man still seems to be downhearted.

Cut to a rikisha with Sojin just getting out. He stops and we move to a closeup of him watching the father and the girl.

Cut back to the girl and her father. The father exits to the cabin, leaving the girl on the scene alone. The girl starts to drape the fish net around her, striking very picturesque poses.

Cut back to Sojin admiring the girl. He exits from the scene and goes on to the set with the girl. He stands admiring her and she assumes a pose, unaware that he is on until she turns and looks down at his feet, then up and sees that it is Sojin. She dislikes him very much, which we can tell from her looks, and he just starts to fondle her hair, which is hanging, when she runs off, leaving him alone. An expression comes on the face of Sojin partly of hatred, then he recovers himself and tries to smile it off.

Cut to the interior of the cabin. The girl rushes in to her father. He says to her, "Why are you so excited? What's the matter?" She tells him in pantomime that old Sojin is out there. The old man immediately tries to calm the girl and says he will go out and have a talk with Sojin. He exits.

Bring the old man on to Sojin. Sojin extends his hand and tries to be very suave. They shake hands and Sojin says, "Well, your note is due today." The old man says he can't pay. Sojin says to the old man, "There is one way out – your daughter." The old man gives him a look and just shakes his head and says, "That could never be." Sojin starts laying down the law to the old man.

The girl comes running into the set, takes her father in her arms and moves him aside, then she tells Sojin that she wouldn't marry him if he were the last man on earth, and tells him to get the hell away from there. Sojin says "Everything will be ready for the marriage at three o'clock tomorrow – just think that over." He starts to make an exit in a very dignified manner and his feet slip on some fish and he does a pratt fall. He gets up very dignified and the girl laughs at him as he makes a very dignified exit.

Take Sojin into another set where he walks to his rikisha, and there is a big pickerel hanging to his fanny. He is walking away from the camera, then he stops, looks back with a look of contempt and snaps his fingers and exits into his rikisha.

In the rikisha he sits down, takes it big and jumps up with a yell.

His head goes through the top of the rikisha and the coolie turns around and starts running with the rikisha. We have a running insert of Sojin trying to pull the fish off his fanny. Fade out.

Cut back to the battleship, a group of sailors standing around and the mailman passing out mail.

Cut to closeup of Stan reading a letter, getting over that he has just received same. In the folds of the letter which he opens, to his surprise he brings forth a $50.00 bill. He goes on reading the letter, which we see is from his parents. It states in the letter that "this is the balance of your Uncle Henry's will and it will be the last you receive." Get over while he is reading, that there is a slight breeze blowing. While he is reading, holding the letter in one hand and the bill in the other, the breeze takes the bill from his hand and blows it off into another set. Stan, realizing what has happened, takes it big and starts chasing after his $50.00.

The bill blows into a set where the captain is standing with his back to the camera, and sticks to the captain's fanny. Stan comes dashing in, sees the bill on the captain's fanny, goes to reach for it and hesitates, realizing it is his superior officer, and tries to contrive a way to get the bill. While Stan is thinking, the captain moves out of the set on a slow walk. Stan gets over "Oh, my God," and starts after the captain, making attempts to get the bill off the captain's fanny. After three or four reaches, the captain turns and nearly catches Stan, who salutes and acts very innocent as if nothing had happened. The captain continues his pace. Work this up as much as possible.

The captain comes to a stop near the rail. Stan realizes it is impossible to reach the bill with his hand, gets an idea and exits.

Cut to another set; Stan enters, getting a long fishing pole with extra large hook at the end of the line. He climbs a mast and works his way out directly over the captain. He stretches out the string and starts casting and trying to hook the bill below on the captain's fanny. He makes four or five snags with the hook, not hooking the bill, but the hook comes a little too close to the captain's fanny and pricks him. Stan gets the hook out of the set before the captain can see it. The captain takes this and turns, looking around wondering what stuck him. Not seeing anyone, he goes on looking out to sea. Stan tries once more, repeating the same action of sticking the captain, who takes it much bigger this time. Stan makes another attempt at the bill, and luckily this time removes it from the captain's fanny with the hook. The bill floats in the air at the end of the string, which is about twenty feet long, and Stan begins to reel it as if pulling in a fish.

Cut to Hardy standing on the upper deck with a large telescope in hand looking off toward the island, focusing on some object. The floating bill comes directly in front of the lens through which Hardy is looking.

Cut to a shot shooting down a funnel showing the bill fluttering nervously in the wind.

Stan removes the bill from in front of the telescope. Hardy without seeing its departure removes the telescope from his eye and looks around very quickly as if startled. He looks at the lens, turns the thing around examining it, puts his hand to his head getting over "My God, I must be ill; I'm seeing money." He again places the telescope to his eye and looks through. The waving bill comes through once more. Hardy takes the telescope from his eye, this time seeing the bill at the end of the string. He looks off and sees Stan reeling in the bill toward him. He takes this, jumps from his perch and runs along the deck toward Stan.

By this time Stan has the bill within his reach. He grabs it from the hook, looks at it and heaves a sigh of relief.

Hardy rushes in just in time to see Stan removing the bill from the hook, grabs the fishing pole from Stan, pulls the string in, looks at the hook and with a silly expression speaks title to Stan, "What do you use for bait?"

Stan shows Babe the letter and Babe says to him, "We're going on shore leave today and a man with all that money in China isn't safe; you need some protection. Let me show you around." Much to Stan's surprise, Hardy takes the bill away and tells him, "I'll take care of this until we get on shore." Stan, boob-like, thanks him very much. Hardy gets over a look as if to say, "What a time I'll have spending this fifty."

Cut to title to the effect that the money lender arrives for his answer.

We discover Sojin, the father and the girl on. Sojin has his watch in his hand, explaining that the time is up. The girl refuses to become his wife and the old man backs her up in this assertion.

Cut to closeup of the girl. She looks off and her face brightens up, and we see that she sees something that pleases her.

Cut to a squad of gobs. They march by the set and the girl exits and goes into the set where they are marching. She walks alongside of Stan, throws her arms around him and plants a big kiss on his lips. He feels embarrassed and tries to shake her away.

Cut to Sojin, who sees this and gets over his hatred for Stan, fearing that he may lose the girl. He gets over to the old man, "I will not be thwarted," and flies into a rage, telling the old man that he is determined to marry the girl.

Back to the marching gobs; the girl is walking alongside with Stan, and he tells her he will come over to see her as soon as they are dismissed. She waves after him and they march off the set.

Lap dissolve to the sailors coming into the town. They are dismissed and scatter in all directions, leaving Hardy and Stan alone in the set. They get their bearings, look around and exit, going into the store set.

Bring Stan and Hardy to the store. They see shoes and sandals lying on the steps. Babe walks right out of his shoes, leaving them on the steps, and enters the store. Stan follows. Hold it for a couple of feet, then we see Stan come flying out through the swinging door, then two Chinks come out and point at his feet. Babe comes out and says, "You damn fool, don't you know you're in China? Take off your shoes – it's the custom of the country." Stan takes his shoes off and he has one toe hanging out of the stocking. He leaves his shoes there and goes into the store.

In the store Stan purchases a trinket and then says, "Give me five dollars worth of fireworks." The Chinaman looks at him, picks up the five, puts on his hat and pantomimes "Take them all," and walks out. Stan is very much surprised to see the fellow leave, and starts filling his blouse with fireworks.

Babe is hungry. He wants Stan to go over to another part of the marketplace or store where they can buy something to eat. They cross over to another part of the store and sit at a table. Stan says, "I'm not very hungry." Babe gets over the fact that he is very hungry. They look at the menu, which is written in Chinese characters. A waiter comes on and Stan tries to talk to him, but the waiter shakes his head. Stan points to some characters, just two or three, and says "I'll take that; I'm not very hungry." Babe takes the menu, and pointing to a lot of characters says, "Give me all that." The waiter exits.

Stan shows Hardy the little chain and heart that he bought. The waiter comes in with one tray loaded with food and another tray with a little pot of tea. The pot of tea he places in front of Hardy, and the big tray of food in front of Stan. Hardy takes it big while he looks at the tray in front of Stan. He then looks at the waiter and says, "Is this all I get?" pointing to his pot of tea. The waiter points to the menu and pantomimes that all those characters mean the pot of tea, and the few characters mean the big tray of food. Hardy says, "Nuts, bring me a hot dog." The waiter shakes his head. Hardy tries to pantomime a dog, standing up and putting his hand at his fanny as if shaking his tail, barks and says "Dog – hot." The waiter says "No savvy." Then Hardy gets a pencil and draws a picture of a dog, calls the waiter's attention and says, "Look." The waiter looks and shakes his head, then Hardy barks like a dog. Then Hardy takes a match out and holds it to his toe and jumps with the pain and says "Hot! Hot dog. Bow-wow." The waiter with a vague knowing look, says "Me savvy." He goes over to the corner of the room and picks up a dog.

Back to Hardy and Stan watching. The Chink says "Hot dog, me savvy," and exits with the dog.

Stan has been eating his big dinner and when he sees the Chink exit with the dog, a thought dawns on him that maybe he has been eating dog meat. He looks at Babe and Babe looks at him. Stan puts his right hand to his head and his left hand on his stomach, gets up and says, "This is enough for me, and exits, followed by Babe.

They come outside. Stan gets two right shoes and Babe gets two left shoes and they start away.

Cut to their feet walking in a pan shot. They stop and see that they have on the wrong shoes and start changing. They hear some people cheering over in a place and they exit and peek in the doorway.

Inside we see a jujutsu wrestler who is naked except for a little coolie coat. He is standing with his back against the wall, getting reach to make a rush.

Babe precedes Stan into this place. Stan thinks they are all dressed that way and he is not going to be fooled this time, so he takes off his pants, hangs them up and makes his entrance into the place with just his jacket, showing his bare legs.

Shoot to the interior of the place; Stan thinking that he is in the right, makes a very proud and dignified entrance. He goes to Babe, sees Babe with his pants on and says, "Hurry up and get those pants off; it's the custom here." Babe looks and sees Stan without his pants and is horrified. Babe calls Stan's attention to all the people in the gallery who are looking at him. Stan looks up and sees them and is embarrassed. Then Babe grabs him by the arm and drags him out to the set where Stan's pants are hanging, gives him the pants and says, "Put them on and get out of here." Stan starts to put on his pants and Babe drags him off the set.

Cut to Sojin around the corner of the girl's cabin. He whistles and two of his henchmen appear, and they all go into the cabin.

Cut to a rikisha coming to the cabin. Stan gets out and moves over to a set near the cabin and starts to give the Chinese love call to the girl.

Cut back to Babe; he produces a bag of bananas from behind the seat and starts to break one off.

Back to Stan "coo-cooing."

Back to Babe peeling the bananas and throwing the skins in front and all around the coolie. He hears Stan coo-cooing. He coo-coos back to Stan, acting a little bit effeminate, giving an imitation of the girl answering Stan's love call. This should be good for about three cuts. Babe gets disgusted at hearing Stan coo-cooing and he starts eating bananas very fast, throwing the skins in front and back of the coolie. The coolie is unaware of the banana skins landing at his feet.

Cut to the rear of the cabin showing Sojin and his henchmen coming out with the girl. The girl manages to utter a scream. They exit.

Stan takes it and calls to Babe, who has heard the scream. Stan runs into the cabin and discovers the old man bound and gagged. Hardy looks up over the top of the rikisha and sees Sojin, the henchmen and the girl running away in another rikisha and the girl hollering for help. Hardy hollers for Stan.

Cut to the cabin. The old man is telling Stan about Sojin taking the girl. The old man and Stan exit.

They come to the rikisha where Hardy is and give the coolie a smash on the fanny with a stick and tell him to hurry. They all jump in the rikisha and the coolie starts to go. His feet hit the banana skins and he does a 108, making a complete circle and landing on his back with a thud, letting go of the rikisha, which tips up, throwing out Babe, Stan and the old man. Babe and Stan right the rikisha, leaving the old man on the ground. The coolie starts to pull the rikisha away. The old man starts to push it from the back, and when he strikes the banana skins he does a 108. the coolie runs away with the rikisha, leaving the old man trying to get up and doing two or three falls on the banana skins.

In another setup the rikisha with the girl comes around the corner and off. Stan and hardy come around the same shot with their rikisha in pursuit.

Sojin's rikisha gets to the bottom of a hill and the girl puts her arms out yelling for help. Stan and Babe see her from their rikisha. The rikisha with the girl goes up over the hill and off the net.

Stan and Hardy come to the hill and get halfway up. The coolie loses control of the rikisha and it goes down, all turned over at the bottom of the hill. The coolie comes running back and says, "Me no pull fat boy up hill." Babe takes it big.

Babe tries to get the rikisha together again and Stan runs on up the hill, leaving Babe and the coolie.

Babe gets a big stick and is prodding the coolie in the fanny to get him to pull him up the hill.

Cut to the exterior of Sojin's home. The rikisha with Sojin and the girl comes on. The gates open and they enter, and the gates are immediately closed.

Stan arrives outside the gate, banging on it. In back of him a little inner door in the gate opens and a big arm reaches out, grabs him by the neck and swishes him in and the door is immediately slammed behind him.

Cut to Babe in the rikisha. He gets almost to the top of the hill when the shafts pull loose. The coolie goes on his face and the rikisha starts down the hill backwards with Babe hollering for help. It goes through the village street, missing Chinamen running right and left. It cuts into a vegetable wagon, vegetables going through the air, coming down and completely covering Babe. He scrambles from beneath them, jumps to his feet and tears out of the set.

Cut to the interior of living room in Sojin's palace. This is a large set about 28 feet wide, with big pilasters in the middle, a fountain in the center and a big chandelier practical for two men to swing on. A balcony runs around three sides of the room, with a smaller balcony on one end, the balconies practical for fighting.

When the scene opens, four girls dressed in geisha costume are lolling around the fountain. Sojin makes his entrance from the back of the set holding the girl by the wrist. Two of his henchmen come up in the rear. Sojin is showing the girl the big living room and he gives instructions to the geisha girls to get off the set.

Then cut to the hallway and we see Stan struggling with the two guards. They exit out of the set and into the living room.

The girl and Sojin see Stan. She starts to go toward Stan and Stan starts toward her. His hands are bound behind him and he is held by the shoulders by the two guards. Sojin tells his two guardsmen to take the girl back through the door. They exit with the girl through the door backstage, leaving Sojin alone at the back of the stage and Stan and his two guards up in front.

Sojin comes down toward Stan, seats himself in a big chair and starts to torment Stan with words. While he is talking to Stan, we cut to a back shot of Stan showing that he is cutting the thong that binds his hands on the sword of one of his guards.

Cut back to closeup of Sojin telling Stan what he is going to do with him, then back to closeup of Stan taking it.

Switch to the back of Stan, where he is getting his bonds severed on the sword of the guardsman, then cut to a full shot of Sojin where he waves his arm to the upper balcony, where the girl is brought out by the two guards who took her off. She is now upstairs with the two guardsmen, leaving the rest of the people downstairs.

Semi-closeup of the girl on the balcony pleading to Stan for help.

Back to a shot of Sojin and Stan, where Sojin says, "She is mine – all mine!"

Cut to a shot in back of Stan showing that he is loose. Then cut to long shot where Stan knocks each of his guards on their fannies; he takes a running jump, steps on the lap of Sojin, then onto his shoulder and then to his head. Sojin has some kind of a Chinese head-dress on the order of a crown, so that when Stan steps on his head, this is jammed down over his face. Stan leaps up and grabs the rail of the balcony, runs along the side of the balcony a la Doug Fairbanks, makes a leap from the balcony to the chandelier, does a swing on the chandelier to the balcony and catches one of the guards by wrapping his legs around the guard's neck. He then swings back and the fellow comes right off the balcony, with Stan's legs wrapped around him, and when they get out over the center of the room Stan drops him into a big jardinière, leaving his feet sticking out.

The other guard goes to grab the girl to take her into the back door of the balcony. The girl puts up a fight and runs over near the edge of the balcony, so that when Stan swings back again he wraps his legs around the other guard's neck, pulls him off the balcony and drops him into the fountain. He then swings back and takes the girl in the arms.

By this time Sojin has the crown off his head and is urging the guards to get Stan. He sees one guard sneak up alongside the balcony and Stan is watching another guard sneaking up on the other side. Stan is backing away from the guard he sees, and in backing away, a Roman candle protruding from the back of his blouse gets lighted from a candle that is standing in front of a Buddha. The Roman candle starts spitting fire balls in back of Stan, who thinks somebody is shooting at him. He turns around quickly to see what it is, and several balls of fire shoot from the Roman candle. The guards all run in different directions.

Stan realizes that the fireworks in his blouse will help to save him. He stoops to light a boomerang firework and throws it out at

Sojin, who ducks, and the boomerang comes around and hits Stan in the fanny (cartoon shot).

The chandelier is now swinging. Sojin, full of determination to get the girl, jumps up the side of the balcony, leaps for the chandelier and swings over to the place where Stan is, but his feet miss and he turns around, then he swings back with his fanny toward Stan. Stan takes a pinwheel and puts it on Sojin's fanny and the girl lights the fuse, and we see Sojin swinging back and forth with a beautiful display of fireworks on his fanny. These fireballs hit the guardsmen below and Sojin drops in the fountain with his fanny on fire.

The chandelier swings back. Stan with the girl in his arms makes a leap, gets on the chandelier and they go over to the other side of the balcony. Once Stan has landed on the other section of the balcony, he takes his remaining fireworks and starts shooting.

There is a Chink half dressed watching Stan from behind a pilaster. He runs over and gets a Chinese suit of armor, buts it on and comes out with a big knife. He is sneaking around under the balcony when Stan looks down and sees him and drops a Roman candle down into the suit of armor. Eyemo shot of this Chink with the balls of fire coming from the Roman dandle inside the suit of armor. He ends up by jumping into the fountain on top of Sojin, who is just getting out.

Stan shoots the balance of his fireworks and sees what he thinks is a secret door and dashes through with the girl. The minute he gets through, the door closes and he finds he is in a small room with heavy iron bars on the window. The henchmen come up and try to get in the door. Stan looks out the barred window and sees Babe Hardy and a couple of sailors.

Cut to a shot of Babe and the sailors saying "How the hell can we get in this place?"

Cut back to the boy and girl in the room. Then cut to the balcony where the henchmen are trying to batter their way into the room.

Back to the room; Stan yells to Babe and the sailors but they cannot hear him. He looks around the room, sees a mirror, takes a candle and starts to write on the mirror, "Help, help, help." He writes this backwards, then reflects the mirror to the side of a wall where Babe and the two sailors read it. They look up and see Stan. Cut to a long shot of the boy and girl at the window.

Babe and the sailors call the rest of the Marines and about 40 Marines come running up to the wall. They try to get in the gate, can't make it, then Babe says, "Zouave style," and they do the wall-scaling of the Zouaves. They get in formation for the wall scaling. Babe is one of the bottom men for the formation and the men start to get up over the wall, leaving Babe as the last man. Two of the marines put their guns down to take Babe up over the wall. Babe can't reach the gun. He makes a couple of jumps for it. At last he gets it but his weight is too much for the Marines and they both do a double twister off the wall, landing on Babe's stomach.

The Marines come tearing through the big set, into the hall, rescue the boy and girl, Chinks scattering in all directions. They come out with the boy and girl, cut through the gate to the street.

The father comes on puffing, all out of breath, and sees his daughter in the safe protection of Uncle Sam's Marines.

The whole crowd walks off with the boy and girl and start marching across a bridge. When they get to the center of the bridge, the weight of the crowd is too much for the bridge and it starts to bend down in the center, and continues down like an elevator until everyone is covered up to their necks in water. While they are all looking around in great surprise, cut to closeup of the girl and Stan; they look at each other and smile. Fade out.

DUCK SOUP

Production history: Production S-17. Script finished September 15, 1926; filmed Monday September 20 through Saturday Oct. 2, 1926. Copyrighted January 13, 1927, by Pathé (LU 23526). Released March 13, 1927. Two reels.

Produced by Hal Roach. Directed by Fred L. Guiol. Photographed by Floyd Jackman. Edited by Richard Currier. Gowns by [William] Lambert. Supervising Director, F. Richard Jones. Titles by H.M. Walker. Story based on a sketch by Arthur Jefferson (uncredited).

With Stan Laurel (James Hives), Oliver Hardy (Marmaduke Maltravers), Madeline Hurlock (Lady Tarbotham), William Austin (Lord Tarbotham), James A. Marcus (Colonel Blood), Bob Kortman (Forest Ranger), William Courtright (Colonel Blood's Butler), Laura La Varnie (Colonel Blood's Maid), Stuart Holmes (Train Conductor).

Two vagrants, trying to elude a forest ranger trying to recruit them to fight a fire, escape into a palatial home which they soon learn has been vacated by the owner (a big-game hunter) and his servants. Their private oasis is short-lived, however, when a well-to-do couple inquire about renting the place, forcing the vagrants to masquerade as the owner and his maid. They escort the couple around the house as best they can, until the hunter returns for his bow and arrow, prompting a fracas and the eventual unmasking of the vagrants, who are duly impressed into service as firefighters.

In case you were mystified by this film's title, "duck soup" was a slang phrase popular in the 1920s, referring to a task that is easy to accomplish. It was used again as the title of an excellent Marx Brothers feature for Paramount in 1933. Edgar Kennedy appeared in that film, and starred in yet a third *Duck Soup*, this one an RKO two-reeler made in 1942.

The *Duck Soup* under discussion here was the second film in which Laurel and Hardy appeared for Hal Roach. It was lost until the early 1980s, at which point a Belgian print, with titles in French and Dutch, turned up. It yielded a number of surprises, the main one being that Laurel and Hardy are teamed throughout the film and also exhibit a number of the character traits we recognize in the mature films. The script also provides some surprises, mainly that Stan Laurel's onscreen partner was intended to be an actor named Sid Crossley; we can be grateful that, for whatever reason, Crossley did not appear in the film and was replaced by Babe Hardy. Crossley appeared in two dozen American films – some of them short comedies such as the Stan Laurel solo film *Dr. Pyckle and Mr. Pryde* and the Hal Roach films *Starvation Blues* and *Loud Soup*, but by late 1929 he was back in his native England, and continued to work in films there through 1942. He died at 74 in Troon, Cornwall, on November 1, 1960.

Dated September 15, 1926, this script is a reworking of a sketch that Stan Laurel's

STAN LAUREL
James Hives

BABE HARDY
Marmaduke Maltravers

SYD CROSSLEY
Suggested for Maltravers

JAMES A. MARCUS
Colonel Blood

WILLIAM AUSTIN
Lord Tarbotham

MADELINE HURLOCK
Lady Tarbotham

BOB KORTMAN
Forest Ranger

WILLIAM COURTRIGHT
Colonel Blood's Butler

LAURA LA VARNIE
Colonel Blood's Maid

father, Arthur "A.J." Jefferson, had written in 1905. The film script bears the same title of the original sketch – and also includes a number of misplaced apostrophes ("does'nt, "do'nt," etc.), something which Stan Laurel did for his entire life in his typed correspondence. For those reasons, I suspect that he is the primary author of this script. In A.J.'s original, the two hoboes are named Flash Harry and Lightfoot Jim. In the 1926 script, they are Marmaduke Maltravers (the role intended for Crossley) and James Hives (Stan). While perusing this script, the reader may substitute "Babe" for "Sid." The "old and peppery retired Army Colonel" named Colonel Blood in the Roach script was Colonel Pepper in A.J.'s original sketch. The well-to-do couple who inquire about renting the Colonel's home, and force Laurel and Hardy to masquerade as the owner and his housekeeper, are named Lord and Lady Tarbotham in the Roach script but were Percy and Lydia Fitzhuggins in the 1905 original.

Actress Madeline Hurlock, frequently cast in Mack Sennett comedies, made her only appearance in a Roach film with *Duck Soup* (possibly as a trade for Sennett's use of Babe Hardy in his short *Crazy to Act*, filmed around the same time). She received most of the publicity for the film from the releasing company, the Pathé Exchange, but didn't have as many scenes in the picture as Stan and Babe. Lord Tarbotham was originally slated to be played by Stuart Holmes, a suave Chicago-born actor who would amass close to 600 film credits between 1909 and 1964, but the role went to William Austin, who would appear in 1932 as Ollie's roommate in *County Hospital*, but whose best remembered film role of nearly 100 is probably Alfred, the butler to Bruce Wayne in Columbia's 1943 *Batman* serial.

The elaborate opening sequence in which the vagrants dream of a lavish meal before being rudely awakened does not exist in the available copies, although since the source materials do show a good deal of wear, particularly at what is now the start of the film, there's the chance that it may have been the original first scene.

Also missing is the scripted scene in which Colonel Blood's servants show him the advertisement in the newspaper. The film as it now exists opens with the gag of the painting sailing through the air and landing on Colonel Blood's head. The part of the maid, suggested in the script for "Ma Lavarnie," is played by Laura La Varnie (1853-1939), a Missouri-born actress who appeared in more than 80 films between 1913 and 1930, notably two starring Mabel Normand: Mack Sennett's *Mickey* and Hal Roach's *Raggedy Rose* (co-written by Stan). She was also in the cast of *The Honorable Mr. Buggs*, a Roach short in which Babe appeared. The butler is played by William Courtright, who was memorable as Uncle Bernal in Laurel and Hardy's 1929 short *That's My Wife*.

One wonders if any of the "title to the effect" suggestions in the script were retained in the original English-language prints of the film. The video transfers we have today from various companies have four different sets of titles. Dave Lord Heath's splendid website "Another Nice Mess" (www.lordheath.com) contains a page devoted to *Duck Soup* in which all four groups are replicated. I am culpable for the "Kirch DVD Print" titles (but not for the misspellings!), which I wrote for a 1983 35mm theatrical reissue of the film presented by John W. Quinn. These were partly taken from the script, and partly translated from the French titles. The titles in other home-video editions which refer to "Mr. Laurel and Mr. Hardy" would never have been used in original copies, as there was not as yet the idea of teaming Stan and Babe at the Roach lot. The next few scripts will prove this.

It's interesting that the lead forest ranger was supposed to be a "type like Tiny Sandford" because his name is spelled correctly in the script (on Roach film credits it was always given as "Sanford"), and because in the film the role is played by Bob Kortman, a frequent cast member in B-Westerns and the owner of the meanest, most haunted eyes in the history of movies. Speaking of eyes, the "burned eyebrow" gag is in the film, but much more briefly.

The bicycle scene is not quite as elaborate in the film. A group of forest rangers chase after the two vagrants in a car, but the action soon concentrates on the bicycle careening downhill; in the film, two buses replace the streetcars suggested in the script. Also, while the vagrants find the two bicycles parked at a curb, there's no indication in the film that this is by a Western Union office.

The scene with Colonel Blood on the train, pulling the emergency brake and exclaiming that he's forgotten his bow and arrow, comes earlier in the film than in the script, appearing just after the vagrants realize that they are the sole proprietors of the mansion for the weekend.

There are a couple of nice gags in the film which aren't in the script. One is a running gag of an insert close-up showing an index finger pushing the button for the doorbell of the Colonel's mansion. Over the course of the film, this is done by Lord Tarbotham, Colonel Blood, a moving man, and the forest ranger who has bedeviled the vagrants. Another gag comes when Babe, masquerading as Colonel Blood, invites the Tarbothams to sit down and make themselves comfortable in the living room. Since Babe now has no place to sit, Stan as "Agnes" brings in a chair – which is clearly too small for Babe's ample size. After Babe glowers at him, Stan exits and returns with a much larger chair.

Duck Soup is one of the most enjoyable of the early L&H silents, and one wishes that Stan, Babe and the creative crew at the Roach lot could have built steadily on this foundation, but it would take several more films before the effortless teamwork shown here would again be on display.

HOME FROM THE HONEYMOON . . . ALL STAR.

[Script has S-17 penciled in, although this was officially marked as S-14.]

CHARACTERS

MARMADUKE MALTRAVERS	. . .	Sid Crossley.
JAMES HIVES	. . .	Stan Laurel.
COLONEL BLOOD	. . .	James Marcus.
LORD TARBOTHAM	. . .	Stuart Holmes.
LADY TARBOTHAM	. . .	Madeline Hurlock.

INCIDENTAL CHARACTERS . . . The Butler – His Wife – the Transfer Man – Forest Ranger – Bums etc.

LOCATION . . . Los Angeles.

. . . .

WHAT THE STORY IS ABOUT:

The story concerns an old and peppery retired Army Colonel who is about to leave his palatial home to go to Africa on a prolonged hunting trip.

Before he leaves he advertises his home to rent furnished, and leaves the renting of the place to his Butler and Maid who are man and wife.

After his departure the two servants decide that there is no hurry about renting the place and they decide that they will lock the house up and go away for the week-end.

Whilst they are deciding to go away, two bums – motivated by a Forest Ranger – enter the house and by chance overhear the servants' plans. They decide that this is a God-send in that they can get free board and lodgings over the week-end.

The servants leave and the bums take possession.

A young married couple arrive in town on their honeymoon, but are unable to find any hotel accommodation. They read the Colonel's advertisement in the paper and decide that it would be an ideal arrangement to rent the place furnished.

They start for the house.

In the meantime the two bums are making themselves very much at home. They are enjoying a big meal when the honeymooners arrive and ring the door bell.

The two bums sense the situation and realize that their only safety – the Ranger being outside – will be to impersonate the Colonel and his maid.

This they do. The young couple are admitted.

The comedy then centers round the renting of the house – the selling of the Colonel's Rolls-Royce – the young wife asking the Colonel's permission to retain the services of the maid- the wife wanting to take a bath and insisting that the maid assist her – and so forth.

This finishes with the young husband asking the phoney Colonel if they can have immediate possession. The phoney Colonel says that it will be alright with him, but asks whether it will be alright for him to pack up and remove a few family heirlooms that are very dear to him. The young couple agree to this and leave the two bums to pack.

The two bums get busy with the packing, but before doing so they telephone for a transfer. Whilst thus engaged they hear the front door bell ring. The phoney maid, thinking that this is the transfer man, runs to open the door. When the door opens she discovers to her horror that it is Colonel Blood who has returned for his bow and arrow.

She admits the Colonel and locks him in a closet. The phoney maid then runs upstairs and tells the other bum that the real Colonel is locked in the closet. The Colonel begins to hammer and kick on the door.

The young husband – hearing the racket – runs downstairs and asks the phoney Colonel what it is all about. The phoney Colonel explains that the man downstairs is a certain Mr. Hookworm with

whom he had had a law suit. Mr. Hookworm had lost and gone insane
and that he had now undoubtedly escaped from an asylum.

The young husband – horrified to think that there is a madman
in the house which he has rented for his honeymoon – is about to
protest, when Colonel Blood – who has escaped from the closet –
enters the scene.

The outraged Colonel demands an explanation, and the young
husband – feeling that he is now the lessee of the house – decides to
take the floor. He reprimands the old Colonel for his violence at which
the old man fairly foams at the mouth with rage. The young husband
persists in calling the Colonel – Mr. Hookworm, which infuriates him
still further. The last straw is when the young husband tells the
Colonel that he is mad because the phoney Colonel told him so.

At this the Colonel goes mad with rage. He accuses the crowd of
being a gang of crooks and indicates the young husband as the
ringleader. He starts to chase him – followed by the wife. The chase
leads them from one part of the house to another. The maid enters with
a transfer man and they commence to carry the things out of the room.

At the last the Ranger enters and arrests the two bums.

We fade out on the two bums whirling round on the end of a fire
hose nozzle – fighting a forest fire on the edge of the town.

....

HOME FROM THE HONEYMOON ... ... ALL STAR.

INTRODUCTORY TITLE to the effect:
    A GENTLEMAN AND A GENTLEMAN'S GENTLEMAN.

FADE IN on the interior of an elaborate hotel suite. We see Stan
and Sidney sound asleep in twin beds.
    The door opens and a hotel waiter in a white suit enters. He is
pushing before him a large serving wagon on which there is a great
deal of expensive and rich looking food. He crosses softly to the
windows and raises the shades allowing the morning sunlight to fall

directly onto the two beds. he then crosses to Stan and politely
awakens him. As Stan wakes introduce him with a title to the effect:

A GENTLEMAN'S GENTLEMAN
Stan Laurel.

The waiter then places a tray across Stan's lap, and as he goes to
get the other tray Stan wakes up Sid. As Sid wakes up give him an
introductory title to the effect:

A GENTLEMAN
Sid Crossley.

The waiter then places the second tray across Sid's knees. He
then hands Sid a card and a pencil which Sid signs with a flourish and
returns it to the waiter, who after enquiring if there is anything else
he can do, makes a quick exit.

Sid picks up his knife and fork and prepares to enjoy a hearty
breakfast.

>   NOTE . . . It is very important to have these trays
>   fixed with the most expensive and appetizing food
>   possible. This also applies to the service.

Stan speaks a title to the effect:

PARDON ME, SIR, WON'T YOU SHOWER BEFORE
BREAKFAST, SIR . . . .

Sid gets over in pantomime . . . That's a good idea, Hives, I will!
He thereupon slips out of bed and exits in the direction of the
Bathroom . . . taking off his pyjama coat as he goes.

Go to a CLOSE UP of Sid in the bath room. His coat is off and he
pantomimes getting out of his pyjama pants. He then steps back into
the shower – rubs his hands in pleasurable expectation, turns on the
water, the water starts pouring all over him – Sid enjoys it immensely,
rubbing himself vigorously all over. Play this for a few feet then LAP
DISSOLVE to –

A CLOSE UP of Sid sitting on a Park bench – the water from a
sprinkler is spraying over him and he is going through exactly the
same business as when we saw him last in the shower bath.

CUT to a MEDIUM SHOT and show the whole Park bench. Stan is
asleep on the other side, the sprinkler awakens Stan. He looks and

sees Sid still rubbing himself under the sprinkler – takes it – and touches Sid and wakes him up. Sidney wakes up – looks round – takes in the situation and moves out of reach of the shower. He looks indignantly at Stan and speaks title to the effect:

WHY IN HELL DIDN'T YOU LET ME EAT MY
BREAKFAST BEFORE I TOOK MY SHOWER?

Stan gives him a double takem and a dumb look – not knowing what it's all about. Then speaks title back to the effect:

BREAKFAST SIR! WHY WE 'AV'NT SEEN A BREAKFAST
FOR THREE DAYS – YESTERDAY, TODAY AND TOMORROW!

Across from the bench we see the Lake. There is a well-dressed youngster (Fauntleroy type) with his nurse at the lake side. The boy has about half a loaf of bread in his hand from which he is breaking off small pieces and throwing them to the gold fish. Stan and Sid enter the scene and watch him longingly- getting over the idea that they envy the fish their luck. They hold it a minute and suddenly the boy tosses the whole chunk of bread into the lake as the nurse tells him that he cannot stay there all day and drags him from the scene.

Stan and Sid follow the bread with their eyes into the Lake.

INSERT the loaf of bread. A lot of fish leap on it from all directions and the loaf sinks abruptly. Stan and Sid look at each other sadly and tighten their belts. Sid speaks soliloquy title to the effect (looking Heavenward):

OH! WOULD I WERE A FISH!

FADE OUT.

FADE IN on the dining room of Colonel Blood's home. We see the Colonel just finishing breakfast. A maid is on (Ma Lavarnie) waiting at table.

Butler enters and speaks title to the Colonel to the effect:

IS THIS ADVERTISEMENT ALL RIGHT, SIR?

And he hands the Colonel a newspaper – indicating an item in the "Want Ad" section.

The Colonel adjusts his monocle and looks at paper.
SHOW INSERT of Paper – want ad. section . . . to the effect:

> FOR RENT... A palatial residence completely
> furnished. The owner, Colonel Blood, who is
> leaving for a shooting trip in Africa, desires to
> rent same to suitable and reliable tenant. The
> right party can have immediate possession.
> For all particulars apply ... the Cedars,
> Poinsettia Grove, Beverly Hills.

The Colonel indicates his approval and then starts to point out to the servant several pieces of valuable furniture that he wants put in storage.
The Colonel finally draws the servant's attention to an oil painting on the wall.

> NOTE . . . This painting is about 2.6 x 3.6. It represents
> the Colonel in his uniform. His sword is drawn and he
> is leading his men heroically to the attack. In the
> background we see cannons – shells bursting and dead
> men. There is a tablet on the frame with wording to
> the effect: "The Charge of the Thirsty First."

The Colonel gets over that this picture is one of his most valued possessions, and he tells the servant to take it down at once and put it in the store room.
The Maid enters and speaks title to Colonel to the effect:

YOUR TAXI IS WAITING, SIR!

The Colonel exits to the HALL. We see several grips and pieces of hand luggage. The Taxi Driver enters and starts to carry baggage out, including suitcases, golf clubs, gun cases, fishing rods and other hunting equipment. The Colonel starts to fix himself up in front of a hall mirror.
CUT BACK to the dining room. We see the servant standing on a chair which isn't quite high enough for him to get the picture off the nail. He is apparently having quite a lot of trouble. He then puts one foot on the back of the chair in an effort to reach up higher. The chair flops right over and he falls – pulling the picture off the wall which flies out of his hand thru' the air and out of the scene.
SHOW the picture going thru' the air and CUT to the Hall –

showing the picture landing on the Colonel's head.

Go to a CLOSE UP of the Colonel showing his head through the canvas, and as he looks in the mirror we see the funny picture – of a big head on a little body. He tears the picture off in a rage and makes an exit to the dining room.

CUT to the dining room. We see the Butler with his back to the Colonel looking around for the picture. The Colonel enters and in a great rage makes a swift kick at the Butler's fanny. The Maid passes through the scene just in time to receive the kick intended for the Butler. The shock is so great to her that it throws her wig back, exposing her bald head. She gives the Colonel a dirty look. Treat this scene the same as Ma Lavarnie did in Raggedy Rose.

NOTE . . . The reason for using this gag is for an excuse for Stan to get a woman's wig when he dresses up as the Maid.

Everybody is all embarrassed – the Butler trying to tell the Maid what's happened. She discovers it and straightens wig. The Colonel exits for the Hall.

CUT to the Hall. The Taxi Driver is waiting. He speaks title to the Colonel to the effect:

YOU'VE ONLY TEN MINUTES TO CATCH THE TRAIN, SIR!

The Colonel hurriedly grabs his coat and hat. The Maid and Butler enter the Hall. The Colonel bids them a hurried farewell – starts to make a dignified exit – trips over the remains of the picture frame and falls. He jumps up in a rage – grabs up a piece of the frame (a corner piece) and throws it at the Butler. Owing to its shape it flies through the air like a boomerang. We follow it with the camera. Show it miss the Butler and return to strike the Colonel on the back of the head as he starts to exit. He falls headlong down the front steps landing in a heap on the sidewalk. As he lands we –

CUT BACK to the Butler and the Maid in the interior of the hall. They are holding up their hands in relief at the Colonel's departure.

FADE OUT.

FADE IN on Park Bench. We see Stan and Sid on. They are reading the remains of a newspaper. Stan is reading the funnies and laughing uproariously which annoys Sid who is interested in an item on the front page. Sid speaks title to the effect:

MY GOOD HIVES – KINDLY RESTRAIN YOUR UNSEEMLY
MIRTH. CAN'T YOU SEE I AM OCCUPIED.

Sid looks back to the paper.
CUT TO an insert of the front page of the newspaper to the effect:
(Bold type headline)

BIG FIRES THREATEN NATIONAL FORESTS.
The Big Fires which have been raging for the past week are
now beyond control, and the Chief Forest Ranger has issued a
request for 5,000 men to check the blaze which now threatens
millions of dollars of governmenttimber reserves.
To meet this demand Forest Ranger McFidgett has been
authorized to round up all the vagrants and bums in the City
and vicinity . . .

CUT BACK to Sid. He shows the paper to Stan who glances at it.
Sid then speaks title to the effect:

POOR FELLOWS! POOR FELLOWS! AND SUCH
SULTRY WEATHER!

Stan agrees with him. They then look out of the scene . . .
CUT to a bunch of Bums being rounded up by several Forest
Rangers. One Bum Character tries to get away. A Ranger (Type like
Tiny Sandford) grabs him by the back of the neck and swings him
around and around in the air – in the manner of wringing a chicken's
neck (use dummy). Tiny then throws the character in line and starts
looking around for more Bums.
CUT BACK to Sid and Stan. Stan looks kind of worried, but Sid
tries to carry it off nonchalantly – intending to bluff out the situation.
He takes a cigar case – leather telescopic kind, well-worn and with his
monogram faintly visible – picks out a cigar stub – pantomimes to
Stan to give him a light. Stan starts looking for a match. Tiny
Sandford walks into the scene and stands beside Sid. Stan finds a
match – strikes it – turns to light Sid's cigar. He sees Tiny and his
hands start to tremble so that he accidentally sets fire to Sid's
eyebrow – burning it off. Sid takes it – holding his hand over his eye –
starts to bawl Stan out. He then removes his hand from his eye and
we see that he has not the sign of an eyebrow left. Very annoyed, he
adjusts his monocle. He turns and sees Tiny – takes it and

pantomimes – looking at his wrist watch. Then he turns to Stan and
for the benefit of Tiny speaks title to the effect:

COME HIVES – WE HAVE AN APPOINTMENT AT THE BANK . . .

They arise from the bench and start to walk out of the scene,
followed by Tiny.

GO TO a WALKING PAN SHOT of the three of them. Stan and Sid
feeling rather nervous being followed by the Ranger gradually
increase their speed and finally break into a run. They turn a corner
and for a moment elude the Ranger.

CUT TO the EXTERIOR of a Western Union Telegraph Office. We
see two or three bicycles leaning against the wall. Sid and Stan run
into the scene. Sid gets a quick idea – grabs one of the bicycles and
pantomimes Stan to sit on the handlebars. Just as they are pulling out
of the scene the Ranger enters and exits after them.

CUT TO another set-up. Sid and Stan on bicycle. Ranger runs in –
jumps on the running board of a Ford that is standing there and
orders the driver to follow the two men on the bicycle. They exit out of
the scene.

CUT TO Side and Stan riding at great speed. Stan speaks title to
the effect:

THIS IS MY FIRST TIME ON A BIKE, SIR!

Sid speaks title back to the effect:

ME TOO!

Stan takes this big. Just then they barely miss an automobile. Sid
looks back out of the scene . . .

CUT TO the Ranger on the running board of the Ford coming
right after them. Sid starts to pedal like hell and starts up a hill. As
they get towards the top the hill the speed slackens and Sid appears
to be pedaling with great effort. They finally reach the top of the hill
and Sid makes one final effort to pedal, and the force is so great that
the chain snaps . . . just as they start down the other side of the hill.
They now start to gain speed – Sid pedaling forward and then
backwards in an effort to find some way of checking the machine.
Stan unaware of what has happened speaks title to Sid to the effect:

PARDON ME, SIR, BUT ARE WE NOT TRAVELLING
A LITTLE FAST, SIR? [Penciled in: It strikes me that we are
travelling a little too fast, Sir.]

Sid gives him a sickly grin and points to the chainless sprocket.
Stan looks down and takes it big. By this time the machine is half way
down the hill and travelling at a high rate of speed. In the background
we see the Ranger following in the Ford.

CUT AROUND TO a shot – Sid's back in the foreground and we see
at the foot of the hill two street cars pull into the scene from opposite
directions at right-angles to the road down which the machine is
travelling. The street cars stop – slightly overlapping and completely
blocking the whole street. People start to get on and off, but as the
bicycle nears the bottom of the hill the cars start to pull away, and
just as it looks as if the men on the bicycle are about to crash into the
two cars they separate – leaving a narrow space between them just
large enough to admit the passage of the bicycle. (Make CLUSE UPS of
Stan and Sid – giving a look of fear – to help suspense and thrill.)

CUT TO another street intersection. We see a traffic cop on duty –
arms outstretched – back to the bicycle blocking traffic in that
direction. It looks like the bike is going to hit him square in the back.
But at the crucial moment he turns – arms outstretched – and the bike
whizzes by him to which he is utterly oblivious . . followed by Ford.

> NOTE . . .   During this routine make cuts of Sid's
> feet sliding along the ground as he tries
> to check bike – show Sid's boots burning.

CUT to a corner. We are now in an exclusive residential district.
The bike comes into the scene and quite suddenly the back wheel
collapses. The bike slides along like this for a few feet getting over the
effect of a horse sitting down. It finally collapses throwing Stan and
Sid to the ground. As they get up, they see the Ford turning the corner
and in a desperate effort to make a get-away they climb through a
French window of a palatial looking house – this being the home of
Colonel Blood. The Ford drives up – Ranger sees the bike laying in the
road – starts searching for Stan and Sid getting over the idea . . .
"They must be here somewhere." He dismisses the Ford which pulls
out of the scene and continues his search for the two men. He is by
this time in a very ugly mood.

CUT TO Interior of Living room. We see Stan and Sid looking

through the French windows – they are watching the Forest Ranger.

CUT TO a shot of the stairs. We see the Butler and his wife, dressed for the street and carrying a little grip, coming down the stairs.

CUT BACK to Stan and Sid. They hear them and quickly hide. The Butler's wife enters the living room – crosses to the French window – turns the key in the lock and puts it in her pocket. She turns and speaks title to the Butler to the effect:

> D'YOU THINK IT'S SAFE FOR US TO LEAVE THE
> HOUSE 'TIL MONDAY?

The Butler comes back with title to the effect:

> WHY SURE! THE COLONEL'S AWAY FOR SIX
> MONTHS AND IT DOES'NT MATTER WHETHER
> THE HOUSE IS RENTED TODAY OR NEXT WEEK!

CUT TO Stan and Sid in hiding. They get over that they have heard the conversation.

CUT BACK to the Butler and wife. They are just making their exit through the front door. As the door closes, Stan and Sid come out of hiding and start towards the Hall. As they get to the stair case the front door suddenly opens. Stan and Sid beat it in different directions and the Butler re-enters to fix the lock. He then exits again – closing the door after him.

CUT TO Stan and Sid in funny position wherever they landed. Sid gets up quickly – rushes to the front door – looks through the little wicket – sees a Rolls-Royce in front of the house with the Butler at the wheel and the old lady putting a grip in the back seat.

GO TO a CLOSE UP . . . The old lady walks into the scene gives the Butler a dirty look and pantomimes . . . Move over! The Butler does so – getting over his disgust – and the old lady gets in and takes the wheel. They drive out of the scene.

[Penciled in note on script: Note: Scene here as The Butler puts up notice on front door - at home Monday.]

BACK TO Stan and Sid. Sid speaks title to Stan to the effect:

> HIVES! WE ARE IN LUCK. SOLE OWNERS
> AND OCCUPIERS FOR THE WEEK-END . . . .

Sid assumes an attitude of swaggering superiority and speaks another title to the effect:

HIVES! PREPARE MY BREAKFAST. I'LL
HAVE MY SHOWER LATER.

Sid gives him a dirty look.

FADE OUT.

FADE IN on a table covered with every conceivable variety of expensive food. Go round table with an Eyemo showing different kinds of food. Hands come into the scene with fork and spoons – picking up helpings of food off dish, and follow it with Eyemo being placed on another plate. After food has been deposited on empty plate – follow it again to another dish of food – repeat action again getting over by suggestion that two people are helping themselves lavishly to the lunch. Then CUT TO a dish containing pieces of cold chicken. A hand comes into the scene and starts to pick up a leg between finger and thumb. Another hand comes into the scene from an opposite direction holding a knife. He gives the first hand a smart rap on the knuckles which makes the hand drop the chicken leg – getting over that the rap hurt. The hand goes out of the scene and re-enters with a pair of sugar tongs with which it delicately picks up the leg and exits from the scene.

MOVE BACK WITH CAMERA and show Stan and Sid eating ravenously . . getting over that they are having the time of their lives.

CUT TO the EXTERIOR of the House. A Taxi drives into the scene and pulls up in front of the front door.

CUT BACK to Stan and Sid. They get over that they hear the Taxi stop. They look at each other a moment. Stan starts to get panicky. Sid calms him down by hitting him over the head with a chicken leg and pantomimes . . . Keep calm. He then exits in the direction of the front door. Stan grabs the four corners of the table cloth and yanks the whole breakfast completely off the table and follows Sid. Sid peeks through the wicket and we . . .

CUT TO the EXTERIOR. We see the Dude get out of the Taxi and hand his wife out. Give them a CLOSE UP with an introductory title to the effect:

LORD AND LADY TARBOTHAM – JUST ARRIVED

IN TOWN ON THEIR HONEYMOON . . .

The Dude looks at a newspaper that he is holding and speaks title to his wife to the effect:

THIS MUST BE THE PLACE THAT IS ADVERTISED
FOR RENT, DARLING.

CUT BACK to Sid. He hears this – takes it. Stan looks at him – still panicky – and speaks titles to the effect"

WHO IS IT, SIR? THE COLONEL?

Sid speaks title back to Stan to the effect:

NO, HIVES! FROM NOW ON I'M THE COLONEL.
AND TO KEEP UP APPEARANCES YOU'RE THE MAID. . . .

Stan starts to protest but Sid grabs him by the seat of the pants and runs him rapidly up the stairs, and into the Butler's bedroom. On the bed we see the maid's clothes and a wig with a little white cap pinned onto same, just as she threw them off before leaving. Sid pantomimes to Stan to put them on as quickly as possible and then makes a quick exit.
CUT TO the front door. The Dude by this time is impatiently ringing the bell.
CUT BACK to Hall. Sid enters the scene down the stairs – tying the girdle of the Colonel's elaborate silk dressing gown. On his head he is wearing the Colonel's little round velvet smoking cap – it has a long silk tassel which hangs at a jaunty angle over Sid's ear. He goes to the living room – takes a cigar from the humidor – lights it – apparently stalling for time.
CUT BACK to the Dude. He is still ringing the bell, his impatience growing.
CUT BACK to Sid. He enters the Hall and stops the foot of the stairs. Pantomimes – calling up to Stan . . . Hurry! Stan enters the scene down the stairs. Sid gets over his delight at Stan's make-up. He pantomimes to Stan to enter the door and exits in the direction of the living room.
CUT TO Stan. He goes to the door and opens it. He makes a courtesy to the Dude. The Dude speaks title to the effect:

I WOULD LIKE TO SEE COLONEL BLOOD.

Stan indicates that they enter which they do. He closes the door after them and pantomimes . . . This way, Sir! Stan takes the lead – the Dude and the wife follow him into the living room. Stan slips on a rug on the polished floor, does a brodie, the shock of which causes a vase to fall off a bracket on Sid's head. Sid takes it – gives Stan a dirty look. Stan gets to his feet all embarrassed and in pantomime introduces the Dude to Sid . . . COLONEL BLOOD!

The Dude shakes hands with Sid and introduces his wife, which Sid acknowledges with an exaggerated bow . . . He pantomimes . . . Be seated! He then sits himself in a big easy chair, while Stan, being a little nervous and not knowing quite what to do, starts to busy himself with a feather duster. The Dude then speaks title to Sid to the effect:

WELL COLONEL! MY WIFE AND I HAVE JUST ARRIVED
HERE ON OUR HONEYMOON. AND ALL THE HOTELS
BEING FILLED MY LITTLE WIFIE CONCEIVED THE
BRILLIANT IDEA OF RENTING A PLACE FURNISHED.
AND HERE WE ARE!

The Colonel speaks title to the effect:

IF THE PLACE SUITS YOU, IT'S PERFECTLY
AGREEABLE WITH ME.

The Dude replies in a title to the effect:

SPLENDID! I'D LIKE TO SEE THE BILLIARD
ROOM, COLONEL. [Penciled in on original script:
BY THE WAY, COLONEL, HAVE YOU A BILLIARD ROOM?]

Sid takes it and gives a dumb look at Stan – getting over the idea . . . Where in hell is the billiard room? Stan gives a bewildered look back – getting over the idea . . . Well, I haven't got it! Sid quickly decides to bluff it through – stands up and in a dignified manner pantomimes to the Dude to follow him. The Dude, feeling very elated at the success of his wife's idea, gives her a kiss, pats her on the back and follows Sid out of the room. Stan – getting over the idea that he doesn't want to be left alone starts after Sid when the Dude's wife calls to him. He stops all embarrassed and the Dude's wife pantomimes . . .

Come over here! This he does very nervously. The Dude's wife speaks title to the effect:

AND WHAT'S YOUR NAME?

Stan becomes flustered and bashfully speaks title:

H'AGNIS!

The woman gets over the idea . . . Oh what a pretty name. She speaks title to the effect:

HOW LONG HAVE YOU BEEN HERE?

Stan getting more embarrassed and not thinking speaks title to the effect:

ABOUT TWO HOURS!

The woman takes it. Stan realizing his mistake tries to cover it with a laugh and the woman thinking that Stan will have his little bit of fun starts to laugh too . . . getting over that she is highly amused.
CUT TO the UPPER HALL . . . We show Sid showing the Dude different pictures and trophies hanging on the walls. As the Dude is looking at these things the Colonel opens a door quickly – looks inside and shuts it – getting over the idea each time . . . Where the hell is the billiard room. Each time he closes a door the Dude turns towards him – almost catching him in the act. [Penciled in on original script: This sequence will be enhanced by the addition of a sequence starting from here – Dude's wife asks Stan how many rooms there are?]
CUT BACK downstairs. Woman speaks title to the effect:

WOULD YOU MIND SHOWING ME THE BEDROOM?

Stan pantomimes for her to follow him and they exit from the scene.
CUT BACK UPSTAIRS. We see Sid – very much discouraged at being unable to find the billiard room. He comes to a door at the end of the Hall which leads to a small balcony overlooking the garden. He looks out and around – the Dude looking over his shoulder. Sid finally turns to the Dude and speaks title to the effect:

ISN'T IT STRANGE! I NEVER COULD FIND THAT
BILLIARD ROOM.

The Dude speaks title back to Side to the effect:

WELL, DON'T WORRY, OLD CHAP! I CAN'T PLAY ANYWAY!

CUT TO the BEDROOM. The door opens and Stan enters the scene
followed by the woman. [Penciled in on original script: Note: Shot of
Stan on stairs, pants come down.] We see that both Stan's pant legs
are down about his ankles. The woman, however, is so busy with her
lorgnette that she does not see this. Stan is also unconscious of what
has happened. He starts showing her around the room. (Work this up
for suspense.) Stan suddenly sees himself in a full-length mirror –
takes it – and starts to pull up the legs of his pants. He gets them
adjusted just in time to avoid the Dude and Sid, who have just entered
the scene, from seeing the pants. Stan then starts to roll his stockings
– unaware that the Dude and Sid are standing behind him. The Dude
takes this and is very embarrassed and crosses to his wife. He gets
over in pantomime to her that if she likes the place he will complete
the details of the lease with the Colonel. She gets over that she does.
The Dude then speaks title to Sid to the effect:

I SHOULD LIKE, COLONEL, TO HAVE IMMEDIATE
POSSESSION.

Sid acquiesces and motions for the Dude to follow him
downstairs. The Dude's wife speaks title to the effect:

COLONEL, WITH YOUR PERMISSION, I WOULD
LIKE TO HAVE AGNIS REMAIN WITH US . . .

Both Sid and Stan take this. Sid regains his composure and again
acquiesces. The Dude being more elated than ever crosses to his wife
and kisses her again – getting over the idea . . . What a brain you
have! Stan pleads with Sid in pantomime that he doesn't want to do it.
Sid replies by giving him a swift kick in the fanny whereupon his
pants fall down again. Stan takes it big and jumps behind a chair just
in time to escape the eyes of the Dude and his wife who turn towards
him. The Dude then follows Sid out of the room. Stan quickly adjusts
his pants again whilst the woman is removing her hat before the

mirror. The woman then speaks title to Stan to the effect:

AGNIS! FIX MY BATH.

Stan takes it big – all embarrassed and exits in the direction of the bath room.

CUT TO the BATH ROOM. Stan enters scene. Fixes the plug in the bath – leans over the tub and turns on the faucet. He has, however, turned the wrong faucet and the water from the shower pours down over the back of his head. Stan takes this in big surprise and keeping his head away from the shower, he turns it off. He then leans over the tub as he did at first and turns on another faucet – the wrong one again. This time there is a gush of boiling water from the shower which envelopes him in a cloud of steam. He takes this big and dashes out of the bathroom into the bedroom – just in time to see the woman stepping out of her dress. Stan takes this big and dashes back into the bath room – closing the door after him.

CLOSE UP of Stan in the bath room. He is in a cold sweat.

CUT BACK to a CLOSE UP of the woman sitting at a vanity dressing table. Shoot in such a manner that she appears to be naked. She turns – looking towards the bathroom and in pantomime speaks title . . . Agnis!

CUT BACK to BATHROOM . . . Stan hears this and starts to shine in desperation. He makes two or three attempts to open the door but each time his heart fails him.

CUT BACK to the WOMAN . . . This time she speaks title much louder:

AGNIS!

She listens a second a speaks title again louder still . . .

AGNIS!

NOTE . . . These titles should be made to start small and quickly expand to fill the screen.

CUT BACK to BATHROOM. Stan is nearly mad with panic as he hears the woman calling him.

BACK TO the WOMAN . . . Using the Eyemo and still giving the impression that she has no clothes on we follow her from the vanity dressing table to the door of the bath room.

CUT TO the BATH ROOM . . . Stan takes a peep – sees her coming towards the bath room door and gets more panicky than ever.

> NOTE . . . Make a scene of Stan in the bath room the first time the woman calls to him. In this scene he takes a peek through the keyhole and sees what he believes to be a naked woman.

CUT BACK TO THE BED ROOM . . . Close up of the woman at the bath room door – still apparently naked. She calls again in pantomime . . . Agnis! She then knocks at the door. Not hearing any response she pulls a kimono up into place over her shoulders – opens the door and enters.

CUT TO INTERIOR OF BATH ROOM . . . Woman enters the scene and sees Stan with his head buried to the shoulders in the bath of water – giving the impression of an ostrich trying to hide. The woman gives a very surprised look and taps Stan on the back. Stan gestures with his hand for her to get away and we see bubbles coming to the surface of the water as though he were trying to say something. She finally pulls Stan out and to his feet. Stan has his eyes closed. The woman starts to shake him getting over . . . What's the matter with you? Stan finally opens his eyes very much surprised to see that she is decently covered in a kimono and very much relieved he tries to alibi his strange actions. He speaks title to the effect:

I WAS JUST LOOKING FOR THE SOAP.

He gets all giggly and makes a quick exit. The woman then turns the key in the door.

CUT TO a shot of a train coming at a high rate of speed.

CUT TO the INTERIOR of a Pullman. We see Colonel Blood surrounded by his baggage – he is getting over the idea that he is looking for something in his various grips etc; his search increases in tempo until it reaches a climax and he reaches up and jerks the communication cord savagely.

CUT to the EXTERIOR of the Train. We see it come to an abrupt halt.

CUT BACK to INTERIOR. We see the passengers in a variety of funny positions caused by the sudden stop of the train. We see the Colonel standing on his head in a hand bag – the mouth of which has snapped to round his neck. He starts to struggle to his feet when the Conductor enters. The Conductor speaks title in pantomime . . . Who pulled that cord? . . . One of the passengers indicates the Colonel who is still struggling trying to remove the bag. The Conductor rushes to him – yanks the bag off his head and starts to bawl him out – getting over . . . What do you mean by stopping this train! The Colonel speaks title to the effect:

> I'VE GOT TO GET OFF! I'VE FORGOTTEN
> MY BOW AND ARROW . . .

The Conductor takes this with a bewildered look as the Colonel starts to gather up all his baggage and makes an exit – the passengers giving him dirty looks as he goes out. The Conductor watches him out of the scene and in Pantomime gets over that the Colonel has got off the train. He then reaches up – pulls the cord and the train starts.

CUT TO the INTERIOR of the LIVING ROOM . . . Stan, Sid and the Dude are on at a table. The Dude is passing money across the table to Sid. Stan is very much interested in the passing of the money . . .

> NOTE ... There is a routine of business here between the three men that will be figured out when actually shooting.

After the transaction the Dude speaks title to the effect:

> THERE YOU ARE COLONEL! THREE MONTHS'
> RENT IN ADVANCE . . .

The Colonel gets over his satisfaction and starts to put the money in his pocket. Stan gives him a look – getting over . . . Where do I come in? Sid looks at him once – getting over the idea . . . Hives! You are forgetting yourself. The Dude in the meantime has noticed a photo on the table – it is the Colonel's Rolls-Royce car. He picks it up and examines it. And in pantomime gets over to Sid . . . Is this your car? Sid very nonchalantly indicates . . . Yes! The Dude speaks title to the effect:

> YOU HAVEN'T ANY HORSES, HAVE YOU, COLONEL?

Sid replies with a title to the effect:

> SORRY, BUT I'M OUT OF HORSES.

Stan takes this – leans over and whispers in Sid's ear a title to the effect:

GO ON! SELL HIM ONE!

Sid gives Stan a dirty look and whispers something in his ear. Stan takes this and exits. Sid then speaks title to the Dude to the effect:

BEFORE I LEAVE, I SHOULD LIKE TO PICK
A FEW OF MY FAMILY HEIRLOOMS . . .

And he indicates with a sweep of his hand one or two objects in the room. The Dude gets over the idea . . . It's quite alright with me! The Dude hesitates a moment and then speaks title to the effect:

IF I SHOULD WISH TO EXTEND MY LEASE,
I SUPPOSE IT COULD BE ARRANGED . . .

Sid gets over that that would be perfectly alright with him. He then speaks title to the effect:

MY DEAR CHAP, I WANT YOU TO FEEL THAT
THIS PLACE IS AS MUCH YOURS AS IT IS MINE . . .

The Dude gets over his delight and what a splendid fellow he thinks Sid is. He shakes hands with Sid and makes an exit.

Stan comes walking through the LIVING ROOM. He has on a cape and hat. He is just about to exit when Sid calls him back. Sid gets over . . . Where are you going? Stan speaks a title to the effect:

I'M GOING TO GET A TRANSFER.

Sid gives him a dirty look and points to the telephone. Stan gives him a dumb look – crosses to the phone.

CUT TO a shot of a TAXI going at a high rate of speed.

CUT TO INTERIOR of same. Show Colonel Blood. He is in a very grouchy mood – his whole trip having been ruined by having forgotten his bow and arrow.

CUT BACK to the LIVING ROOM . . . Sid and the Dude are on. In the center of the room are two or three large trunks. One has the lid shut. Get over the appearance of the trunk being jammed full by showing odds and ends of drapes etc. sticking out between the lid and the trunk. The other has the lid open and Sid is busy throwing in silver ware etc. The Dude is looking on in dumb amazement. The trunk is finally filled. Sid has trouble in closing the lid so he pantomimes the Dude to come to his assistance – which he does. Finally the trunk is forced to close and locked. The Dude straightens up and starts to walk away. We see the Dude's coat tails are firmly shut in the box. The Dude continues to walk away unaware that he is caught – the coat tails tear away at the waist giving the impression that the Dude is wearing an Eton jacket – he doesn't know this.

NOTE. . . The value of this gag will be increased if the Dude can wear light shepherd plaid pants.

The Dude discovers that his collar – during his struggle with the trunk – has come off the front collar button on one side. He gets over the idea to Sid that he is going upstairs to fix his collar and starts towards the Hall. As he reaches the archway, Stan enters the scene dragging a large trunk. The Dude falls right over this. As the Dude is picking himself up, Sid reprimands Stan for his carelessness. The Dude intervenes – getting over the idea . . . Don't blame the girl! It's all my fault! He then makes an exit up stairs. Stan starts to fill this trunk with more silverware etc; from the living room, while Sid puts on the Colonel's silk hat, fur coat and white silk muffler – stuffing his pockets with cigars from the humidor. At this point the Tempo begins to get fast as they are anxious to make their get-a-way.

CUT TO an INSERT of a DOOR BELL ringing.

CUT BACK to Sid and Stan . . . Sid speaks title to Stan to the effect:

QUICK! THE TRANSFER MAN!

Stan exits to the front door while Sid continues to pack.

CUT TO the FRONT DOOR . . .

NOTE . . . The center panel of this door should be made to open inwards there being, in reality, one door within the other . . . See Stan Laurel.

Stan opens the door and we see the real Colonel Blood standing there. Stan – at first surprised because he expected the transfer man – is fussed and makes a little courtesy [curtsy]. Stan's attitude here is one of not knowing who the Colonel is but that he had better invite him in. Stan politely pantomimes the Colonel to enter. The Colonel, who is by this time a little bewildered, enters the Hall. Stan closes the door behind him while the Colonel continues to stare at him. He then

commences to stare round the hall – still bewildered. He suddenly
sees through the arch of the living room, Sid packing one of the
trunks. Sid passes back and forth across the arch without once
looking at the Colonel. Sid re-enters the scene again with the Colonel's
bow and arrow.

CUT TO Stan and the Colonel. By this time the Colonel has a wild-
eyed expression – realizing that his house is being robbed. Stan sees
his expression. A thought suddenly dawns on him that it might be the
Colonel. He turns and looks at a picture on the wall – a large head of
Colonel Blood – this verifies his suspicion, and realizing something
must be done quickly he makes one leap at the Colonel which knocks
the Colonel staggering backwards into a closet which is located at the
foot of the stairs. Stan closes and locks the door.

CUT TO the INTERIOR of CLOSET . . . The Colonel is in a terrible
rage. He starts hammering and kicking at the door. Sid rushes into
the hall. Stan runs to him and pantomimes to him that the Colonel has
returned and is locked in the closet. Sid takes this big . . .

CUT UPSTAIRS to the BEDROOM . . . The Dude is trying to fix his
collar before a mirror. His wife enters to him and gets over in
pantomime . . . What's that terrible noise downstairs. They stop and
listen. . .

CUT TO the INTERIOR of the CLOSET . . . The Colonel is still
hammering and kicking at the door.

CUT BACK TO the Dude and his wife. They make a hurried exit in
the direction of the stairs.

CUT TO the LOWER HALL. Stan and Sid on. Stan is running up
and down – Sid is trying to calm him. The Dude and his wife enter
down the stairs all excited, getting over . . . What's all this noise and
excitement? Sid motions to him to keep calm and follow him – gives
Stan orders to keep the Colonel in the closet – and leads the way into
the living room. Stan crosses to the closet – by this time the door is
beginning to give – getting loose on the hinges. Stan with great
difficulty is pushing against the door trying to keep the Colonel in

CUT TO the LIVING ROOM . . . Sid is on – talking to the Dude and
his wife – all very excited. He is explaining the situation in pantomime
and speaks title to the effect:

THIS MR. HOOKWORM AND I HAD A LAWSUIT
OVER THIS HOUSE. HE LOST AND WENT INSANE . . .

The Dude and his wife take this big.

CUT TO the HALL . . . Stan has his back to the door – still trying to hold the Colonel in.

CUT TO the INTERIOR of the CLOSET . . . The Colonel is in a terrible rage. [Crossed out: He suddenly feels in his back pocket and pulls out a gun. With an insane grin he points the gun at the lock and pulls the trigger.] He draws back – raises his foot and takes one terrific kick at the door. His foot goes clear through the panel of the door.

CUT TO the EXTERIOR of the CLOSET . . . We see the foot come through the door and land squarely on Stan's fanny. It lifts Stan clear over the banisters and right out of the scene. The door falls out – the Colonel enters, standing on the threshold and looking like an infuriated Bull. He exits to the dining room.

CUT TO the DINING ROOM . . . Colonel enters – holds it a second while he looks them all over. He is in such a rage that he cannot speak. Finally he breaks out with a title to the effect:

YOU THIEVES AND ROBBERS! WHAT ARE YOU DOING IN MY HOUSE?

The Dude and his wife take this, but Sid gets over the idea in pantomime . . . There you are! I told you so! The Dude decides that as he is now the lessee of the house it is up to him to take the matter in hand and order this lunatic out of the house. He adjusts his monocle and steps up to the Colonel and speaks title to the effect:

NOW LOOK HERE, MR. HOOKWORM –

The Colonel takes this with a dumbfounded look. The Dude then continues his title:

IF YOU DON'T LEAVE THIS HOUSE QUIETLY I'LL HAVE YOU TAKEN BACK TO THE ASYLUM.

This absolutely staggers the Colonel – his eyes literally pop out on his cheeks with rage. He gets over in pantomime . . . Asylum – Me! He pats his chest. He is nearly distracted with rage and speaks title:

DON'T YOU DARE "HOOKWORM" ME! I'M COLONEL BLOOD!

AND he bangs his fist on the table – emphasizing the statement.

The Dude gives him a look of pity and shakes his head sadly. Sid then pantomimes . . . Poor fellow! The Dude indicates Sid and speaks title:

NOW MY DEAR MR. HOOKWORM, DON'T BE SILLY!
THIS IS COLONEL BLOOD; HE TOLD ME SO.

This almost floors the Colonel. He suddenly bursts out with a wild maniacal laugh . . . HA! HA! HA! The Dude takes this and he too, breaks into a stupid laugh, thinking he has the Colonel in a good humor. Sid then laughs – echoed by Stan. Suddenly the Colonel stops laughing – realizing that they are making fun of him. He dives for a drawer in the buffet, opens it and pulls out a large gun – breaks the gun and commences to load it with big shells. The others take this and realizing that the situation is getting serious they get nervous. The wife faints and Stan catches her. The Dude getting very bold and thinking that he is going to stop all this nonsense picks up a feather duster. Sid gets over . . . this is no place for me! And makes an exit. The Dude crosses over to the Colonel – who by this time has the gun all fixed. He starts to threaten the Colonel with the feather duster. The Colonel starts to back up – preparing to take a good aim at the Dude. The Dude follows him up feeling that the Colonel wouldn't dare shoot. The Wife comes to – sees the Dude and the Colonel – she screams to the Dude to be careful – Stan starts to exit – the Colonel fires blowing all the feathers out of the feather duster into the air and leaving only the stick in the Dude's hand. The Wife screams and faints again – Stan dashing back to her just in time to catch her again. The Colonel starts to chase the Dude about the room while Stan is doing a Leon Errol with the wife. The Dude exits followed by the Colonel who is firing wildly at him as he runs. Stan and the wife do a Brodie – the wife comes to just in time to see her husband being chased thru the arch. She screams and starts after him.
    CUT TO the HALL . . . The Colonel chases the Dude up the stairs. The wife enters and follows.

>   NOTE . . . The Colonel in making a shot, at the Dude,
>   who is half way up the stairs, hits the newel post of
>   the stair case – knocking it away. As the wife enters
>   she grabs this and exits up the stairs after the Colonel.

    CUT TO an INSERT of the DOOR BELL . . .
    CUT TO A SHOT OF STAN . . . entering the hall from the dining room. Sid enters from the living room in a great hurry – pantomimes

to Stan to open the door to the transfer man. Stan rushes to the door. Sid exits to the living room to continue packing. By this time the room is pretty well stripped – carpets up – trophies off the wall etc.

CUT TO the FRONT DOOR . . . Stan opens the door, then enters. NOTE . . . This is an eccentric character. Type like Harry Bowen. The Dude comes rushing down the stairs followed by the Colonel and the wife. The Dude bumps into the transfer man – knocking him flat. He staggers up – the Colonel fires a shot at the Dude – hits the transfer man in the fanny and he does another flop. He gets up again just in time to receive a blow on the head from the wife who had just made a swing at the Colonel. This staggers the transfer man – he is in a daze.

CUT Shooting from the hall into the LIVING ROOM . . . The Dude in the lead chases around followed by the Colonel and the wife – Sid ducking the shots but still packing.

CUT BACK to Stan . . . He grabs the transfer man by the hand and makes a dash for the living room. The Dude, followed by the Colonel and wife, come tearing out of the side arch. They collide with Stan and the transfer man and all fall in a heap – they all get up & start chasing around not knowing who's who, finally they get into their original formation again & the dude followed by the Colonel & wife start up the stairs again, Stan & the transfer man enter the living room and start to lift up the trunks.

CUT UPSTAIRS to a shot . . . The Dude is on. He creeps towards a door in the hall down stage. The Colonel enters from the door behind him and the wife enters from around the corner behind the Colonel. The Dude looks in the room – the Colonel raises his gun to fire at him – the wife hits the Colonel on the head with a club – the Colonel's gun goes off, hitting the Dude in the fanny – he does a brodie.

CUT DOWNSTAIRS to the HALL . . . The transfer man is staggering beneath the weight of an enormous trunk. He trips and falls and as he does the trunk breaks away and all the silver ware falls out. Stan and Sid run in – start to grab up the silver ware. Stan exits with an armful in the direction of the front door – Sid helping the transfer man from beneath the pile of stuff.

CUT TO the EXTERIOR of the HOUSE . . . Stan enters the scene and starts to throw the silver ware in the truck. As he does so the Forest Ranger walks into the scene. Stan sees him – gives a big takem, but recovers himself and makes a flippant exit to the house –leaving the Ranger with a suspicious look on his face.

CUT TO the EXTERIOR of the HOUSE . . . Stan enters the scene and starts to place the silverware in the truck. The Forest Ranger

enters the scene – starts looking Stan up and down suspiciously. Stan
starts to go and sees the Ranger – takes it big but quickly recovers
himself. He gets coy and tries to act like a flapper. He turns to exit –
his skirt gets caught on a hook on the wagon and comes off. Stan is
unconscious of this and walks up to the front door – giving little coy
looks back to the Ranger. The Ranger just stands looking at Stan and
he gets over with an expression that he is wise. . . Stan is just about to
enter the house – Sid meets him and hands him some more stuff to
put on the wagon and exits. Stan feeling pretty confident that he has
bluffed the Ranger starts back to the wagon. As he does this the
Ranger comes walking towards him. Stan suddenly stops and
hesitates – he suddenly realizes that the Ranger is wise to him. He
discovers his dress gone and knowing that the game is up he starts
backing towards the house – the Ranger still approaching him. He
suddenly drops everything and turns and beats it. As he enters the
hall he falls over the transfer man who is just picking himself up. He
continues into the living room. Sid is on – locking a trunk. As Stan
flies past him – Sid speaks title:

WHERE ARE YOU GOING?

Stan speaks title back:

I'M NOT STAYING FOR THE MAIN EVENT!

Sid takes this and turns. As he does he comes face to face with
the Ranger. He takes it so big that he falls back over the trunk. The
Ranger scrambles over after him. Sid gets up and runs. He joins Stan
in the Hall running thru the hall with the Ranger after them. By this
time the Dude, the Colonel and the Wife come running down the stairs
and they all meet at the bottom. There should be a general rally with
the transfer man getting the worst of it. Everybody swings at
somebody else – the transfer man always getting it in the neck.
    The Forest Ranger grabs Stan and Sid by the seat of the pants
and as he starts to yank them out lap dissolve to:
    A SET UP . . . We get over that it is the outskirts of the Town. Men
are on with hoses – buckets – blankets apparently fighting a forest
fire. Smoke is coming into the scene over foreground. Sid and Stan are
being dragged into the foreground by the ranger. The Ranger points
out over the foreground getting over . . . LOOK!
    CUT TO A STOCK SHOT of a FOREST FIRE (See Currier)

BACK TO STAN and SID . . . They take it getting over that the fire is hotter than hell. The ranger shoves an enormous hose nozzle into their hands getting over . . . now get busy. He leaves the scene. Stan tries to work the stop-cock on the nozzle – no water comes out – he looks down the nozzle.

CUT to the Ranger . . . We see him turning on the fire hydrant. Show a shot of the hose filling and whipping around like a snake.

CUT to a LONG SHOT . . . We see Stan and Sid being whirled around in the air at the end of the hose.

. . . . . FADE OUT.

. . . .

September 15th. . . .

SLIPPING WIVES

Production history: Production S-18. Script finished October 18, 1926. Filmed Wednesday, October 20 through Wednesday, November 3, 1926. Copyrighted January 17, 1927, by Pathé (LU 23555). Released April 3. Two reels.

Produced by Hal Roach. Directed by Fred L. Guiol. Photographed by George Stevens. Edited by Richard Currier. Costumes by [William] Lambert. Titles by H.M. Walker. Supervising Director, F. Richard Jones. Assistant Director, Lewis R. Foster (uncredited). Story by Hal Roach (uncredited).

With Priscilla Dean (The Wife), Herbert Rawlinson (Leon, the Artist Husband), Stan Laurel (Ferdinand Flamingo/"Lionel Ironsides"), Oliver Hardy (Jarvis, the butler), Albert Conti (Hon. Winchester Squirtz).

A young woman is feeling very neglected by her husband, an artist, who is so preoccupied by his work that he hardly notices her. A family friend suggests that she hire a man to romance her and thus make the husband jealous. Conveniently, at that moment a rather brainless fellow comes to the door to deliver some paint. He instantly arouses the wrath of the butler, but is nevertheless enlisted to become the romantic rival to the husband. At a dinner party, the "rival" is introduced as a famous author, and is compelled to act out the exciting story of Samson and Delilah. His attempts to feign affection for the wife and make the husband jealous are unsuccessful, because he thinks the family friend is the husband and vice versa. Ultimately, the husband learns of the ruse and secretly forgives the delivery man, but the butler chases him out of the house, armed with a shotgun.

Laurel and Hardy's transition from two actors working in the same film into a harmonious team did not happen in an unbroken progression. They have only a couple of scenes together in *Slipping Wives*, and they are marked by Hardy's utter hatred of Laurel. In the first scene, paint delivery man Stan arrives at the front door of the artist's home, and butler Babe insists that he go to the servants' entrance at the back of the house. Stan refuses, and he and Babe begin to tussle, with the result that Babe is soon covered in white paint. This prompts his utter disgust with Stan's mere existence, which is later expressed through a violent bathtub scrubbing and a chase in which Hardy wields a shotgun.

The title may be a parody of *Foolish Wives*, Erich von Stroheim's notorious feature film of 1922. The film gives "the Artist" a name, Leon, but none to the wife. Stan's character changes from "Clive Dashwood" in the script to "Ferdinand Flamingo" in the film. Stan's nom de plume of "Lionel Ironsides" in the film was "Oliver Ironsides" in the script; one wonders if this was changed to avoid confusion with Mr. Hardy. The butler, named "Jarvis" in the film, was merely "James" in the script.

The film inserts some witty introductory titles, no doubt from the fertile mind of

PRISCILLA DEAN
The Wife

ALBERT CONTI
Hon. Winchester Squirtz

STAN LAUREL
Ferdinand Flamingo

OLIVER HARDY
Jarvis, the Butler

HERBERT RAWLINSON
Leon, the Artist Husband

Beanie Walker:

The Artist – He wanted to do something big – So he painted an elephant –

The Wife – Her birthday – Nineteen for the fourth time –

The Butler – Very proud of his ancestors – Most of them could hang by their tails –

Ferdinand Flamingo – Out of the nowhere – Going nowhere – Delivering paint –

The scene of butler Babe giving Stan a bath is not quite as long in the movie as it is in the script, but is still their most sustained scene together. The scripted gag with Stan being hidden in the ironing board closet does not appear in the film. Stan's pantomime of Samson and Delilah may have been inspired by Charlie Chaplin's pantomime of the story of David and Goliath in his 1923 film *The Pilgrim*.

The script's suggested alternate ending was used in the film, enhanced with a title wherein the policeman tells Babe, "You nearly blew my brains out!," then turns to reveal that the posterior portion of his trousers was the recipient of Hardy's rifle shot. This gag was also used in *Wrong Again* and *A Chump at Oxford*.

Babe appears without his mustache here. In the mature L&H films, this would only happen again when Babe was playing duplicate roles: in Brats as his young son, in *Twice*

Leon has learned of his wife's ruse, but Jarvis has not.

Leon thinks that his houseguest is not being shown the proper hospitality by his butler.

Two as his own sister, and in *Thicker Than Water* as a hybrid of himself and Stan.

Priscilla Dean was one of the fading stars that Roach employed for his "All-Star" series (one of which, *Wife Tamers*, starred Lionel Barrymore during a temporary career lull). She has wonderfully expressive eyes, and in her scenes with Stan she demonstrates some excellent comedy instincts. Her film career began when she acted in some Biograph one-reelers at the age of 14, in 1912; she was just shy of 30 in *Slipping Wives*. She was no stranger to slapstick comedy, having appeared in several shorts with Eddie Lyons and Lee Moran in 1916-17 for Universal. She graduated to dramatic features for that studio, starring in *The Virgin of Stamboul, Outside the Law, Under Two Flags*, and others. Just before *Slipping Wives*, she had starred in *Birds of Prey* for Columbia, still considered a "Poverty Row" studio. She made two other Hal Roach shorts, *The Honorable Mr. Buggs* (which also featured Babe as a butler) and *All for Nothing*, starring Charley Chase. She appeared in four talkie features, then married aviator Leslie Arnold and retired from film work; she died at 91 in Leonia, New Jersey.

Affable Herbert Rawlinson as the artist doesn't exactly burn up the screen, but he was popular enough to make more than 200 films from 1911 through 1927. He, too, had starred in features for Universal and had worked for Columbia just before *Slipping Wives*. Not long after making this Roach short, he left movies for four years, then returned to the screen in 1931 and continued in supporting roles in Westerns, serials and television shows. He died at 67 in Los Angeles on July 12, 1953, the day after completing his role in Ed Wood's epic feature *Jail Bait*.

Albert Conti is quite charming as the family friend. He was born in Austria-Hungary in 1887. His first film work came when he was 35, with roles in Erich von Stroheim's *Merry-Go-Round* and *The Merry Widow*. Prior to *Slipping Wives*, he'd had prominent roles in the 1925 Rudolph Valentino feature *The Eagle* and the Norma Talmadge version of *Camille* (1926). Although most of his roles in films were small and several were uncredited, he worked prolifically as an actor until joining MGM's wardrobe department in 1942; he continued there for twenty years. He died in Hollywood on January 18, 1967, eleven days before his 80th birthday.

The basic situation of *Slipping Wives* formed the story for Laurel and Hardy's 1935 short *The Fixer Uppers*. There, Charles Middleton was the preoccupied artist, Mae Busch the neglected wife, and it fell to Ollie to arouse the jealousy of her husband. Ollie did this all too well, because in the L&H remake, Middleton challenges him to a duel to the death!

PREMIS...

ALL STAR. S 18.
DIRECTOR .. FRED GUIOL

. . . . . .

CHARACTERS

THE NEGLECTED WIFE	. . .	PRICILLA DEANE.
THE HUSBAND	. . .	HERBERT RAWLINSON.
THE FRIEND OF THE FAMILY	. . .	ALBERT CONTI.
THE BUTLER	. . .	BABE HARDY.
CLIVE DASHWOOD	. . .	STAN LAUREL.

. . .

THE STORY CONCERNS: -
The Wife of a famous young Artist who is so wrapped up in his career that he unconsciously neglects her. He really loves her, and although she is aware of this, nevertheless she is deeply hurt at his attitude.

A Friend of the family – aware of the situation – advises the Wife that her only remedy is to make her Husband jealous. To effect this he conceives the idea of hiring a man to make love to her in her Husband's presence.

At this point the Comic arrives to deliver paint. The Friend sees him and suggests to the Wife that here is the man they require. The Wife makes the proposition to Stan who after a little hesitation accepts. The Friend, meanwhile has walked into another room, and Stan is under the impression that HE IS THE HUSBAND.

The Wife hands Stan over to the Butler – with orders to dress him for the occasion. In this sequence Stan and the Butler become bitter enemies.

That evening Stan is introduced to the Husband and the Friend as a prominent author – the introduction is performed in such a way as to leave Stan still under the impression that the Friend is the Husband. In this sequence Stan gets a little cock-eyed and is put to bed.

Later on complications arise by Stan seeing the Husband go into his Wife's bedroom . . . as he is still sure that the Husband is the Friend.

We go into a chase wherein the Butler participates – finally ending in a general rally. The Husband and Wife effect a reconciliation while Stan and the Butler get into trouble with a Cop outside.

. . . .

ALL STAR . . . S 18.
DIRECTOR . . . Fred Guiol.

. . . . .

FOREWORD TITLE to the effect: -
ONCE UPON A TIME THERE WAS A FAMOUS YOUNG ARTIST WHO REALLY LOVED HIS WIFE, BUT –

FADE IN . . . On the DINING ROOM of the Artist's Home. We see the Artist and his Wife finishing breakfast. The Artist is buried in a newspaper.

CLOSE UP . . . of Artist with introductory title to the effect – getting over his profession.

CUT TO INSERT . . . of newspaper. There is an article to the effect that he – the Artist – has just commenced work upon a painting that he hopes will make him internationally famous.

BACK TO . . . The Artist. He is concentrating on the newspaper and his mental attitude is that he is totally oblivious to his surroundings and anything not connected with his work.

CLOSE UP ... of Wife. Introductory title to the effect that she is the neglected Wife – suffering at the expense of her Husband's career.

TWO FIGURE SHOT . . . The Wife smiles sweetly and speaks title:

DO YOU KNOW WHAT DAY THIS IS, DARLING?

The Artist – without looking at her – glances at wrist watch and speaks title absent-mindedly:

NINE-THIRTY!

> NOTE . . . To help this gag – it must be established in
> the Wife's introductory title that it is her Birthday.

The Wife takes this – very much hurt at his neglect. She tries
however to overcome her resentment because she realizes that it is
his work that causes his attitude, and that he does really love her. At
this point the Butler enters and speaks title:

MR. SQUIRTZ TO SEE YOU SIR!

The Artist rises and starts towards door. His Wife also rises, and
as he is about to exit she smiles sweetly and speaks title:

HAVEN'T YOU FORGOTTEN SOMETHING, DARLING?

The Artist turns absent-mindedly – looks towards table – sees
newspaper and picks it up. He pantomimes his thanks to his Wife and
exits.

CLOSE UP . . . of Wife. She takes this and – as she hoped for a kiss
– she is deeply hurt. She sinks into a chair and commences to cry.

CUT TO THE INTERIOR . . . of the Artist's Studio. This is a very
luxurious set – getting over the general atmosphere of a successful
artist's studio. There are several beautiful semi-nude models on.
(NOTE. . . Use Morgan Dancers.) Off to one side we see a large half-
completed painting. Standing off from it and admiring it is the Friend
of the Family.

CLOSE UP . . . of the Friend of the Family with introductory title
to the effect:

MR. SQUIRTZ – A FRIEND OF THE FAMILY.

ANOTHER SHOT . . . The Artist enters the scene and crosses to
his Friend. He speaks title:

AH! GOOD MORNING, SQUIRTZ!

The Girls – back of the Artist – hear this – smile sweetly and in
chorus speak title:

GOOD MORNING, SIR!

The Artist takes this big. He gives the girls a look and they curtsy to him. He commences to discuss the picture with his Friend. He turns to the girls – gives them an order and they take up their positions on a dais. The Friend looks at his wrist-watch – gets over the idea that he must be on the way – pantomimes goodbye and picks up his silk hat. We see that the hat was laying on the artist's palette on the top of a stool. As the Friend exits we see that the palette has stuck to the top of his hat which he has placed on his head. The Artist starts to look for his palette – can't figure where he left it – he turns and sees it on his Friend's head. He calls to the Friend and gets over in pantomime that he wants his palette. The Friend takes off his hat and to his great surprise sees that the palette is stuck on top. He apologizes for his carelessness and hands the palette back to the Artist.

> NOTE . . . When the Friend removes the palette from the top of his silk hat show that he has a little difficulty in doing it. Also show insert of hat leaving alette and lots of sticky, gooey paint. This is to plant another gag that follows later.

The Friend exits from the Studio.

CUT TO THE DINING ROOM . . . We see the Wife still seated in the chair. She is wiping her eyes and still crying a little. Back stage through an archway we see the Friend going thru the scene. He turns and sees the Wife and stops. He then enters the room and crosses to her. The Wife quickly dries her eyes and tries to smile. The Friend shakes hands with her and gets over the idea . . . Why! What's the matter? She gets over in pantomime that her Husband is neglecting her. The Friend shakes his head getting over his sympathy. He sets his hat on a small occasional table – sits down beside her and starts to give her advice. He talks to her a moment, she getting over that she is deeply interested in what he is saying. Work this up and finish with a title to the effect:

-- AND THE THING TO DO IS TO MAKE HIM JEALOUS!

The Wife takes this and gets over the idea that she agrees, but that she is in the dark as to how to go about it. The Friend talks for a moment and then speaks title:--

-- AND WHAT WE MUST DO IS TO BRIBE A MAN TO MAKE

LOVE TO YOU IN THE PRESENCE OF YOUR HUSBAND.

The Wife takes this – thinks a moment and then turns to the
Friend. She speaks title: --

WHY DON'T YOU DO IT!

The Friend takes this big and then comes back with title: --

ME! I WOULDN'T DARE. YOUR HUSBAND WOULD
MURDER ME.

She continues to insist so that finally he begins to think it over.
CUT TO INSERT OF DOOR BELL RINGING.
CUT TO INTERIOR OF HALL WAY . . . Butler enters and opens the
front door. Stan is discovered.
CLOSE UP OF STAN . . . with introductory title: --

CLIVE DASHWOOD – WITH ARTISTIC ASPIRATIONS.
HE DELIVERS PAINT.

TWO FIGURE SHOT . . . STAN AND THE BUTLER. Stan gets over
that he is delivering paint. In one hand he is carrying a quart can of
WHITE PAINT – there is handle and lid on the can. Under the other
arm there is a package of tubes containing oil paints. The Butler very
pompously indicates that Stan go round to the servant's entrance in
the rear. Stan in a very dignified manner refuses and tries and tries to
force the Butler to accept delivery of the package. The Butler refuses
and still insists that Stan go round to the back. The argument
becomes heated and as the Butler still refuses to accept the paint Stan
decides to take it in himself. The Butler pushes him out. A struggle
ensues. During the struggle the can of paint falls to the floor – the lid
comes off – the paint runs out – the Butler slips in it – does a brodie
and his face is buried in the thick of it.
CUT TO THE INTERIOR OF THE DINING ROOM . . . The Wife and
the Friend hear the commotion and exit in that direction.
BACK TO HALLWAY . . . Stan and the Butler on. The Butler is
still on the floor – trying to wipe the paint out of his eyes. Stan is
gathering up the tubes of paint. The Wife and the Friend enter the
Scene. They take it. The Wife speaks title:

JAMES! STOP PLAYING AND SEE WHAT THE YOUNG
GENTLEMAN WANTS.

The Butler is by this time on his feet, and having seen his
mistress, he is standing at attention. The Thick white paint is running
slowly off his chin making a funny picture. He speaks title:

I THINK HE WISHES TO DELIVER SOME PAINT, MADAM!

The Butler exits from the scene. The Wife indicates to Stan that
he put the paint on the table – this he does.

CUT TO TWO FIGURE SHOT OF FRIEND AND WIFE . . . The Friend
is looking off at Stan attentively – he is getting an idea. He beckons to
the Wife who crosses to him. He whispers to her – indicating Stan. She
shakes her head, indicating . . No! The Friend argues a moment and
then speaks title:

WE COULD DRESS HIM UP – AND HE LOOKS DUMB
ENOUGH TO DO ANYTHING.

The Wife gets over the idea that the plan might work. The Friend
exits into the Dining Room to get his hat. The Wife thinks a moment
and exits in the direction of Stan.

TWO FIGURE SHOT OF WIFE AND STAN . . . The Wife smiles
sweetly at Stan and speaks title:

WOULD YOU LIKE TO EARN SOME MONEY?

Stan indicates that he would. The Wife then speaks title to Stan:

-- AND I WANT YOU TO MAKE MY HUSBAND
JEALOUS BY PRETENDING TO MAKE LOVE TO ME.

Stan takes this big. He looks at the Wife and then looks off at
Friend – he thinks that he is the Husband.

CLOSE SHOT OF FRIEND . . . He is fussing at himself before a
mirror.

BACK TO STAN AND WIFE . . . Stan turns to Wife and very
emphatically pantomimes . . . No! I will not. The Wife pleads with him
a moment and then speaks title:

I'LL PAY YOU WELL!

Stan looks at the Wife – she gives him a prop smile. He begins to weaken and the Wife seeing this – urges him to accept the proposition. Finally Stan smiles and indicates . . . Yes! The Wife looks at Stan – gets an idea and calls the Butler. The Butler enters. The Wife speaks title to him: --

JAMES! DRESS THIS GENTLEMAN FOR DINNER.
HE IS OUR GUEST FOR THE WEEK-END.

This almost floors the Butler. He hesitates The Wife looks at him sharply and he indicates . . . This way Sir! They exit up the stairs. The Wife exits in the direction of the Dining room.

CUT TO INTERIOR OF DINING ROOM . . . Wife and Friend on. The Wife gets over that the plan is working out – the Friend reassures her that everything will be all right and prepares to leave. He picks up his silk hat and places it on his head. We see that the little table on which it was placed has stuck to the crown of his hat – with the four legs sticking straight up into the air. He is unaware of this and starts to exit. The Wife sees this and takes it big, but before she can stop him he crosses the threshold of the door – the legs of the table strike the lintel and the table is knocked off, taking the whole crown of the hat with it, and we see a very funny picture of the Friend making a very dignified exit with only the brim of his hat on his head.

CUT UPSTAIRS TO THE INTERIOR OF A BEDROOM . . . Stan and the Butler on. The Butler is busy laying out a Tuxedo, collar, shirt etc. Stan is standing near the bed watching the Butler. He sees a smoking set on which is a cigar humidor. He opens it – takes out a cigar – smells it and puts it in his mouth. He reaches in his pocket for a match and is about to strike it on the beautiful, highly polished bed when the Butler sees him – lets out a yell – dives for him and grabs him just in time. Stan looks at him in surprise. The Butler produces a cigarette lighter (Dunhill Type) from his pocket – lights it and hands it to Stan. Stan lights the cigar – blows out the lighter and very nonchalantly tosses it through the open window. The Butler looks at him dumbfounded. Stan pays no attention but starts to take off his coat. The Butler recovers and indicating the clothes laid out on the bed speaks a title:

BEFORE YOU PUT ON THE MASTER'S CLOTHES

YOU'VE GOT TO TAKE A BATH.

The Butler exits in the direction of the bathroom. Stan thinks a minute and then follows him.
CUT TO INTERIOR OF BATHROOM . . . The Butler is on and fixing the plug in the bath. He turns on the water as Stan enters the scene. He stands there watching the Butler. The Butler turns – sees Stan and pantomimes . . . Come on! Hurry. Stan shakes his head and speaks title:

NO! I JUST HAD ONE ONLY LAST SATURDAY.

The Butler starts to reach for Stan who exits hurriedly into the bedroom. The Butler follows him.
CUT TO INTERIOR OF BEDROOM . . . Stan and the Butler do a little chase round the room. The Butler finally catches Stan and carries him – kicking and struggling into the Bathroom.
CUT TO INTERIOR OF BATHROOM . . . The Butler enters – carrying Stan who is still struggling violently.
The Butler slips on a bath mat – does a brodie and falls into the bath. Stan drops on the floor. The Butler – foaming at the mouth – jumps out of the bath – makes a swing at Stan, misses him and does another flop into the Bath. Stan tries to get out of the bathroom but the door is locked.
NOTE . . . When the Butler carries Stan into the Bathroom, he tucks him under one arm while he locks the door and puts the key into his pocket.
The Butler scrambles out of the Bath – makes a dive for Stan – grabs him by the collar and the seat of the pants – swings him over the bath – shoves him into the bath – and then jerks him up and down in the way a woman rinses clothes. He then sits him up – grabs the soap and starts to lather Stan's head. Business of soap getting in his eyes etc. Stan gives a helpless gesture and starts to whine.

FADE OUT.

GO TO A TITLE . . .

AFTER DINNER – AND THE PLOT THICKENS TO
SLOW MUSIC . . .

FADE IN ON THE LOWER HALL . . . Wife and Butler on. The Butler has a semblance of a black eye. Wife speaks title to him: -

IS OUR GUEST READY?

The Butler – with an air of guilt and swallowing nervously speaks title: -

HE – HE LEFT THE HOUSE AN HOUR AGO BUT
SAID HEWOULD BE BACK.

The Wife takes this big – is a little anxious and speaks title: -

WELL – AS SOON AS HE ARRIVES, SHOW HIM IN.

She exits in the direction of the Living Room. The Butler feels his black eye tenderly – shakes his head and exits from the scene.

CUT TO THE INTERIOR OF THE KITCHEN . . . The Butler enters – thinks a moment, scratching his head – and goes to the ironing-board closet. He opens the closet and we see an ironing board flat against the wall. He grabs the top of it and yanks it down. We then discover Stan laying face downward flat on the board. He grabs him by the back of the collar and slides him right off onto the floor. Stan gets up a little dazed. The Butler grabs him again and yanks him over to the kitchen door.

CUT TO THE DINING ROOM . . . The Butler enters dragging Stan. He pauses by the arch – peeps into the Living Room and sees the Husband, the Wife, and the Friend. The Friend is playing the piano – the Husband is seated in a chair, smoking his pipe in deep thought. The Wife is seated near the table, anxiously looking at her wrist watch. They are all unconsciously facing the arch. They all simultaneously look in another direction. The Butler – seeing his opportunity – makes a dash across the Dining room in the direction of the Hall. Just as they are about to exit, the Friend, the Wife and the Husband turn again in the direction of the arch – just missing seeing the Butler and Stan.

CUT TO THE HALL . . . The Butler opens the front door – rings the bell – slams the door.

CUT TO THE INTERIOR OF THE LIVING ROOM . . . The Wife hears the bell and the door slam – takes it and gets over the idea . . . Thank Heaven, he's come! The Butler appears in the archway and announces

. . . A gentleman to see you! They all turn in the direction of the arch.

CUT TO TWO FIGURE SHOT OF WIFE AND HUSBAND . . . Wife speaks title to the effect: -

DARLING - I HAVE A SURPRISE FOR YOU. I HAVE
INVITED A FAMOUS NOVELIST TO SPEND THE WEEK END.

The Husband closes the book he is reading and gets to his feet - looking off in the direction of the arch.

CUT TO THE ARCH . . . Stan makes an entrance.

CUT BACK TO ARTIST AND WIFE . . . The Husband is looking off expectantly - the Wife smiles sweetly and makes an exit.

CUT TO THE ARCH . . . The Wife enters - shakes hand with Stan - takes him by the arm and leads him out of the scene. The Butler exits.

INTERIOR OF LIVING ROOM . . . The Wife enters from the Arch with Stan. She turns to the Friend and the Artist and - indicating Stan - speaks title: -

GENTLEMEN! I WANT TO PRESENT MR. OLIVER IRONSIDES
-- THE FAMOUS WRITER OF SEA STORIES.

The Artist shakes hands with Stan and as Stan turns away, the Artist gives him a look of mingled disgust and disappointment - picks up his book - sits down and commences to read where he left off. Stan crosses to shake hands with the Friend - Stan's attitude here is that he is not altogether pleased to meet him as he thinks that HE is the Husband - having already seen him with the Wife earlier in the day. Get this point over strongly. On the top of the piano is a large photo of the Friend. Stan glances at it - then at the Friend - he then gets over that now he is perfectly sure that the man he is now shaking hands with his the Husband. The Wife smiles at Stan and she indicates that he sit beside her on the couch. Stan gives the Friend a nervous glance - hesitates a moment and sits down. An embarrassing silence ensues and Stan is uncomfortable beneath the fixed stare of three pairs of eyes. Stan begins to squirm and the Wife - feeling the situation - breaks it up with a title: -

OH MR. IRONSIDES - DO TELL US ALL ABOUT YOUR
LATEST NOVEL!

Stan gives her a double-takem - realizes the position is in - tries to get out of it but, as the Wife continues to urge him, he decides to make a stab at it. He starts off nervously but gathers courage as he goes along. He speaks title:

> MY LATEST NOVEL IS BASED ON THE STORY OF
> SAMSON AND DELILAH . . .

CLOSEUP OF ARTIST . . . He takes this and gives Stan a disgusted look getting over . . . Good God!

CLOSE SHOT OF FRIEND AND WIFE . . . They take it to each other getting over the idea . . . Now we have torn it.

CUT TO MEDIUM SHOT . . . Stan rises dramatically to explain his story. The Friend leans back in his chair and just as Stan passes him he crosses one leg over the other. Stan sees the movement of the foot from the corner of his eye and quickly draws in his fanny as though expecting a swift kick.

CUT TO THE ARCH . . . Stan enters – walks up the steps beneath the arch and turns to face the audience. He bows – smiles and speaks title:

> NOW AS YOU KNOW SAMSON WAS A VERY STRONG MAN –

He turns his back on his audience – pulls out his starched shirt front giving the impression of an enormous chest – ruffles out his hair – blows out his cheeks – frowns terribly and turns – making the picture of a strong man. He holds it a moment then struts up and down doing various pantomime to get over strength. Finally he snatches up a wooden pedestal, goes to break it across his knee – hurts his knee but fails to break the pedestal. Takes it – rubs his knee and throws the pedestal out of the scene. Follow the pedestal out of the scene. It crowns the Butler who is standing in the Hall watching Stan.

BACK TO STAN . . . He comes out of his character and speaks title: -

> THEN ONE NIGHT SAMSON STEPPED OUT AND SO THE
> NEXT DAY HE WAS VERY SLEEPY . . .

He immediately gets back into character – yawns – stretches his arms and begins to look round on the floor – like a dog trying to find some place to lie down. He goes around in a circle and finally lies down and goes to sleep – striking a funny pose. He jumps to his feet – gets out of his character and speaks another title: -

THEN CAME DELILAH. SHE WAS A LADY BARBER.

CUT BEHIND THE ARCH . . . The Butler is on – ready to cut Stan's throat. Stan enters the scene and starts to fix himself as Delilah. Stan – all ready – prepares to enter. The Butler gives him a swift kick in the fanny which knocks him out of character. Stan settles himself – gives the Butler a dirty look – and exits.

BACK TO THE ARCH . . . Stan enters and in pantomime gets over the character of Delilah. He walks across the arch – trips over the imaginary form of Samson – gives it a takem – looks jumps back over him again – gets an idea – looks around cautiously – tiptoes over to the imaginary Samson – lifts up his hair piece by piece – pantomimes a pair of scissors with his fingers – and goes through the motions of cutting off Samson's hair. He throws it to the floor. Strikes a pose – snaps his fingers – laughs dramatically . . . Ha! Ha! and exits. He then runs right back with a little jump – getting over that the Butler has kicked him in the fanny again – and takes up the position again of Samson asleep. He then pantomimes Samson's awakening. He sees the imaginary hair on the floor – gives it a double-takem – feels his head – gets over that his hair is gone – staggers to his feet – tries to walk but his knees wobble under him. He gets over that all his strength is gone and finally falls to the floor. He gets over his despair with intense dramatic emotion. He jumps to his feet out of character and speaks another title:

THEN CAME TWENTY THOUSAND PHILADELPHIANS –

Stan makes a quick exit. He then runs in and cut several times – waving his arms – shouting and gesturing others to follow – getting over the idea of a crowd of men. He pantomimes a crowd around Samson – and he – as the leader – giving them orders as to how they shall seize the imaginary Samson. Finally he drags the imaginary body up and off Raspberry and all. (See Frank Butler.) Stan steps out of character again and speaks title:

THEY THEN TOOK HIM TO THE TEMPLE OF ADENOIDS . . .

He makes a quick exit.

CUT BEHIND THE ARCH . . . Stan enters from the arch. The Butler draws back his foot as tho to kick a football. Stan sees him from the corner of his eyes and gives him his heel in the stomach – pushing the Butler onto his fanny. Stan exits.

BACK TO THE ARCHWAY . . . Stan – pantomiming a crowd enters – dragging the imaginary Samson. He props the imaginary body against one of the pillars of the arch and goes thru the motions of tying him to the pillar. He then takes the place of the prisoner – kicking at the imaginary crowd and struggling violently. He then takes the place of the imaginary leader of the mob – who goes thru the motions of sticking his fingers in the prisoner's eyes and blinding him. He then takes the place of Samson and gets over the idea that each eye has been poked out by closing each one. As the second eye closes the Butler's hand comes round the corner of the arch and viciously pokes Stan in the eye with his finger. Stan takes it and opens both eyes and after giving the Butler a dirty look, he closes his eyes again and continues his pantomime. He struggles to break away from his bonds. Stan gets out of the Samson character – runs across to the other side of the arch – and pantomimes the mob, jeering and laughing at Samson's helplessness. He then runs back and takes up the position of Samson at the pillar. He continues to struggle and then, realizing that he is helpless offers up a bum prayer (See Myer's picture). He suddenly gives a big takem – getting over that his strength is returning. He breaks his bonds with a violent gesture and starts to grope about him blindly. He lets out a scream of triumphant rage. He jumps out of character and runs across to other side where he pantomimes a terrified mob trying to escape the imaginary Samson. He runs back and takes the place of Samson still groping blindly. By this time – we the audience see that Stan is standing just in front of, but midway between, two tall brass standards upon the top of which are brass jardinières containing ferns. Stan gropes blindly with his arms outstretched and pantomimes the idea that he can feel the pillars of the temple – one on either side. He gets set – gets over the idea that he is gathering himself for one final effort – steps back and thrusts out his arms with all his strength. The step back has brought him in line with the brass standards – his hands strike them – they crash outwards and fall – one jardinière flies up into the air and lands on the Butler's head – knocking him down. The other one crowns Stan and lays him out.

NOTE . . . . MAKE CLOSE UPS AND WHATEVER SHOTS

MAY BE NECESSARY OF HUSBAND, WIFE AND
FRIEND WATCHING STAN WITH DEAD PANS
AND WHATEVER EXPRESSIONS MAY BE
NECESSARY TO HELP THE SEQUENCE.

CUT TO INTERIOR OF LIVING ROOM . . . Friend – Husband and
Wife. The Friend and the Husband – getting over their disgust – rise
and exit. The Wife runs out of the scene in Stan's direction.

CUT TO THE ARCH . . . Stan is just coming to when the Wife
enters the scene. She helps him up and leads him out of the scene in
the direction of the living room.

BACK TO LIVING ROOM . . . Stan and Wife enter the scene. The
Wife supports Stan to the couch – they sit down. The Wife gets over
her impatience – looks at her wrist-watch – looks at Stan. At that
moment the Husband enters the scene, deep in thought and carrying
a portfolio of sketches. He sits down in a chair – opens the portfolio
and starts to examine sketches. He is in such a position that Stan
can't see him. The Wife sees him and, wanting to make the most of the
opportunity, grabs Stan's hand and puts it round her waist, pulls his
head down onto her shoulder and whispers title: -

MAKE A FUSS OF ME.

Stan takes it – a little surprised – pulls away from her. The Wife
grabs him and pulls him back. Stan – looks around – and seeing that
they are apparently alone, gets over the idea . . . Gee! This is great. He
starts to reciprocate her attentions. The Wife – in Stan's arms –
glances towards her Husband to see how he his taking it. To her
disgust he hasn't even seen it but is still deeply engrossed in his book.
At that moment the Friend passes thru the scene. Stan sees him –
thinks it's the Husband – and jumps away from the Wife. The Wife
pulls him to her again – trying to draw the Husband's attention to the
situation. At that moment the Friend enters the scene again – Stan
sees him and once more jumps away. The Wife looks at the Friend and
gives him a helpless, disgusted look. The Friend looks at Stan and
beckons to him to follow him. He starts to exit in the direction of the
Dining Room. Stan looks at the Wife – looks at the Friend – and gets
over that the Friend's invitation has made him very nervous. His
mental attitude that for all he knows he may be taking him out to
shoot him for having made love to his Wife. Finally he summons up
courage and follows the Friend out of the scene.

CUT TO THE INTERIOR OF THE DINING ROOM . . . Friend enters the scene followed by Stan. Stan getting more and more nervous. The Friend crosses to a large china closet. (Note . . . This is the type of closet which stands up on four legs – two doors which when opened will permit of the audience seeing a person's legs beneath the open doors.) Friend opens the doors which hide him from view of the audience. Stan – seeing this – gets more nervous than ever and prepares himself to make a quick exit. He suddenly sees the contents of the closet and gives it a double takem. The Friend's hand comes out and beckons Stan to come closer. Stan smiles broadly and exits behind the closet door.

CUT TO AN INSERT OF THE TWO PAIRS OF LEGS . . . We see that there is a wooden bar joining the front legs of the closet. We see Stan put one foot up on the bar – then the Friend puts his up. They take their feet off the Bar. Then Stan puts his up again – this time his foot is a little wobbly and he has a little difficulty in finding it.

CUT TO THE INTERIOR OF THE LIVING ROOM . . . . Wife and Husband on. The Wife crosses to her Husband – sits on the arm of his chair and slips her arm round his neck. Her attitude is that she wishes that he would show her a little attention. She starts to stroke her Husband's hair – closes the book and generally invites him to pay her a little attention. The Husband snaps out of his absent-mindedness and smiles at her – taking her hand and stroking it.

CUT BACK TO AN INSERT OF THE TWO PAIRS OF LEGS . . . We see Stan make a determined effort to put his foot on the bar. The bar breaks and Stan falls flat on his ear so that we see him beneath the closet door. We now see that Stan has acquired a modest bun. We move back and we see the Friend close the closet and help Stan to his feet. Stan is feeling rather good and starts toward the living room. The Friend follows him.

CUT TO THE LIVING ROOM . . . Stan enters. He is just in time to see the Husband and Wife in a fond embrace – they kiss each other. Stan takes this – quickly turns and pushes the Friend back into the living room so that he won't see what is going on – still under the impression that he – the Friend is the Husband. He then attracts the Wife's attention and pantomimes – indicating the Friend – and gets over to the Wife . . . Be careful! He nearly saw you. The Husband nonchalantly crosses to a humidor. The Wife gives Stan a bewildered look. The Friend enters the room – the Wife rises and crosses to the Friend to ascertain what is the matter with Stan. Stan crosses to the Husband.

CUT TO A TWO FIGURE SHOT OF HUSBAND AND STAN . . . Stan takes a cigar lights it – digs the Husband in the ribs with his elbow – gives him a knowing look and confidentially whispers in his ear: -

ISN'T SHE A KNOCKOUT! SHE'S NUTS ABOUT ME TOO.

The Husband takes this dumbfounded. Stan glances over at the Wife – turns and whispers another title: -

JUST ANOTHER CASE OF WHERE THE BEST
MAN WINS!

This staggers the Husband.

CUT TO THE WIFE AND FRIEND . . . They have been watching Stan and the Husband, and seeing the Husband's reaction are in a state of intense nervousness as to what Stan may have been telling him. They get over the idea to each other that something must be done quickly.

CUT BACK TO STAN AND THE HUSBAND . . . The Husband thinks a moment and then gets over the idea that there is something wrong and quickly decides to see how far it will go. He smiles and pats Stan on the back to encourage him. Stan by this time is pretty pleased with himself.

CUT BACK TO FRIEND AND WIFE . . . Wife excitedly whispers title: -

GET MY HUSBAND AWAY AND I WILL GET RID OF HIM . . .

and she indicates Stan. The Friend exits from the scene; bring him on to Stan and the Husband. He pantomimes to the Husband that he wants to speak to him. The Husband excuses himself to Stan and follows the Friend out of the scene. Stan exits in the direction of the Wife.

CUT TO SHOT OF STAN AND WIFE . . . Stan puts his arms round her a couple of times – she pushes him off. Stan starts to make violent love to her – mauling her. She gets panicky and speaks title: -

THIS HAS GONE FAR ENOUGH – LEAVE THE HOUSE!

Stan pays no attention but grabs her again. She rings for the Butler. In the meantime Stan falls asleep on the Wife's shoulder. She pushes him off and he flops over assuming a funny position on the couch. The Butler enters the scene and the Wife – indicating Stan, speaks title:

PUT THIS FELLOW OUT!

She exits from the room. The Butler takes this – looks at the sleeping Stan – and gets over his satisfaction at the job in hand. He rubs his hands and approaches Stan.

TWO FIGURE SHOT OF STAN AND BUTLER . . . Butler tries to wake Stan. Stan sleepily pushes him away, getting over the idea . . . Get to Hell out of hear and leave me alone. The Butler shakes him violently dragging him to his feet. Stan – very sleepy and dazed – makes a wild swing at the Butler – misses him and does a terrible nose-dive and falls fast asleep again on the floor. The Butler grabs him by the seat of the pants and commences to drag him from the room.

At this point the Husband enters the scene. He sees Stan's condition and gets over in pantomime to the Butler . . . what are you going to do with him? The Butler gets over . . . I'm going to throw him out. The Husband – his mental attitude is that he would like to see just how far Stan would go – speaks title:

YOU HAD BETTER PUT HIM TO BED IN YOUR
ROOM – JAMES.

The Husband exits. The Butler takes this big and looks at Stan in disgust. He drags Stan to his feet again. Stan – sleepy and dazed – gets annoyed – makes a wild swing at the Butler – misses him and does a terrible nose-dive. The Butler drags him to his feet – Stan tries to resist and they go into a struggle.

FADE OUT . . .

GO TO A TITLE . . .

THEN CAME MIDNIGHT – OR THEREABOUTS.

FADE IN ON THE INTERIOR OF THE HUSBAND'S BEDROOM . . . We see the Husband – in pyjamas and lounging robe – sitting under a lamp and reading. From time to time he gets over the idea that he is listening.

CUT TO INTERIOR OF WIFE'S BEDROOM . . . We see the Wife in very attractive negligee. She is fixing her hair before the mirror. Cut to a small kitten playing on the floor – the kitten is playing with a long silk stocking.

CUT TO A SHOT SHOWING THE KITTEN ENTERING THE STOCKING.

CUT BACK TO WIFE . . . She is looking into a hand mirror. Suddenly she gives a big takem as she sees a long white stocking crawling slowly across the floor – getting over the impression of a long white snake – the kitten being inside. She screams.

CUT TO INTERIOR OF HUSBAND'S BEDROOM . . . . A flash – he hears the scream.

CUT TO THE INTERIOR OF FRIEND'S BEDROOM . . . HE HEARS the scream and sits upright in bed.

CUT TO INTERIOR OF BUTLER'S . . . We see the Butler and Stan asleep in the Butler's double bed – a close shot. The Butler's arm is extended under Stan's chin and with his hand he is holding onto the bedrail – thus imprisoning Stan in a sort of stranglehold. Stan hears the scream – tries to sit up and feels the Butler's arm holding him down.

CUT BACK TO THE WIFE . . . The stocking does a porpoise leap at her. She screams again.

CUT BACK TO BUTLER'S BEDROOM . . . Stan hears the scream – tries to free his neck from the Butler's arm – but finds that he can't without waking him.

CUT BACK TO WIFE'S ROOM . . . She goes to the door and opens it. She looks in the direction of her Husband's bedroom and speaks title: -

DARLING!

CUT BACK TO BUTLER'S ROOM . . . Stan hears this – gets over that he thinks she is calling for him. He makes another effort to escape, but fails. He thinks a moment – gets an idea – reaches up to the pillow with his free arm – pulls out a small feather and drops it on the Butler's nose. The Butler feels this – his face twitches and finally he removes his hand from the bedrail to brush off the feather – as though it were a fly. Stan – the moment he does this – sits up – slips the pillow where his body had been. The Butler's arm immediately falls across it and he grasps the bedrail again firmly with his hand.

Stan slips out of bed and goes to the door and looks out.

CUT TO THE HALLWAY ... We see the Husband tip-toe out of his room in the direction of his Wife's bedroom. Stan sees this – takes it big – and tiptoes cautiously after the Husband. The Husband enters his Wife's room and closes the door.

CUT TO INTERIOR OF WIFE'S BEDROOM .... The Husband enters and closes the door behind him. He looks at his Wife and then round the room. His mental attitude is one of suspicion – getting over the idea that he expected to find Stan there. The Wife points to the stocking that is running round in circles. The Husband picks it up and shakes out the kitten. He relaxes – his attitude being that his suspicions were unfounded and that he feels rather a heel for having suspected his Wife.

CUT BACK TO THE HALLWAY ... We see Stan peeking cautiously thru the keyhole. He sees the Husband and the Wife kissing each other goodnight. He takes this big. At that moment the Friend exits from his room – looking out. The room is opposite the Wife's. Stan sees him – gives him a double takem – gives him a sickly smile and starts back towards his own room – he exits into the Butler's room. The Friend satisfied that he has gone – re-enters his room and closes the door. Stan pops his head out of his room and seeing that the coast is clear, quickly tiptoes back to the Wife's bedroom. He quietly opens the door and looks in.

CUT BACK TO THE INTERIOR OF THE WIFE'S BEDROOM ... As Stan looks in the Wife and Husband break away from their embrace. Stan whispers title: -

LOOK OUT! HER HUSBAND IS OUTSIDE!

Stan exits – closing the door quickly. The Husband takes this. He looks at his Wife suspiciously – speaking title: -

WHAT'S THE MEANING OF THIS?

She starts to explain to him ...

CUT TO THE HALLWAY ... Stan listening outside the door. Friend quickly enters from his room – Stan startled does a little jump. The Friend – thinking that things are going too far, speaks title: -

WHAT ARE YOU DOING HERE?

Stan – feeling that he is caught in a delicate situation – whispers title: -

THAT GUY'S IN THERE WITH YOUR WIFE!

The Friend takes this big – staggered. He gasps and speaks title: -

MY WIFE –

CUT BACK TO WIFE'S BEDROOM . . . The Wife is still explaining. She finishes with title: -

AND SO I ENGAGED HIM TO MAKE YOU JEALOUS.

The Husband goes into an assumed rage (we do not let the audience know that this attitude is to convince the Wife that he IS jealous) as he realizes that he has been to blame for neglecting his Wife. He rushes to a drawer – pulls out a gun and pantomimes the idea . . . I'm going to kill the man who has wrecked my home!
CUT BACK TO HALLWAY . . . Friend and Stan on. Friend speaks title: -

THAT MAN IS HER HUSBAND!

He indicates the Husband in the bedroom. Stan takes this. At this moment the door opens and the Husband rushes out. He is in a terrible rage. Stan and the Friend fall over each other in an effort to get out of his way. Stan and the Friend start to run down the hall – Stan does a flop and the Friend falls over him. Just as the Friend is getting to his feet the Husband fires a shot which hits the Friend in the fanny. The Friend leaps into the air – holding his fanny, and makes a wild dash for his room. The Wife comes out of her room and just as the Husband fires another shot at Stan she screams and runs back.
CUT TO THE BUTLER'S ROOM . . . The Butler sits up in bed – wondering what all the uproar is about.
CUT TO THE HALL . . . Stan and the Husband on the run. The Husband finally corners Stan. He drops his menacing attitude and calms Stan who is expecting to be shot. He whispers a hurried title: -

GET OUT OF HERE QUICK! I DON'T WANT TO SHOOT YOU.

I'M MAKING MY WIFE THINK THAT I'M JEALOUS.

At this point the Wife comes running out of her room. The Husband sees her and quickly assumes the attitude of the outraged husband. He fires another shot – deliberately wide of Stan. Stan – for the Wife's benefit – takes this. He falls to the floor with his hands pressed to his side – getting over that he is shot. He winks to the Husband and starts to do a dying scene. The Wife thinking that he is really shot – screams – puts her hands over her eyes and runs back into the bedroom. At this moment – whilst the Husband is still menacing Stan for the Wife's benefit – the Butler runs out of his room – takes in the situation of the enraged Husband. He rushes over to the Husband and gets over in pantomime . . . Leave him to me, Sir. I'll fix him. He runs into his room and dashes back with a shot gun. He levels it at Stan – Stan takes it on the run – and before the Husband can stop, the Butler is after him. Stan makes a wild dash into the Wife's bedroom, followed by the Butler and the Husband who is by this time terrified that the Butler is really going to kill Stan.

CUT TO THE WIFE'S BEDROOM . . . Stan enters on the run – terrified – he doesn't know which way to turn and leaps into bed and pulls the covers up over his head. The Butler and the Husband run in. Stan and the Wife sit up in bed simultaneously. The Butler does a belly flop – the gun goes off in the direction of the bed – the bed breaks away to the floor. Stan scrambles out on the run.

CUT TO THE FRIEND'S BEDROOM . . . The Friend is on rubbing his fanny. He sits down in a chair but jumps up again quickly – getting over that his fanny hurts him. He gets a large soft cushion – places it beneath his fanny and sits down cautiously. He gives a sigh of relief and relaxes.

CUT DOWNSTAIRS . . . We see Stan running down the stairs, followed by the Butler and the Husband. Stan does a trip and falls – the Butler takes aim at Stan as he gets up and just as he is about to fire the Husband runs up behind him and with his arm he jerks up the barrel of the gun. Both barrels go off in the direction of the ceiling.

CUT DIRECTLY TO THE FRIEND'S BEDROOM . . . He is sitting in the chair. As the gun goes off downstairs we see a puff of smoke beneath the chair – followed by a great cloud of feathers as the shots tear the pillows to pieces.

CUT DOWNSTAIRS . . . The chase is still on. Stan dashes out of the front door – followed by the Butler. The Wife enters the scene and grabs the Husband – putting her arms round his neck. The Husband assumes the role of the forgiving husband – winks to the audience and kisses her. At this moment the front door opens. Babe enters – his collar is torn off – his clothes ripped and he has two black eyes – giving the impression that Stan has beaten him up. Suddenly Stan is shoved thru the door – he is also torn up and he, too, has black eyes. Stan stands there making a funny picture. A Cop enters behind him and gets over in pantomime the idea . . . If there's any more noise I'll kill you both.

FADE OUT . . . .

We suggest another finish . . .

As the Husband kisses the Wife – the door opens and the Butler comes in in the same condition as above – giving the impression that Stan has torn him up. A Cop enters with a shotgun in his hand (the one that the Butler had exited with). He throws the gun down and roughly warns the Butler about carrying firearms. As he turns to make his exit – we the audience see that the seat of his pants have been shot away – getting over that the Butler had done this.

FADE OUT . . . .

. . . .

OCTOBER 18th, 1926.

LOVE 'EM AND WEEP

Production history: Production S-19. Working title: *Better Husbands Week*. Written circa mid-November 1926. Filming was supposed to commence on November 25 but took place from Friday, November 26 through Tuesday, December 7, 1926. Retakes shot by Fred Guiol on Wednesday, January 12 and Thursday, January 13, 1927. Copyrighted April 11, 1927 by Pathé (LU 23846). Released June 12, 1927. Two reels.

Produced by Hal Roach. Directed by Fred L. Guiol. Photographed by Floyd Jackman. Edited by Richard Currier. Gowns by [William] Lambert. Supervising Director, F. Richard Jones. Titles by H.M. Walker. Story by Hal Roach, Fred Guiol, and Stan Laurel (all uncredited).

With Mae Busch (Peaches, an actress), Stan Laurel (Romaine Ricketts), Jimmie Finlayson (Titus Tillsbury), Oliver Hardy (Judge Chigger), Charlotte Mineau (Mrs. Aggie Tillsbury), Vivien Oakland (Mrs. Ricketts), Villie Latimer (Old Lady Scandal), Charlie Hall (Tillsbury's Butler), Ed Brandenburg (Waiter), May Wallace (Mrs. Chigger), Leo Sulky (Restaurant Manager), Clara Guiol (Maid).

Prominent businessman Tillsbury is about to have his sterling reputation tarnished when an old flame (Busch) undulates into his office and threatens to expose him as an unfaithful philanderer. Her "evidence" is a photograph from long before Tillsbury's marriage, showing him with "Peaches," both of them wearing bathing suits. It so happens that the unsuspecting Mrs. Tillsbury is giving a dinner party for other moral bastions of the community. Lest Peaches decide to cling to this soirée, Mr. Tillsbury dispatches his faithful secretary, Ricketts (Stan), to her apartment, to keep her at bay until a settlement can be arranged. However, the old flame is burned up by this, and descends upon the Tillsbury home to exact her revenge.

Love 'em and Weep is one of many Hal Roach silent comedies populated by old flames and jealous spouses.

Among the differences between the script and the film are the suggestions for the casting. Vivien Oakland – a vaudeville and Broadway veteran with her husband and partner John T. Murray since 1917, but from 1926 onward concentrating on films – won the part of Stan's wife. This was originally suggested for Gertrude Astor, who would eventually play Ollie's wife in *Come Clean* (1931).

The script suggests for the part of the town gossip Gale Henry, a lanky, loose-limbed and sometimes cross-eyed comedienne who had starred in many short comedies since the Teens. Instead, it went to the much more threatening Villie Latimer, a 46-year-old Tennessee native who specialized in playing harridans in short comedies, among them *Chasing the Chaser* (1925) a Hal Roach comedy written and directed by Stan Laurel and starring a certain bald-headed Scotsman.

And that would be James Henderson Finlayson, a longtime presence at the Hal Roach lot. *Love 'em and Weep* marks the first time that Finlayson, Laurel and Hardy all appeared in the same film; he would become the most memorable of all the L&H supporting players. Born in Larbert, Stirlingshire, Scotland on August 27, 1887, James was studying business management at George Watson College in Edinburgh. There he met Andy Clyde and his actor-producer father John, and joined their theatrical troupe. He came to Broadway with the 1912 hit *Bunty Pulls the Strings*, toured in a vaudeville sketch (*The Concealed Bed*) and began making films in 1916.

In 1919 he signed with Mack Sennett and played crooked bankers, lawyers and other villains; this led to a contract with Hal Roach in 1922. He frequently appeared as a foil to Stan Laurel in his solo Roach comedies of 1923-24. Occasionally, Finlayson starred in the Hal Roach shorts (he is definitely given the spotlight here), but he shone most brightly as a supporting comic. He would ultimately appear in almost 250 films through 1951, 33 of them with Stan and Babe. He passed away at 66 from a heart attack at his Hollywood home on October 9, 1953. His work in *Love 'em and Weep* is outstanding, and he proves that there was more to his artistry than just squinting his right eye and saying "D'ohhh!!"

Two more frequent visitors to the Laurel and Hardy world also make their debuts with the boys in this film. Mae Busch, born in 1891 in Melbourne, Australia, was educated in a convent and appeared in legitimate theater and vaudeville before making her first film in 1912. She worked prominently with Mack Sennett and ultimately starred in several early 1920s features, such as Stroheim's *Foolish Husbands* and the Lon Chaney drama *The Unholy Three*. A nervous breakdown and a bad temper spelled the end of her starring career, but she ultimately appeared in more than 125 films, 13 of them with Stan and Babe. She died of cancer in Woodland Hills, California on

MAE BUSCH
Peaches

STAN LAUREL
Romaine Ricketts

JIMMY FINLAYSON
Titus Tillsbury

OLIVER HARDY
Judge Chigger

CHARLOTTE MINEAU
Mrs. Aggie Tillsbury

April 19, 1946.

Charlie Hall, known affectionately around the Roach lot as "The Little Menace," was a native of Birmingham, England, born there on August 18, 1899. He worked as a carpenter in his hometown, and continued to do so at the Roach lot all through the 1930s and '40s when not working in front of the camera. His first film was the 1923 Stan Laurel short *Mother's Joy*, the first of 300 films in which Charlie would appear through 1956. Along with his 47 L&H films, Charlie can be seen in *College* with Buster Keaton, the Astaire-Rogers musical *The Gay Divorcee*, and comedies starring Wheeler and Woolsey, Leon Errol, and Abbott and Costello. He was working as a prop maker for Warner Bros. when he died at 60 in North Hollywood on December 7, 1959.

While the script for *Love 'em and Weep* specifies that Finlayson is running for Mayor, the film doesn't make that distinction. The "Morgan Dancers" referred to in the script were the Marion Morgan Dancers, who staged elaborate interpretations of

VIVIEN OAKLAND
Mrs. Ricketts

VILLIE LATIMER
Old Lady Scandal

CHARLIE HALL
Tillsbury's Butler

MAY WALLACE
Mrs. Chigger

GALE HENRY
Planned for
Old Lady Scandal

GERTRUDE ASTOR
Planned for
Mrs. Ricketts

classical legends; they were well known in Hollywood and appeared in several films, among them the John Barrymore 1926 feature *Don Juan*.

A "takem" is a surprised reaction, which of course was Finlayson's specialty. A "108" is a particular kind of funny fall in which the participant practically somersaults in mid-air before falling flat on his back; the term seems to have originated with Ben Turpin, who joked about having so many variations on the pratfall that he would call out to his directors, "Which one do you want, number 108?"

I'm not sure which Hal Roach-Mabel Normand film contained the "Gabriel blow your horn title," but Oliver Hardy would repeat the phrase when he took over Finlayson's role for *Chickens Come Home*, the 1931 Laurel and Hardy remake of this picture.

If the gag with Finlayson attempting to get out of the house by buying some cigars was in the original version of *Love 'em and Weep*, it no longer survives. However, it was definitely used in *Chickens Come Home* – where Finlayson, now playing Hardy's butler, supplied the fresh box of cigars that Mr. Hardy didn't really want.

The golf-club gag at the curbside is a highlight of the film, but instead of merely putting as per the script, Stan gives a mighty swing, looks far in the distance for the imaginary golf ball, and jumps into the car as it speeds off.

Babe, as "Judge Chigger," does very little except make polite conversation with May Wallace, who plays his wife. (She would appear in many Our Gang comedies, such as *Love Business*, and she provided the voice of Ollie's sister in *Twice Two*.) Babe wears a large, brushy mustache here, in contrast to none at all in *Slipping Wives*. The only moments that he shares with Stan are a couple of extreme long shots at the very end of the film.

The entire last section of the script was entirely reworked so that when Mae arrives at Finlayson's house, Fin introduces her as Stan's wife. (In the film, Stan's actual wife does not arrive until the very end of the picture.) The scenes with Jimmy and his wife in their bedroom – and the amazing finale involving the butler – were jettisoned in favor of a great gag in which Stan and Finlayson attempt to smuggle the unconscious Mae out of the house by putting her astride Finlayson's back and covering both of them with a long housecoat as Stan escorts his "wife" out the door. (Mae really proved that she could take some strenuous physical-comedy business in these scenes.)

Naturally, this ruse doesn't work – especially when the bent-over Fin looks out from under the "wife's" coat and sees his own little bride glaring at him. (He remarks to her, "I'll bet you suspect something!") By this time, the real Mrs. Laurel has arrived on the scene. Babe begins laughing heartily as Laurel and Finlayson's wives chase them around the front lawn of Finlayson's estate, and receives a wallop from his own wife for showing such merriment. For her part, Mae scampers away with no retribution at all.

S-19

Cast:

Mae Busch – A Gold Digger.
Jim Finlayson – Running for Mayor.
Charlotte Minneau – His Wife.
Stan Laurel – His Secretary.
Gertrude Astor – Stan's Wife.
Gale Henry – a Gossip.
Babe Hardy – Chief of Police [crossed out on original script
    and replaced with "Judge"]
    – Babe's wife.

Open in Finlayson's private office. He is reading and rehearsing a speech which he is going to make during election time. The theme of the speech is "Keep the city clean from vice," etc., getting over that Finlayson is a clean-living, highly respected citizen. He has Stan as his audience, who keeps applauding Finlayson at the wrong time; in other words he is trying to "Yes" Finlayson.

Cut to the outer office, several stenographers on. The door suddenly opens and in walks Mae Busch. The way she is dressed and her manner gets over she is the gold-digger type. One of the girls comes over to her and asks her business. She gets over she wishes to see Finlayson.

The girl exits to Finlayson's office and tells him there is a lady to see him. He is very annoyed at the interruption and tells the girl he is too busy to see anybody. He chases the girl out and slams the door.

She tells Mae that Finlayson can't see her. Mae just pushes the girl aside and makes her entrance to Finlayson's office. Finlayson turns and sees her and has a big takem. She crosses over to Finlayson, puts her arm around him and gives him a big kiss, and speaks title, "Just the same old bald-headed daddy."

Stan takes this and as Jimmy tells him to get out, he makes an embarrassed exit.

Jim indicates for her to sit down in a chair; at the same time he sits down in his swivel chair at the desk. She ignores the chair offered and walks deliberately over and sits on his lap. Jim takes it and finally recovers himself and speaks title, "Well, what do you want?"

She pantomimes, Money." Jimmy gets over "Absolutely nothing doing!" and bangs his fist on the table. Mae then opens her purse and brings out a postal card picture and shows it to Jim. Jim takes a look at it and nearly does a 108.

Cut to insert of the picture and show Jim and Mae in bathing suits on the beach, posed like the Morgan dancers.

Jim then speaks title to her, "That was years ago, before I was married." She comes back with title, "They wouldn't know that – you haven't altered a bit." Jimmy bangs his fist again on the table and says "This is an outrage – you can't get away with that stuff." She holds up the picture admiringly and says, "That would look swell in the morning paper, especially with you running for Mayor." Jimmy comes back with title similar to the "Gabriel blow your horn" title in the Normand picture. Mae gets over, "Well, what are you going to do about it?" Jimmy thinks a minute and speaks title to the effect, "I'll meet you tonight at seven and take you to dinner, and make a settlement."

Mae gets over that's O.K. with her, takes out a long cigarette holder and cigarette and lights it, Jimmy all the time looking at her, giving her the one-eye, disgusted looks, etc.

Cut to the outer office; door opens and in walks Charlotte Mineau, Jimmie's wife. Stan sees her, grabs a bunch of letters off the desk and tears into Finlayson's office.

Cut to Finlayson's office; Stan enters and speaks title, "Your wife's here!" and makes a quick exit.

Jim pushes Mae off his lap, she landing on the floor on her fanny. He picks her up and rushes her wildly into a closet and closes the door just in time as his wife enters.

Jim gives her a "Hello Mama" look, sees the long cigarette holder lying on the floor with the lighted cigarette in it, takes it big, picks it p and starts smoking it. Charlotte looks at him rather surprised to see him smoking. Jimmie alibis about it.

Charlotte then speaks title to the effect, "darling, I've arranged a little supper party for this evening and invited the Chief of Police and his wife and Parson Brown and his wife. Be sure to be home early – they mean so much to you in your campaign."

Jimmy takes this big by taking a big puff on the cigarette. He draws so hard that the cigarette goes clear through the holder, and he gets over it went down his throat.

Charlotte gets over she wants to wash her hands. She crosses to the closet that Mae is hiding in, opens the door and we see a wash basin. Alongside of this is a roll of towel. At the bottom of the towel is standing a laundry basket. Charlotte washes her hands and starts to dry them on the towel, pulling it from the top. Jimmy by this time is in a cold sweat, as he knows that Mae is hiding behind this towel. Charlotte makes another pull on the towel, at the same time looking toward Jim. As she does this, the towel comes off the roller, exposing Mae. Jimmy seeing this does a bum faint to attract his wife's attention.

Charlotte walks over to Jim and picks him up. Jimmy pantomimes in back of her to Mae to close the door, which she does. Jimmie then gets up and gets over to his wife that he feels much better. His wife then exit, getting over, "Don't be late for the supper."

Jimmie crosses to the closet door and opens it. Mae walks out. Jimmie says "I'm sorry, but we'll have to call it off – I have a dinner engagement at my home." Mae looks at him and gets over by shaking her head and telling him that he is to keep the appointment with her. She opens her pocket book, hands him a card and speaks title, "That's where I live – meet me there at seven. And if you don't ---" She then brings the picture out of her pocket book and shows it to Jimmie, and exits.

Jimmie sinks into his chair and presses the bell.

Cut to the outer office. Mae exits through the door and Stan exits to Jim's office.

Cut to Jim's office; Stan enters. Jimmie looks at him and gets over, "You've got to help me out." He hands Stan the card and speaks title to the effect, "Meet her at seven and take her to the Blue Bird Cafe – I'll be over there later."

Stan speaks title, "But what about my wife?" Jim speaks title, "Tell her you're working." Stan gets over it would be useless, and Jim comes back with title, "If you don't you're fired!" Stan picks up the phone and calls his wife.

Cut to Stan's home and introduce his wife, Gertrude Astor, and Gale Henry, the gossip. Gertrude answers the phone.

Back to Stan; he tells her he won't be home as he has to work tonight.

Back to Gertrude; she gets over "Nothing doing."

Back to Stan; he pantomimes to Jim that it's no use. Jim gets over "Let me talk to her." He takes the phone from Stan, talks to Gertrude getting over that Stan has to work and that's final.

Back to Gertrude; she gets over she is satisfied that everything is O.K. She hangs up and gets over to Gale that Stan won't be home as he has to work. Gale gets over "That's a lot of applesauce – don't believe it."

Back to Stan and Jim. Jim is giving Stan a roll of bills. He speaks title to Stan to the effect to buy himself a Tux and take this woman to the cafe and entertain her till he gets there. Stan gets over he is a little worried, and starts counting the money. FADE OUT.

Fade in on the boudoir of Mae's apartment. A maid is on lyaing out evening dress, wrap, etc.

Cut to insert of bell, hand presses button.

Back to the maid; she hears it, crosses to the door of the apartment, opens it, and we see Stan all dressed up in Tuxedo, derby hat and overcoat. He gets over he wants to see Mae. The maid motions for him to enter. As she closes the door she indicates for him to sit down and she exits to tell Mae. Stan gets seated, looking around the apartment.

Alongside of him is a little table upon which is a vase of flowers, and leaning against the vase is an enlarged picture of Jim and Mae, a reproduction of the picture she showed Jim in the office. Stan sees this, takes it and gets over in his own mind it would be a good idea if he got that away from Mae. He looks around cautiously, quietly picks the picture up and puts it in his pocket with a satisfied smile.

Stan is seated in the foreground of the set. Mae enters from the bedroom backstage, in a very light flimsy negligee. She kind of takes it when she sees Stan, as she was expecting Finlayson. She comes down to the foreground to Stan. Stan gives her a double takem and gets up. She demands to know what he is doing there. Stan hands her the card that Jimmy gave him and explains in a title to the effect that Jimmy told him to take her to the cafe and he would be over later. She looks at Stan in a disbelieving manner and walks right over to the phone.

Cut to Finlayson's home; he is seated at the supper table with his wife and friends. Butler enters and speaks title, "Mr. Finlayson wanted on the phone." Jimmy takes it, gets up rather nervously and exits to the telephone.

Cut to Mae on the other end; she starts to bawl him out, then speaks title, "If you double cross me I'm going right over to your joint."

Back to Finlayson; he takes it big and speaks whispered title to the effect that he will keep the appointment and not to do anything rash. He hangs up the phone and discovers that the butler has been standing alongside of him all the time and he is in the know that it was a dame. Jim very embarrassed feels in his pocket, pulls out a $5.00

bill and hands it to the butler, getting over "Not a word to the wife." He exits back to the dining room.

Cut to Mae's apartment; she has just hung up the phone. She crosses over to Stan and says "I'll be ready in ten minutes." She starts to exit. Stan pulls a cigarette out, gets a match and just as Mae is about to enter the bedroom he speaks title to her, "Do you mind if I smoke?" Mae stops in the doorway, turns and looks back at Stan and speaks title, "I don't care if you burn up," and exits. Stan sulks and makes an exit.

Cut to exterior; Stan comes down the steps of the apartment and sits in the car. At this point Gale Henry enters the scene. She passes the car, sees Stan and takes it big. Stan sees her and his hat goes up in the air. Gale starts questioning Stan and he gets all fussed up. She asks him how his wife is, etc., embarrassing him to death.

Stan begins to get so uncomfortable that he accidentally leans on the button of the horn. He takes it.

Cut to the front of the apartment house and we see dames in negligees looking out of every window.

Gale and Stan see this. Gale gives Stan a knowing look.

At this point Mae enters the scene at the top of the apartment steps. Stan sees her and gets over it's all up now. He thinks quick, pulls Gale's head to him and whispers in her ear, at the same time pantomiming with his hand for Mae to go back. Mae doesn't pay any attention, but keeps on coming. She gets to the car, pushes Gale aside, slips into the seat alongside of Stan and puts over title, "let's go, honey." Stan gets all flustered and by mistake puts the gear shift into reverse. Instead of going forward he backs into a Ford and hits it so hard the whole Ford collapses. Stan finally gets it inot the right gear and the car pulls out of the scene.

Gale gets over she is going to find out more about this and hails a passing Taxi and follows.

Lap dissolve to exterior of the cafe. Stan and Mae drive in and stop. Mae is seated on the side of the car next to the curb. Stan crawls all over her trying to get out, stepping all over her, etc. Finally he gets out and opens the door. Mae steps out and they enter the cafe.

Cut to interior of the cafe. Stan and Mae enter and stop at the check room. The check boy helps Stan off with his coat. As he pulls off his overcoat, he pulls off the inner coat too, leaving him in his shirt sleeves. Stan takes Mae by the arm and enters the cafe. Mae discovers it, Stan takes it big and runs back and gets his coat.

By this time the head waiter has shown Mae to her seat and Stan enters on the run. As he crosses the dance floor he slips and does a brodie. A waiter helps him to his feet and seats him at the table with Mae.

Mae speaks title getting over she is not very hungry. The waiter hands her the menu and she starts to order. Each order she gives the waiter, he keeps writing it down. He finally fills up a page and turns over, fills up a second page and turns over to the third. Make cuts of Stan taking this. He looks a bit worried, feels in his pocket and pulls out a $5.00 bill. Mae finishes her order. The waiter then turns to Stan and gets over "What'll you have?" Stan says, "Just a cup of coffee." The waiter exits.

Cut to living room of Finlayson's home. Jim and his wife and the guests are on. Jim has a nervous attitude, keeps looking at his watch, and gets over he has something on his mind; he is trying to figure how to break away. He sees a box of cigars on the table and suddenly has a bright idea. He backs up to the table, gets the box of cigars and holds them in back of him. He then crosses to the window, which is partly open, and throws them out.

Cut to the exterior; the box of cigars lands on a cop's hea, who is just passing by, knocking his hat off.

Back to the interior; Finlayson speaks title to Babe, "How about a cigar, Judge?" Babe acquiesces and Jim goes to the table as if expecting to find the box of cigars there. He starts looking around and gets over to his wife "Where are the cigars?" His wife gets over they were there a little while ago.

Jim feeling that his plan has worked, speaks title to the effect, "I'll go out and get some." He starts for the archway. The butler walks in and speaks title, "An officer to see you, sir." Jim takes it. The cop walks in with the box of cigars in his hand, hands them to Jim and gets over he found them outside. Jim takes the box of cigars and thanks him. The cop salutes them all and makes an exit. Jim feels very foolish, giving sly looks at his wife, who is looking at him suspiciously. He starts to hand the box of cigars to the Judge.

Cut back to the cafe; Stan and Mae on at the table. Mae gets over she is getting impatient waiting for Finlayson. She lifts up her leg, exposing an ankle watch, and looks at the time. She looks at Stan and indicates the watch and gets over, "If he is not here in half an hour I'm going after him." Stan becomes all embarrassed seeing her leg and starts to plead with her not to do anything rash.

Stan then decides to try and humor her. He starts to get affectionate with her, puts his arm around her neck and she throws it off. Work this up until he starts mauling her, Mae getting more annoyed every minute. He puts his arm around her and whispers in her ear, "What time is it?" Mae in a brazen manner brings her ankle up across the other knee. Stan gets over he can't see the time from there, so he takes her ankle and lifts her foot up onto the table to get a good look at the time.

Stan suddenly does a double takem and looks out of the set.

Cut across to another table and we see Gale Henry sitting there looking with a frozen pan at Stan, which breaks into a grin.

Cut back to Stan; he pushes Mae's foot away from him, which places her whole leg on top of the table. She starts struggling to get it off, gives a terrific heave and the whole table comes over. The chairs slip from under them and they are in a heap.

Two waiters rush in, help them to their feet and straighten things up. Mae gets over she is going to phone Finlayson. Stan takes this big. Mae exits and Stan gives a silly grin at Gale as he follows her.

Cut to telephone; Mae enters and picks up the phone. Stan enters and tries to persuade her not to do it.

Cut to Finlayson's home. Insert phone bell ringing.

Cut to living room; Finlayson and the Judge and his wife are on. Finlayson gets over he hears the phone bell, excuses himself and makes an exit.

Cut to the hall; Finlayson's wife is on just answering the phone. Finlayson enters and gives it a takem.

Cut to the cafe, Mae at the phone. She speaks title, "I want to talk to Mr. Finlayson.."

Cut back to Finlayson's wife; she takes it. Finlayson grabs the phone from her and prepares to take the message.

Back to the cafe; Stan grabs the phone from Mae, pushing her aside, and starts talking.

Back to Finlayson, very much relieved to hear Stan's voice.

Back to Stan; he gets over title, "You'll have to hurry – I can't keep her here much longer."

Back to Finlayson; he starts talking in a buisness-like manner. His wife is still standing alongside of him. Finlayson finally speaks title to the effect, "All right, old chap, I'll see you in the morning," and hangs up. He looks at his wife and speaks title, "A dear old pal of mine – we used to bunk together years ago – in fact we were inseparable." He exits to the living room. She gives him a look and follows.

Cut to the living room. Jimmie and the wife enter. The Judge speaks title to Finlayson to the effect, "Sing us one of your old songs,

Jim." Jim ges over he doesn't feel like singing, and speaks title, "The pipes ain't what they used to be." The Judge's wife gets over "Please do," and indicates to Jim's wife to sit down at the piano and play for him.

Finlayson's wife sits at the piano, looks through some music, pulls a sheet of music out and hands it to Jim with a dirty look. Jim takes the copy, looks at it and we go to insert of the title of the song, "You May Be Fast But Your Mama's Going to Slow You Down." Jim gives a big takem and looiks at his wife with an expression conveying "I wonder if she is wise?" His wife strikes a chord and Jim starts to sing.

Cut to the cafe, check room set. Mae is pacing up and down, Stan walking up and down with her trying to quiet her. Mae finally pushes Stan aside, brabs her cape, speaks title to Stan, "I'm going over to get that guy." She starts to exit. Stan tries to pull her back, she gives him a push, knocking him on his fanny, and makes a wild exit. Stan gets up and quickly grabs the phone.

Cut to insert of phone bell; then to the living room of Finlayson's home. Finlayson stops singing, gets over he hears the phone, makes a dash out of the room with his wife after him.

Cut to the hall; Jim and his wife enter. His wife gets to the phone first. She takes the receiver off the hook.

Cut to the cafe; Stan gets over in title, "I want to speak to Mr. Finlayson."

Cut back to Jim and the wife; she hands him the phone and looks at him suspiciously. Jim takes the phone and listens.

Back to Stan; he gets over title, "She's on her way over and I can't stop her."

Back to Finlayson; he hangs up the phone, gives a look of despair and speaks title to his wife, "Wrong number," then realizing his mistake he gets all flustered and exits to the living room, followed by his wife.

Cut to living room; the wife smiles sweetly to the company and sits down at the piano again. Finlayson all fussed can't find the music and picks up another piece without looking. Then he looks at it and gives a big takem. Insert title of song, "Somebody's Coming to My House." The wife starts to play again and Jim starts singing in a very nervous manner.

Cut to exterior of the cafe; Mae is in the car trying to start it. Stan enters from the cafe. Mae glares at him and speaks title, "give me the key." Stan refuses to do so. Mae gets sore, gets out of the car and starts to wrestle with Stan, trying to get her hand in his pocket to get the keys. They fall to the sidewalk and a wrestling match follows. During this Gale enters the scene and stands in the doorway of the cafe looking on. Mae finally gets to her fett, grabs Stan's legs, yanks them up in the air and some money and keys drop out of his pocket. Mae grabs the keys and jumps into the car.

Stan picks himself up, sees Gale out of the corner of his eye, does a double takem and tries to cover up his embarrassment. There is a golf club lying on the sidewalk, which fell from a golf bag attached to the side of the car during the struggle. Stan picks up the golf club and starts putting. As the car starts to pull out, Stan jumps into it and the car exits.

As the car is leaving the scene, Gale watches off in the direction the car went, hails a taxi, gets in and the taxi exits.

Go to running insert of Stan and Mae driving along. Mae has a set expression on her face and is driving like hell, Stan trying to plead with her but she pays no attention to him.

Back to the living room of Finlayson's house. We show him singing and then give a music title with line in the song to the effect, "Papa's jumping with joy." Back to Finlayson; he has a face full of misery.

Back to shot of Stan and Mae driving along, Stan still pleading with her. She turns around, hits him on top of the head and the derby goes down over his eyes. He struggles to get it off.

Back to the living room of the home. Jim has finished the song and by this time he is in a cold sweat. The Judge and his wife applaud Jim. The Judge's wife speaks title to Jim, "Sing another one." Jim gives a helpless gesture and picks up another sheet of music, and as he looks at it he gives another takem.

Insert title of the song, "What'll I Do?"

His wife gets over "What number is this?," and he shows her the copy with a helpless look. She strikes up a chord and starts to play, and Jim starts to sing.

Cut to exterior of Finlayson's home. Stan and Mae drive in. The taxi enters in the background and slows down. As Mae gets out of the car and walks toward the house, followed by Stan, cut to close shot of the taxi; Gale looks through the window and sees them go into Finlayson's house. She speaks hurriedly to the driver and the car pulls out of the scene.

Go to interior of the living room; Finlayson on singing "What'll I Do?" Mae bursts into the room, followed by Stan. Finlayson gives a big takem, thinks quick and speaks title, "Meet Mr. and Mrs. Laurel." Stan gives a big takem. The Judge and his wife stand and bow.

Jim's wife crosses to Mae, helps her off with her coat and says, "Won't you stay a while?" and indicates to Stan to take his coat off.

Stan starts to take his overcoat off and as he does, the picture which he took out of Mae's apartment falls out of the pocket onto the floor, striking Stan on the foot. (This picture is in a silver frame.) Stan sees it, goes to pick it up in a hurry, his foot catches it and slides it right across the room, bumping the foot of the Judge who is sitting talking with his wife. (The picture is face down.)

Cut to the Judge and his wife; he takes it when he feels the picture hit his foot. He looks at a little table alongside him, getting over he thinks the picture dropped from the table. He picks it up without looking at it and places it on the table, and continues talking to his wife.

Cut to Finlayson; he sees it and has another big takem. The Judge and his wife stand up and the Judge speaks title to Jim, "I think we had better be going – it's getting late." He is now standing with his back to the picture.

Finlayson's wife crosses to them and gets over she is sorry they have to go.

Cut to Jim and Mae; he is pantomiming to her not to say a word. Mae is just giving him the icy stare.

The Judge and his wife start to exit, bidding goodnight to everybody. Jim, Stan and Mae are very nervous, and the wife is ushering the Judge and his wife out of the room.

Jim rushes across the room, grabs the picture and quickly puts it under a cushion on the corner of the settee, and gives Stan a dirty look as if Stan had been trying to double-cross him.

Cut to interior of Stan's home. Gale is on telling Stan's wife what she saw, Gertrude getting worked up to a high pitch, nearly going into hysterics. She can't stand it any longer. She grabs her hat and coat and runs out of the room.

Cut back to the living room. Jim, Stan and Mae are on. Jim is pleading in vain for Mae to leave the house. She snaps her fingers in his face, just laughing at him. Jim is about distracted. He finally gets a wild idea to end it all. He rushes to a drawer, pulls a gun, pantomimes to her "If you don't get out, I'll shoot you and then shoot myself." Mae thinks it is on the level, screams and does a faint and falls into Jim's arms.

At this point Jim's wife enters. Jim looks at her helplessly and gets over "She fainted." He places Mae on the settee. The wife comes over and sits down alongside of Mae and starts stroking Mae's forehead and trying to make her comfortable. She reaches around, sees the cushion in the corner of the settee, takes it and places it under Mae's head. This exposes the picture again.

Finlayson sees it, makes a wild dash and sits on it. His wife looks at him with surprise. Cut in insert of Jim's fanny sitting on a lot of broken glass. Back to Jim; he is taking it and pantomimes taking pieces of broken glass out of his fanny.

The wife speaks title to Stan, "I think you better stay here for tonight – you can sleep in the guest room." Stan takes this, so does Jimmie. The wife gets over that Stan and Jim should carry Mae upstairs. She makes a hurried exit.

Jim gets the picture and frame and sticks it up the back of his coat, and he and Stan pick up Mae and start to struggle out with her.

Cut to interior of the taxi; we see Stan's wife all excited and with a wild insane look, pantomiming to the driver to go faster.

Cut to the bedroom; Stan and Jim enter carrying Mae. They place her on the bed, and throw the cover over her.

Cut to the exterior; taxi drives up, Stan's wife jumps out and exits toward the house.

Cut to interior of the hall, Stan and Jim coming down the stairs. The front door opens and in walks Stan's wife. Stan sees her out of the corner of his eye and takes it, but regains control of himself. He walks right over to where his hat and coat are, puts them on and starts bawling Finlayson out, getting over "What do you mean by keeping me working so late – and my dear little wifie waiting at home for me!" Stan has his back to his wife and his getting over that he doesn't know she is there. His wife hearing this grand speech of his softens and looks very proud at Stan. Jim looks at Stan in amazement.

At this point Stan's wife calls to Stan, with arms outstretched. Stan turns and gets over his surprise, says "My darling!" and rushes over to her. Finlayson is still looking dumbfounded. Stan takes his wife in his arms, turns to Finlayson and gives him a final bawling out, getting over "I'm through with you and your wives." Finlayson gives a helpless look, and Stan raises his hat and makes a dignified exit with his wife.

Finlayson goes to the door and looks out into the black night, turns to the camera and gives a helpless gesture and starts to close the door. At this point his wife enters with a glass of water and an ice bag. Jim speaks title to her getting over "They've just left." His wife very much relieved puts the glass of water and ice bag on the table, crosses over to Jim and speaks title, "I'm so glad – never bring anybody like that again." She starts talking with him and they exit up the stairs.

Cut to the bedroom; Jim and his wife enter. She sits down at a dressing table and starts to undo her hair. Jim in a very worried state of mind gets over he is trying to figure out how to get this dame out of the other room. He is standing by the bed, and as he takes his coat off, the picture falls onto the bed. He has an idea and speaks title to his wife, "I forgot to put the cat out." She gets over, "Well, don't be long." Jim makes his exit.

Cut to the hall; Jim crosses to the guest room and looks in the door.

Cut to the interior of the guest room; Mae sitting on the edge of the bed all ruffled up in a daze. Jim enters and pantomimes to her to get out. She starts to bawl him out, getting over she is not going unless she gets some dough. Jim starts to plead with her but she refuses to leave.

Cut back to the wife's bedroom. She crosses to the bed and suddenly sees the picture. She picks it up and looks at it.

Go to insert of the writing on the picture getting over "From your darling Daddy" etc.

An insane look comes into her face; she has the same attitude as Charlotte had in "Should Husbands Pay." She exits to the hall.

Cut to the hall; Charlotte enters and sees Finlayson through the doorway in the guest room on his knees pleading with mae to go. She takes it.

At this point the butler comes walking up the stairs and starts down toward Charlotte with an unconcerned attitude, just as if he were going to his room. Charlotte suddenly sees him and without any warning pushes him right on his fanny, grabs one of his legs and starts pulling on it. The butler motions "Not this leg, the other one." Charlotte grabs the other leg and gives a terrific yank and the wooden leg comes out of the pants.

She flies into the guest room and clunks Finlayson on the head. Finlayson starts taking bows, getting lower and lower to the floor. Charlotte starts after Mae. Mae screams and exits to the hall, Charlotte after her. Charlotte runs her down the stairs, swinging the wooden leg at her.

Cut to lower hall; Mae enters with Charlotte after her, still swinging the wooden leg. As they get to the bottom of the stairs Charlotte takes the top part of the leg and starts hitting Mae in the fanny with the foot. Mae gets over that she thinks Charlotte is kicking her. As she exits through the door, Charlotte after her, fade out.

WITH LOVE AND HISSES

Production history: Production S-21. Outline and final script written February 1927. Filmed Monday, March 14 through Wednesday, March 30, 1927. Copyrighted May 18, 1927, by Pathé (LU 23978). Released August 28. Two reels.

Produced by Hal Roach. Directed by Fred L. Guiol. Titles by H.M. Walker. Story by Hal Roach.

With Stan Laurel (Cuthbert Hope), Oliver Hardy (Top Sergeant Banner), James Finlayson (Captain Bustle), Anita Garvin (Captain Bustle's first girlfriend), Eve Southern (Captain Bustle's second girlfriend), Josephine Dunn (Girlfriend), Frank Brownlee (Major General Rohrer), Jerry Mandy (Hungry Soldier), Will Stanton (Soldier sleeping next to Stan), Charlie Hall (Soldier at station), Viola Richard (Charlie Hall's girl at station), Symona Boniface (Dignified lady at station), Chet Brandenburg (Soldier), Frank Saputo (Soldier).

In this army comedy, Finlayson plays a gruff and short-tempered captain; Hardy is an even gruffer and shorter-tempered sergeant. Both of them are exasperated by one private in particular (Stan), who is childlike, not too bright, and a little effeminate. A trip to camp on a troop train does not go well for any of them, but an attempt at inspection goes even worse. The sergeant leads his soldiers on a long and exhausting hike, until a hidden stream offers a welcome respite. Hardy orders Stan to guard the squad's uniforms while everyone else goes skinny-dipping. Thanks to Stan's inattention and an errant cigarette, the soldiers' clothes are burned to ashes, just at the moment when the Major General is arriving for a camp inspection. The soldiers find a unique way to conceal their nudity and beat a hasty retreat back to camp.

With Love and Hisses gives Laurel and Hardy a significant amount of footage together, although they are once again adversaries and not yet buddies. Babe is certainly much more rough-hewn and surly here, and he's definitely part of the outside world. In later films, he would join Stan as part of the "misfit squad."

For his part, Stan displays not only a childlike quality but also a pronounced effeminacy that was a key part of his character in these early films. His name here is Cuthbert Hope; in *Sailors, Beware!* he is Chester Chase and in *Flying Elephants* he's Little Twinkle Star. At one point during an inspection, Finlayson orders him to "dress right" and put his hand on his hip; Stan mistakes this as a flouncy "nance" gesture and rather enjoys teasing Finlayson with it.

One of the other soldiers on the troop train, a very hungry but generous Italian fellow, is referred to in the script as a "wop." Apologies for this, but these scripts are products of their time and sometimes refer to various ethnic groups by names which today would not be "politically correct." (The name derives from turn of the century Italian immigrants who arrived at Ellis Island with no passports or documentation,

Eve Southern (1898-1972) appeared in about 40 films between 1917 and 1936. She made several shorts for Mack Sennett, but *With Love and Hisses* is her only known credit for Hal Roach, and a rare turn as a blonde.

We don't know the Harold and Gladys to whom Stan sent his good wishes in April 1927, but that's Viola Richard resting on his shoulder.

and were noted by officials as being With Out Papers.) This character is played by Jerry Mandy – actually Gerard Mandia of Utica, New York, so his portrayal of an Italian-American is authentic.

In the script, Captain Finlayson marches down the aisle of the sleeping car trying to determine who hit him in the face with a pie, and is overcome by the odor of the soldiers' feet. Happily, this is not in the film. It was replaced by a bit where Stan, overcome by the garlic and onions being consumed by his Italian friend, puts on a gas mask. In another scripted gag, Stan appears to be in desperate need and is knocking on the door of what looks to be an outhouse – which turns out to be merely a supply room. This also, happily, is not in the film. What does survive is still pretty crude and grimy, with gags depending on body odor and the aforementioned garlic and onions – not to mention nudity.

The scene of Babe chasing Stan through a thicket of brush before discovering the stream was not used in the film. One element that isn't noted in the script is that, while Babe spends several of the early scenes trying to unsuccessfully "roll his own" handmade cigarette, the one which he smokes and tosses away – accidentally setting the soldiers' uniforms ablaze – is factory-made.

The idea of the soldiers sneaking out with the billboard promoting *The Volga Boatman* "to the same tempo as the tune" doesn't really come across in today's copies, although perhaps alert theater organists in 1927 added this musical commentary. The scripted scenes with the bill poster, his girlfriend and his Ford were not used in the film. Nor were the gags of the windstorm, the cactus patch and the revolving billboard. Incidentally, *The Volga Boatman* – starring the future "Hopalong Cassidy,"

Captain Bustle (Finlayson) bids farewell to his girlfriends Anita Garvin and Eve Southern, as Cuthbert Hope (Stan) and Sergeant Banner (Hardy) look on.

Stan was supposed to be guarding the soldiers' uniforms from hazards like the cigarette that Babe carelessly tossed into them.

William Boyd, as Feodor, the title character – was a Cecil B. DeMille film released by Producers Distributing Corporation, so the Hal Roach Studios and the Pathé Exchange were giving some free publicity to a rival company.

---

129   CLASS 4—Comedies and Juvenile

REEL NO.	TITLE	PRODUCER

4540 Code GARGA   **With Love and Hisses**
Kodak Cinegraph
Featuring Stan Laurel and Oliver Hardy

As an exceedingly awkward private in the army, Laurel repeatedly treads on the official toes of the top Sergeant Hardy, who likewise offends the captain of their company. From the time they entrain through the following day up to the time of a formal inspection at Camp Klaxon, which their arrival from a "fatigue detail" completely disrupts, ripples of laughter from the audience will be continuous.

A very good slapstick comedy by this ever popular team of comedians.
1951 feet standard length—on 2 reels
Rental $2.50

4541 Code GARGE   **Flying Elephants**
Kodak Cinegraph
Featuring Stan Laurel and Oliver Hardy

A very amusing conception of life in the Stone Age, although somewhat slapstick. "King Ferdinand" issues a proclamation that males over 13 and under 95 must marry within 24 hours. Hardy, dressed in skins and carrying a club, reads the proclamation and sets out to comply, boasting that it won't take long. He finds that all his prospects have husbands who stand in his way.

Laurel arrives on the scene and after several attempts to win maidens, we find him and Hardy engaged in a very funny combat over the same individual.

Modern touches lend interest to this caveman farce.
1575 feet standard length—on 2 reels
Rental $2.50

4542 Code GARGI   **Do Detectives Think?**
Kodak Cinegraph
Featuring Stan Laurel, Oliver Hardy and James Finlayson

Death is the sentence imposed on a desperate criminal by Judge Foogle. He threatens the judge's life in revenge as he is led from the courtroom.

On learning of his escape, the judge calls for two of the best detectives to guard his home. Laurel and Hardy, who are sent, may be the best but they are a long way from the bravest, and as protectors they leave a lot to be desired.

The criminal intercepts the new butler and takes his place in the house just before the arrival of the detectives, who are delayed because of their lack of courage in passing a cemetery.

Laurel and Hardy are usually in the wrong part of the house when most needed but eventually they capture the criminal quite by accident. They are

To secure subjects of your own choice

Most of the Laurel and Hardy films released by Pathé (everything up to *Flying Elephants*) exist only because they were made available on 16mm "safety film" prints for the non-theatrical market, not long after their initial release. This page is from the 1932 catalog for the Kodascope Library.

An original "corner-block" from 1927. Even after Laurel and Hardy became a sensation with concurrent Roach releases through MGM, the Pathé Exchange neglected to acknowledge Hardy in its advertising.

"With Love and Hisses"
Roach-Pathe
A Grab-Bag of Comics

Type of production..2 reel comedy

Here is something that is a little broader than an evident satire on citizen's training camps. Facial expressions rather than situations and gags contribute to the humor, and in this line of delivery Stan Laurel and Jimmy Finlayson can take a lot of punishment. The point that is most apparently made is that wars can get along without these particular heroes, whose topmost distinction in this free-for-all conflict, is to capture a pullman car on the way to camp. Oliver Hardy makes things easier on the eyes.

In a review published August 28, 1927, *The Film Daily* definitely acknowledges Hardy.

Cast.

Capt ... Type like Jim Finlayson.
Top Sarg .... Type like Babe Hardy.
Dumb Private .... Stan. Laurel.

Foreword title to the effect that the home guards were leaving
for training camp.   Fade in on long shot, platform of railroad depot,
night. Lots of activity going on. General effect of troops leaving,
soldiers kissing sweethearts goodbye, etc.

Cut to set-up on platform. Stan enters with two suitcases and
sets them down. Introduce him with title: "The last of the Six
Hundred."

Cut to another set-up and introduce Hardy as top sergeant. He
takes out a sack of Bull Durham and starts to roll cigarette. Stan
enters the scene. As he passes Hardy he bumps his elbow, knocking
the tobacco out of the paper. Babe takes it, looks at him, starts to
swear at him getting over he's plenty tough. He turns and sees a girl
standing nearby. His expression changes to a sweet smile; he starts to
make another cigarette. As he does so, he crosses over to the girl in a
jovial manner as he is rolling the cigarette with one hand and he pats
the girl on the back. The girl, resenting this, slaps his face, which
causes Babe to drop the cigarette again. The girl exits.

Cut to the exterior of the depot. Taxi drives in. A porter opens
the door and Jim steps out, followed by two swell looking girls who
introduce Jim as Capt. Bustle, a devil with the ladies. He takes the two
girls by the arm and starts with them into the depot.

Go to a moving dolly shot shooting straight on. Jim is putting it
on with one girl on each arm, swinging his swagger stick and so on. As
the dolly pulls back it gradually brings Babe into the scene, and Stan's
suitcases are still in the foreground. Babe suddenly sees Jim and
salutes him. Jim returns the salute and, not seeing the suitcases, does
a brodie over them and lands in a sitting position facing camera. Jim
gets to his feet and gives Babe a dirty look and speaks title, "Report to
me tomorrow A.M." Babe comes to attention and salutes Jim, who
returns the salute, takes the two girls, and makes an exit with a
swaggering attitude, leaving Babe watching them go off with a
bewildered look.

At this point Stan enters and starts to pick up his suitcases as if
nothing has happened. Babe takes this big, crosses to Stan sore as an

owl, and gets over if you hadn't left the suitcases there I wouldn't have gotten into this jam. He speaks title, "Report to me tomorrow A.M." Stan picks up suitcases and exits.

Cut to the steps of the train . . . . . Jim is standing in the steps of the vestibule. Down on the platform the two girls are throwing kisses to him. Jim is doing likewise to them. Babe enters the scene at platform at foot of the steps. He starts to roll another cigarette. Stan enters the scene and starts to enter the coach. He turns and sees the two girls waving and throwing kisses. He starts to return same but suddenly stops, realizing that they don't mean him. He turns and sees Babe standing alongside of him and, thinking maybe Babe is the one the girls are calling to, he nudges Babe's elbow, spilling the tobacco again. Babe turns and is about to bawl Stan out. Stan in pantomime gets over that the girls are waving at him. Babe looks toward the girls and his attitude changes. He becomes all smiles and exits towards them. Stan enters the coach, passing Jim.

Cut to the two girls. Babe enters and starts talking in a jocular manner. The girls freeze up on him, and Babe continues to force his attentions on them.

Cut to Jim giving it the one-eye. He exits towards Babe and the girls. He enters the scene with Babe and the two girls, Babe not aware of his presence. Jim taps him on the shoulder. Babe, thinking it's the other girl, motions with his arm to keep away. Repeat this two or three times. Finally, Jim gets sore and gives him a terrific kick in the fanny. Babe takes it and turns sore as a goat, but in seeing Jim changes his expression and comes to attention. Jim bawls him out and speaks title, "Report to me tomorrow P.M." Babe salutes and exits with blood in his eye, now looking for Stan.

Cut to interior of train. Berths are all down, soldiers are sitting on upper and lower berths, playing ukes, harmonicas, etc. General action. In the background we see Stan trying to put his grips in the lower berth.

Cut to shot of Stan looking helpless. Everyone is telling him there's no room for him. He turns around and sees the open door of a drawing room. Stan enters towards it (cut to the interior of drawing room).

Stan enters, looks the place over, and decides it's great, places his grips down, closes the door, sits down and starts to make himself comfortable.

Cut to exterior of train. We see Babe walking up and down the platform, sore as hell, searching for Stan.

Cut to interior of drawing room. Stan is all comfortable in the drawing room, in front of the window, using the pillows to make himself as comfortable as possible. He is reading a magazine and eating chocolates in a very satisfied manner.

Cut to shot shooting through window towards the platform, Stan in the foreground. Babe enters the scene on platform, still continuing the search. He suddenly turns and looks up towards Stan and takes it.

Cut to shot shooting from platform. We see Stan sitting at window eating chocolates and reading magazine. Babe enters the scene directly to the window, looking at Stan. Stan sees him with a double takem and gives him a big grin. Babe makes a wild exit towards the vestibule. Stay with Stan, who gets over, what's the matter with him?, then settles himself and continues to read.

Cut to interior of drawing room. Babe enters and glares at Stan. Stan looks at him in a dumb manner and offers him a chocolate. Babe knocks the box out of Stan's hand, points at him, and gets over title "Report to me tomorrow afternoon." Tells Stan to get out of here. Stan starts to exit. Babe makes a wild kick at him but misses. Stan exits. Babe shuts the door, picks up the chocolates, and proceeds to make himself comfortable.

Cut to exterior of train. Conductor yells all aboard!! Jim is standing with the two girls, kissing them goodbye. He steps up on the porter's step, thinking he's on the train. He steps, turns towards the girls to give them another waving farewell, and the train pulls out of the scene in back of him. Jim throws the girls a final kiss, turns to make his step on the train and makes a high step into space doing a brodie.

Cut to long shot of train pulling out in distance. Jim gets up and runs after it, finally makes it.

Cut to interior of train. Jim enters all out of breath. We follow him with an Eyemo passing all berths. As Jim passes each berth, the soldiers salute him, Jim returning the salutes all the way up the aisle. As he gets towards the end, Jim is automatically saluting. A big fat soldier sticks his fanny out of a berth. Jim turns and salutes it. Realizing his mistake, he gives it the one-eye and looks to see if anyone saw him do it. He continues walking and as he passes the end berth, a big hob-nailed boot sticks out and strikes him in the face. Jim grabs his face and hobbles into the drawing room.

Cut to interior of drawing room. Babe by this time is on the bed with his boots and leggings off and his belt unbuckled, giving him more room to eat and breathe, and is making himself very comfortable. Jim enters, still holding his face, looks down at his feet and sees candy wrappers, nutshells, banana skins, etc. He takes it big. He looks around and sees Babe eating a big banana. Babe looks around and sees him and takes it big, and jumps to his feet and stands quickly at attention, and as he salutes his pants fall down around his ankles. He quickly pulls them up and continues his salute. Jim orders him out of the drawing room and speaks title, "Report to me tomorrow night." Babe picks up his belongings and makes a hasty exit. Jim makes a kick at him and misses and hits the door with his foot. Jim lets out a yell and we leave him jumping on one foot, holding the other.

Cut to interior of coach. Babe enters, looking around for a berth. He finally picks one out and there are three or four soldiers in the berth. Babe orders them to move over and gets in.

Cut to another lower berth. Stan is in there with three or four other characters. One is a wop. He is sitting in a corner eating salami, garlic and green onions, etc. Stan is looking at him in disgust, getting over that the smell is terrible, and finally opens a window.

Cut to interior of drawing room. Jim is all prepared for bed in long woolen undershirt that reaches to his knees, and heavy woolen socks. He does a quick routine of calisthenics and jumps into bed feeling spry, rubs his head and scratches his head. He opens the window and inhales a big breath of air. We see his chest swell out inflated by using a bladder beneath his shirt. He turns back to camera, makes a funny face and exhales, his chest going back to normal. He gets over, this is the life.

Cut to Stan's berth. The wop is cutting a head of garlic with his knife. He looks over at Stan and gets over he wants to give him something. He reaches in tin cracker box and brings out blackberry pie. Without cleaning the knife, he cuts it in half and hands it to Stan. Stan gets over he sees this, takes the pie and thanks him. When the wop is not looking, Stan smells it, closes his eyes, gets over he can't eat it. He stalls with it a while, then, noticing the open window, and unseen by the wop, throws the pie out the window.

Cut to interior of drawing room. Close up of Jim at the window, peacefully asleep. Pie comes in at the window, hitting Jim in the face. He wakes up and takes it, naturally.

Cut to Stan's berth. Stan is wiping his mouth. The wop looks at him, gets over he must have liked it. Stan gives him a grin. The wop gets over he's big-hearted, and gives him the other half. Stan with a sickly grin thanks him.

Cut to Jim's drawing room. He's got the pie pretty well wiped off and is sore as a boiled owl. Sticks his head out the window to see where it came from.

Cut to Stan's berth. Stan sees his chance to get rid of the pie and throws it out the window.

Cut to Jim's drawing room. He has his head out the window. We see his body flinch. He pulls his head in and as he faces the camera, he's covered with pie. Fade out.

Fade in on title, getting over that they arrived in camp.

Cut to long shot of camp soldiers, all milling around in General activity.

Cut to shot of Stan and Babe. Stan has a trench shovel, a bucket and a mop. Babe is giving him orders, at the same time rolling a cigarette with one hand. Stan turns to exit and as he does so, the mop accidentally hits the cigarette and knocks the tobacco out of his hand. Stan sees this and exits on the run, leaving Babe muttering to himself.

Cut to another set-up; background portrays a roughly made tool-house which has the appearance of an ordinary outhouse. There is a little path worn zig-zaggedly up to the door. Stan enters and walks down this path in the same shot. When he reaches the door, cut to a medium shot. Stan tries to open the door and discovers it's locked. He listens and knocks on the door lightly. He gets over that someone evidently said wait a minute. He puts down his bucket and mop and patiently waits. He finally knocks on the door again and gets over that someone said again wait a minute. He starts pacing up and down, waiting. Stan finally gets sore, walks up to the door and gives it a good hard knock. The door opens and the Quartermaster looks out and gets over, What do you want? Stan hands him the bucket and mop. The Quartermaster pantomimes, bring 'em inside. They exit into the house.

Cut to interior, door in background. We see it's a long supply room – lots of mops, buckets, supplies, etc. and a small wall desk with a high stool. Stan places the bucket, etc., in the corner. The Quartermaster checks them off and Stan exits.

Cut to long shot of camp. Close up of bugler blowing assembly call. We see soldiers coming out of tents, putting on coats, etc., and lining up.

Cut to medium shot, soldiers still coming into the scene and getting in line. Babe and Lieutenant are on. Jim enters, all dressed up. Stan comes into scene with gun and takes his position, being the last one to get in line. Jim takes it and gives him a dirty look. Everything is set now. Jim speaks title, "Right dress." The soldiers all place their left hand on their left hip and turn their heads to the right. A very tall soldier next to Stan, as he fulfills his order, catches Stan on the chin with his elbow. Stan pushes his elbow off with the attitude, what's the idea? The soldier tries to show Stan. We play this business with Stan getting all mixed up. Jim sees Stan and yells at him a title, getting all balled up himself, "Dress right." Stan looks at his uniform and looks at Jim and inquiringly speaks title, "This is all you gave me." Jim takes it. Jim gets sore and walks over to Stan, and standing in front of him he describes the order by placing his own left hand on his left hip and turning his face to the right. He then looks back and Stan gives him a little nance look and places his hand on his hip, very effeminate. He's all embarrassed and does it in such a manner that makes Jim blush. Jim becomes all flustered and exits out of the scene, giving Stan dirty looks as he walks away from him.

Cut to medium shot. Jim shouts an order, "Front." The soldiers all turn front. Jim shouts another order, "Inspect arms." The soldiers unlock their guns for inspection. Jim starts walking down the line, stops at one soldier, takes his gun, inspects it, and throws it back at him. He passes up one or two more, inspects his and throws it back at him.

Cut to Stan set-up. Jim comes in, looks at Stan and takes it. Stan still has his left hand on his hip, gives Jim a nance look. Jim gives a quick look up and down the line and then back of Stan. Tells him to put up his gun for inspection. Stan does it and in pulling the bolt back, it comes off the gun so he has the gun in one hand and the bolt in the other, and doesn't know what to do with it. He looks at Jim inquiringly. Jim takes it. Stan hands him the bolt and the gun. Jim takes them and is trying to figure how to put it together himself. He looks up and discovers that the whole line is watching him. He gets embarrassed and gives an order, "About face," which they do, but Stan makes a complete turn and faces him again.

Jim continues to try to put the bolt in the gun. Stan sees his predicament, walks over to him and tries to help him out. Jim takes it and tells him to back to line with his back to him, which he does. Jim goes back to try and put the bolt back in the gun. Stan looks over his shoulder, sees Jim's predicament, again comes to Jim and tries to help him out again, not knowing himself. Jim takes it again and orders him back to the line, again with his back to him. This time, Jim watches him. Stan turns his head over his shoulder towards Jim. Jim sees this, gets sore, and kicks Stan in the fanny. Stan takes it. Jim goes back to his work. Stan gets sore, steps out of line, and kicks Jim in the fanny, and nonchalantly gets back in the line. Jim looks at him, walks over and kicks him again. Stan turns quickly and kicks Jim again.

This time, the line is starting to turn toward Jim. Jim recovers himself and gets back on his dignity. He finally throws the bolt away and orders, "About face." The whole line turns towards him. Stan makes a complete turn so his back is to Jim. This is too much for him, and he kicks Stan in the fanny. Stan makes a quick turn as if to kick Jim. Jim makes a quick move away from him as a man who is expecting to be goosed. Stan finally gets in line. Jim takes Stan's gun, whirls it around in an awkward manner, and as he swings the gun up into the air and looks into the barrel, a big bunch of rust falls out into his eye, giving him the appearance of a black eye.

This is too much for Jim. He throws the gun back at Stan. Stan throws it back at him. Jim throws it back at Stan. We repeat this till it gets faster and faster; finally Jim throws it so hard that it goes through Stan's hands and hits him in the nose. Stan looks dumbfounded for a minute, then breaks into a cry. Still crying, he leaves the ranks, looking back pointing at Jim, acting like a little boy, getting over that he's going to tell his mother all about it, and quitting the army.

Cut to Jim. By this time he's boiling. He calls Babe over to him, tells him to take them out and drill them till they can't walk. Jim exits. Babe yells at Stan, orders him back into the line. Stan obeys unwillingly and still crying. Babe then calls various men from the line, about eight or ten, the dumbest looking ones, including Stan. He lines them up and marches them out of the scene, Stan still crying and warning Babe he's going to tell his mother.

Cut to another set-up of Jim's tent. Babe enters with his squad, and as they are passing his tent, Jim looks out, wiping his eye with a towel. Stan, being the end man, turns and sees him, breaks from his cry into a big smile, puts his left hand on his hip and starts tripping along. His foot gets caught on Jim's tent rope; he trips and falls, pulling the whole tent down. Stan sees what happens, gets up and runs towards the squad in the background, leaving Jim looking for something to throw at him as we fade out.

Cut to the title that Babe has marched the fannies off the awkward squad.

Fade in on a dusty country road. We see the squad and Babe all dragging their fannies, all dusty, dirty and perspiring. Their coats are open, getting over it's hot as hell. Use walking close-ups amongst the soldiers, getting over the funny types and how miserable they look, and use a shot of their feet to get a funny effect. We see a big rock in the road, and as each one passes, they trip, too tired to pick up their feet.

Cut to full figure shot. Stan starts to get slower and soldiers start passing him. Finally, he's at the end of the squad. He turns and sees a big rock at the end of the road, gets over he can't go any farther, goes over and sits on the rock and the squad passes out of the scene. Close up of Stan. He looks down at his feet with a pained expression.

Cut to insert of the feet. Both feet are pulsating. Back to Stan. He starts to cry again.

Cut to Babe and the rest of the squad. Babe starts looking around for Stan and takes it as he sees Stan in small figure shot, sitting on the rock. Babe halts the soldiers and waves to Stan to come on. Stan in small figure shot waves to him, nothing doing. Babe gets mad. He starts out to get Stan.

Cut to small figure shot. Stan away in the background sitting on a rock. Babe enters on the foreground, walking toward Stan. We see by his manner of walk he intends to murder Stan. He gets about halfway to Stan and –

Cut to Close up of Stan. He's looking towards Babe, half afraid and not knowing just what to do.

Cut to close-up of Babe on a moving shot, showing murder in his eyes, walking towards Stan.

Cut back to Stan. He starts to get off of the rock.

Cut to small figure with Stan in the background; Babe is getting near him. Stan slides off of rock, starts walking backward down the road. Babe stops and makes another motion for Stan to come back to the squad. Stan stops but does not make a move towards Babe. Babe gets sore, picks up rocks, starts throwing them at Stan. He starts to dodge them. Play him just like a kid; finally Babe makes a run at him. Stan ducks him in a lot of brush alongside of the road. We stay with this long shot. We see Babe go into the same direction that Stan did.

Cut to moving shot. Shooting from the road into the thicket of brush. We catch glimpses of Stan now and then running into the direction of the squad, giving the effect of a deer running through brush.

Cut to the squad, standing at ease. Stan comes out of the brush, all in, and sits on another rock right by them.

Cut back to the set-up where we left Babe. We see some movement in the brush and Babe suddenly makes his way out of the brush. We see his face is all scratched with the brush, and parts of his uniform torn. Babe is pulling stickers out of his neck and hair. He looks off in direction of squad.

Cut to shot of squad and Stan sitting on a rock. Back to Babe. He takes this calmly and walks out of the scene towards the squad.

Cut back to Stan. He sees Babe coming and takes it.

Cut to Babe walking toward Stan with murder in his heart, but trying not to show it. He comes into Stan's set-up, bawls him out and does everything but hit him, Stan sheepishly taking everything. Babe turns and looks out of the scene.

Cut to a shot of a beautiful pool, cool and refreshing.

Cut back to Babe. He gets over he has an idea, and looking over at the soldiers, he speaks title to the effect, "Let's all take a swim before we get back to camp." Soldiers all run out of the scene, followed by Babe and Stan.

Cut to a set-up on the edge of a lake. The soldiers enter and start undressing. Stan also starts to undress. Babe yells at him to stop, crosses over to him and reads title to the effect, "You can't go in, you've got to watch these clothes." Stan takes this with great disappointment and breaks into a cry and does the same business he did after Jim hit him in the face with the gun. Babe starts to undress and orders Stan to take off his leggings and shoes. Babe pantomimes to one of the soldiers to give him a cigarette, lights it and takes off his undershirt.

Cut to lower half of Babe. Stan is on his knees taking off Babe's leggings and shoes, crying. Back to Babe, close shot. He pantomimes taking his pants off, brings them into the scene and throws them to Stan, takes a last long draw at the cig, and flips it away.

Cut to insert of cigarette landing in some dry brush near some clothes.

Cut to Babe and with an Eyemo, we do not show any more than from his armpits up. Babe makes a run towards the pool. We follow him until he jumps out of scene.

Cut to an extreme long shot. He does a running jump into the big pool with a splash. He starts swimming around like a big porpoise.

Cut to another extreme long shot. We show soldiers diving, etc., having a great time.

Cut to Stan whining a little bit and he sees soldiers having a good time and starts to get mad, and suddenly makes up his mind he's going to swim too, and starts to undress.

Cut to insert of cigarette Babe threw down; it is smoldering and finally sets fire to a little bit of brush.

Cut back to Stan. He has his clothes off. Cut to him under armpits getting over he's naked. We follow him with an Eyemo and as we come to edge of pool, he jumps out of scene.

Cut back to extreme long shot. He does a funny dive, comes up, and gets over it's great, and does another dive under the water.

Cut to set-up of Babe in the water. Stan comes up alongside of him. He has his back to Babe, starts splashing around trying to swim, Babe looking at him. Stan then decides to float, lying on his back, and looks straight up into Babe's face. Stan takes it and gives Babe a prop smile and speaks title, "Ain't it great?" Babe takes it and attempts to grab Stan by the throat. Stan turns over and goes under the water like a mud hen. Babe follows him under the water.

Go to a long shot. Stan's head pops up in the background, and Babe comes up in another part of the scene. He sees Stan and dives under the water again. So does Stan. Hold it for a second, and Stan pops up in another part of the water. Then Babe pops up a distance from him. We repeat this two or three times.

Cut to a close shot. Stan's head comes up out of the water, and as he does Babe also comes up near him, back to back, both looking for the other. Suddenly they turn and see each other, and both duck down again.

During this little chase sequence in the water, make cuts of the clothes burning up.

Cut to title getting over that some big General is coming to the camp to review the home guards, and it is to be quite an event.

Cut to shot of the camp, Finlayson strutting around, talking to several women and swanking. A big car drives in with a General and a couple of his aides. We get over the regular military proceedings of Jim meeting the General. Jim calls to one of his Lieutenants and gives him an order. The Lieutenant in turn gives an order to the bugler, and the bugler blows an assembly call. Soldiers rush in from different parts and start lining up.

Cut to the pool. We show the boys all having a good time.

Cut back to the bugler, still blowing the assembly call.

Back to the pool, and they all take it and hold it. Babe gives them an order, and they all start to leave the pool in a hurry.

Back to the camp, soldiers still rushing in from different directions. They finally get set, but the outfit looks a bit short and straggly. The Lieutenant looks them over and crosses over to Jim and whispers title in his ear, getting over that some of the troops are missing. Finlayson gives it a look, and tells the bugler to give the second and last call. The bugler does so.

Cut back to the pool. Babe and the soldiers run into the set-up where their uniforms were, and as they look down we cut to insert of the smoldering ashes, just showing buttons, belt buckles, etc., and around this the bare feet of the soldiers. Back to Babe and the soldiers for their takem.

Cut to the pool. Stan is swimming towards shore. He finally gets out, and runs to get his uniform.

Bring him into the set-up where the soldiers are. They just stand looking at him. Stan gets over he realizes what happened and is just about to explain. Babe looks out of the scene, and we cut to a couple of girls on horseback coming along the road. Babe gets panicky. The others see it and start to run in all directions to hide. About four of them run behind a bush, and the other four, including Babe and Stan, run out of the scene.

Bring them into a set-up where there is a signboard with a poster of "The Volga Boatman." Babe and Stan and the other two enter and run behind the board.

Cut to the two girls on the horses. They come toward the board. Cut to shot behind the board. They are all getting very nervous. Back to the girls. One of the horses starts to get restless and wheels around. We get over that it is liable to suddenly make a run around the back of the board.

Cut back of the board. Babe quickly gives an order to pull up the braces of the board. His idea is to make the board free so they can turn it in any direction and always be covered.

Cut to insert of the braces being pulled out of the ground.

Cut back to close shot of the four of them, and we see the board fall backwards on their heads, and their heads go through. They straighten the board up, and we cut to the other side and show that the four heads are in the position of the four characters on the poster towing the boat. The girls come to the scene, stop their horses, look at the poster and start conversing about it. One of the girls, pointing to Babe's face, laughs and speaks title, "Isn't that a funny face? I have an Airedale at home that looks just like it." The other girl laughs.

Cut to Babe and Stan. Babe gives Stan a quick dirty look and Stan gives him a grin.

The girls look at the board again. Stan has to hold it. They then wheel their horses around and look in the direction of the pool. One points and starts talking.

Cut back to the board. Babe motions to Stan and the others to try and sneak out. They all look toward the girls to see that they are not looking, and start sneaking out with the board, to the same tempo as the tune of "The Volga Boatman." They exit out of the scene.

Take them into another set-up, sneaking along. Play this for a few feet, and get over they are getting tired with this heavy billboard. They finally set it down.

Go to close-up of Babe and Stan. Babe gives Stan a dirty look and speaks title, "You're the cause of this." Stan looks at him innocently and speaks title, "Yes sir, what time do I have to report?" This burns Babe up.

Cut away and show a bull bellowing.

Cut back to the board. They all take it, looking off in the direction of the bull.

Cut back to the bull. He starts snorting and kicking up the ground, preparing to make a rush.

Back to the board. They are all taking it big. They suddenly pick up the board and start to run. Stay with this for a few feet, and suddenly a Ford truck drives into the scene in the background and starts down the road. The signboard stops.

Cut to a medium shot. The Ford drives in, and we get over it is a colored bill poster and his girl. He takes out a bucket of paste and a painter's stepladder, sets up the ladder and takes out some bills, putting them on the shelf of the ladder, then dips a brush into the paste, goes up the ladder and starts pasting just above the boys' heads. They are all taking it. After giving it a good pasting and just missing their faces, he turns away from the board and starts unfolding one of the bills. He's having a little trouble unfolding them, and Babe motions for the boys to pull out of the scene. They start to tiptoe, again to the tempo of "The Volga Boatman."

Cut to the girl in the Ford. She just watches the board with open mouth, too scared to speak.

Cut to the bill poster. He has the bill all opened up, and he turns to smack it onto the board. As he does so, he falls into space. As he lands, the girl starts up the Ford and pulls out. The bill poster sits up, bewildered, and looks out of the scene.

Cut to the board, still moving.

The bill poster jumps to his feet, turns and runs out of the scene in the direction of the Ford.

Cut to set- up on the road, the Ford halfway down the road. The bill poster enters the scene on the run, and we stay with him until he passes the Ford and gets out of the scene.

Cut back to the billboard, still creeping along.

Cut back to the camp, Finlayson pacing up and down, and the General and visitors all waiting. Finlayson orders the bugler to give another call, which he does.

Cut back to the signboard. The boys take it again and start moving toward the camp.

Cut to a shot, and by using a wind machine, get the effect of a windstorm starting. We see dust and leaves flying, the brush waving and tumbleweeds rolling.

Cut to the signboard. They are beginning to feel the effects of the windstorm. We play this scene, shooting back from in front of the board, which is becoming unmanageable. Another gust of wind starts running them backwards. Carry them out of that set and bring them into a set-up where there is a cactus patch. They enter on the run with their backs to the cactus, and all do a brodie right into it. They finally get up, all taking it, the wind still blowing them around.

Move back to small figure shot, and we see the board start to circle around like a top.

Come to close-up of their faces, using Eyemo shot going around with them, and have Babe speaking titles to Stan.

Cut back to small figure shot, the signboard still revolving, and it goes out of the scene in a waltzing effect.

Cut back to the camp. Finlayson orders the bugler to blow another call. The bugler starts to do it. Jim decides to take the bugle and blow it himself. He blows a blast in one direction, then blows a blast to the front, each time taking the bugle down and looking sore. The General walks in alongside of him. Jim turns and blows a big blast right in the General's ear. The General's hat flies up in the air, and he holds his ear, giving Jim a dirty look. Jim hands the bugle back to the bugler.

Cut back to set-up with the signboard. The wind by this time is abated, and the board is standing still. Babe is again picking on Stan, blaming him for their predicament.

Cut to shot of a skunk. It enters in back of the board.

Cut to shot shooting in back of the board, and we see the skunk run in and stop around the feet of the soldiers.

Cut to close shot of Babe and Stan, Babe still bawling Stan out. He stops abruptly, getting over he smells something.

He looks at Stan. Stan gives him an inquiring look. Then Stan smells something and looks at the other two. As he starts to look back at Babe, bring the skunk around in front of the signboard and Stan sees it. Babe sees it at the same time. They simultaneously turn to each other and give it a nod.

Cut to shot of the skunk. It starts walking around toward the board. The boys start backing away and exit out of the scene on the run.

Bring them into another set-up on the run. Cut to insert of their feet, and we show them passing over a big bees' nest. Show a couple of the feet trip over the nest, and they pass out of the scene. We stay with the bee nest, and show thousands of bees taking it big. They all look off in the direction of the board, give it the one-eye, and all make an exit.

Cut to a shot of the board running along, and cartoon a big swarm of bees coming into the scene and catching up with the signboard about the height of the boys' fannies, and exit behind the board. The boys start jumping around, doing all kinds of contortions, and more bees come into the scene.

Cut to the camp. Finlayson by this time is drilling the soldiers, and after each order is fulfilled, the guests all applaud. Finlayson looks at the General with a pleased expression, and the General gives him a look of disgust. Finlayson takes it, then starts to give another order.

Cut to long shot. In the background, the boys enter with the board, on the run. By this time it is covered with bees. They come running down, passing the guests. Be careful to have the guests on the front side of the board. The guests start taking it, waving the bees away from them. The board continues past Finlayson and the General, leaving bees on them. They run through the ranks of soldiers, who drop their guns and start fighting the bees off. During this commotion we fade out.

Go to title, to the effect, "All's Well That Ends Well."

Fade in on the company, all intact, Finlayson giving them an order. They all stand at attention. The General walks down the ranks, reviewing them. As we come to the awkward squad, they all have pained expressions. As the General looks down the rear of the line, we show they all have swollen fannies. Fade out.

JIMMY FINLAYSON
Cyrus Brittle

STAN LAUREL
Brittle's Lawyer

OLIVER HARDY
Brittle's Butler

NOAH YOUNG
Brother-in-Law

CHARLOTTE MINEAU
The New Mrs. Brittle

EDNA MARIAN
Mrs. Brittle's Daughter

KAY DESLYS
Suggested in Script

DAVID BUTLER
Suggested in Script

STAN LAUREL
As Butler's "Wife"

SUGAR DADDIES

Production history: Production S-1. Written early-mid May 1927. Filmed Thursday, May 26 through Friday, May 27, 1927. No filming on the 28th through the 30th (Memorial Day, a vacation day). Shooting resumed May 31, finishing on June 3, 1927. Copyrighted August 17, 1927, by Metro-Goldwyn-Mayer Distributing Corp. (LP 24291). Released September 10. Two reels.

Produced by Hal Roach. Directed by Fred L. Guiol. Photographed by George Stevens. Titles by H.M. Walker.

With James Finlayson (Cyrus Brittle), Stan Laurel (Brittle's lawyer), Oliver Hardy (Brittle's butler), Charlotte Mineau (The new Mrs. Brittle), Noah Young (Mrs. Brittle's brother), Edna Marian (Mrs. Brittle's daughter), Sam Lufkin (Ticket-taker at Fun House), Dorothy Coburn (Girl in the Fun House), Eugene Pallette (Husband mistaken for Brittle's butler), Villie Latimer (Tall wife), Charlie Hall, Jack Hill, Sam Lufkin, Clara Guiol (Hotel extras), Ray Cooke (Bellboy).

Wealthy businessman Cyrus Brittle is too fond of booze and women – with the result that he awakens one morning with a colossal hangover, and his butler informing him that he got married the night before. Brittle immediately wants out of the romantic entanglement, but his angry and threatening new in-laws, wanting to attach some of Cyrus's loot, have other ideas. Mr. Brittle's lawyer and butler help him escape to a beachfront hotel, but the new wife, her murderous brother and her daughter trail him. In an effort to escape, the lawyer climbs on Mr. Brittle's back, dons a lengthy housecoat and a wig, and poses as the butler's very tall wife. Brittle's new relations chase the hapless trio through a number of boardwalk attractions.

The scripts for the early films in which Laurel and Hardy appear (they're not quite "Laurel and Hardy movies" just yet) vary greatly. The unfilmed "Sojin" story ran to 21 pages; *Duck Soup* was 19 pages; *Slipping Wives* took up 17; *Love 'em and Weep* made it to 12. It appears that, as Hal Roach, Supervisor Leo McCarey, Fred Guiol and Stan and Babe themselves were becoming more aware of the Laurel and Hardy chemistry, the scripts were becoming shorter and less detailed. *Sugar Daddies* takes the reliance on improvisation into a whole new realm, with a script that runs only two single-spaced, legal-sized pages.

The script suggests that Stan should play Finlayson's butler and that his lawyer should be portrayed by Babe. One wonders if any footage was shot with the boys in these roles before somebody decided that they should switch places. (At one point, Stan as the lawyer "speaks" a title that would have been appropriate for Babe: "A fine mess you've made of things!")

The butler that Hardy plays here is a much nicer one than the one he portrayed in *Slipping Wives*. Although he has an opening scene in which he is determined to snatch Stan's hat from his head (such things are not worn indoors), he is generally much nicer

Cyrus's new brother-in-law (Noah Young) demands $50,000 to annul the marriage (to Charlotte Mineau, second from left). Cyrus's new stepdaughter (Edna Marian, left) and butler (Babe) fear the worst.

to Stan, especially in the later scenes when they're both dedicated to keeping Finlayson away from his lethal brother-in-law. Hardy also has his toothbrush mustache again, freed from the burden of whiskers he wore in *Duck Soup* and *With Love and Hisses* – and trimmed more daintily than his mustache in *Do Detectives Think?*, shot exactly one month before *Sugar Daddies*.

The script states that Finlayson's bride should be played by Kay Deslys, who would later provide memorable turns as a good-time girl attracted to Stan's Adam's-apple in *We Faw Down*, as Mrs. Hardy in *Should Married Men Go Home* and *Perfect Day*, and as the lady who refers to Ollie as "Mister Whiteman" in *Below Zero*. If we are to believe her stated birth date of September 28, 1899, Miss Deslys would have been 27 when *Sugar Daddies* was filmed in late May and early June of 1927.

The script further suggests that Charlotte Mineau play the part of Finlayson's mother-in-law. She was 41 at the time of filming, closer to Finlayson's age of 39. Probably for that reason, Miss Mineau's role was changed to that of Finlayson's new bride. The role intended for Kay Deslys went instead to the lovely, 20-year-old Edna Marian; it would have been ridiculous for Finlayson to protest a marriage to her, so she became his new stepdaughter.

One wonders why the part of the menacing brother-in-law wasn't originally proposed for Noah Young, who had been a mainstay of the Roach lot in the late Teens

Cyrus's attorney demonstrates just what kind of a legal mind he has.

and early Twenties. Certainly he provides more of a threat than David Butler, a pleasant 32-year-old actor, later a prolific film and TV director. Right around this time, Butler was supporting Max Davidson in a Roach short, *Should Second Husbands Come First?*, but he would almost immediately thereafter forsake acting for the megaphone and the canvas chair.

Roughly two-thirds of the action in the film is either nonexistent or barely hinted at in the script. Stan's introductory scene in his office is nowhere to be found, nor his arrival at Finlayson's doorstep (which provides some nice interplay with Babe). Nor do we find the scene of Stan reading Noah Young the riot act, which prompts Young to demand $50,000 for nullifying the marriage – and to demonstrate his trusty revolver.

Two paragraphs of the script's first page are devoted to a rather complex routine involving Finlayson, a line of automobiles and a bathing beauty parade. No doubt this would have been expensive as well as unnecessary to the story, so it was neatly replaced with a close-up of a newspaper story:

WILD SCREAMS OF CHORUS GIRLS
FEATURE RIOTOUS MIDNIGHT PARTY
Millionaire Cyrus Brittle last night dropped twenty-seven
chorus girls off the Sutter Street Bridge in a frantic effort
to find one who wouldn't splash.

A meeting of the opposing parties brings dramatic results.

The film does in fact have the proposed gag of the family driving to Finlayson's beachfront hotel in an ambulance. (Noah Young tells the driver, "Wait here – I'll have a customer for you!") It does not include the idea of Finlayson on the phone with a gold-digging bathing beauty. Incidentally, the fantastically ornate hotel lobby was probably a pre-existing structure – one can hardly imagine it being created with the budget for a two-reel comedy – but nevertheless, Roach art directors Harry Hopkins and Ted Driscoll were capable of designing some very impressive sets in this late-silent period.

The entire last section of the film is barely hinted at in the script. The gag of Finlayson in a stooping position, with Stan on his back and disguising as his very tall wife had just been used in *Love 'em and Weep* (and would show up again in 1931's *Chickens Come Home*); evidently it went over well with audiences. Most of these climactic scenes were shot at the real attractions of the Long Beach Pike amusement park, and they clearly contained more potential for comedy than anticipated in the script, which merely states, "we play another routine for what it is worth."

The ornate hotel lobby may or may not have been a Roach studio creation. In any event, the later Hal Roach silents often featured very impressive sets.

Actual amusement park attractions provide most of the thrills in the final scenes.

Gonzaga, ao lado de Sam Hardy, James Finlayson e Stan Laurel, comediantes da Hal Roach.

Between takes with Brazilian film journalist Adhemar Gonzaga, later an actor, screenwriter, producer and director.

Promotional artwork.

S-1.

Cast:-

An Old Millionaire	– Jim Finlayson
His Secretary	– Babe Hardy
His Butler	– Stan Laurel
The Girl	– Type like Kay Deslys
Her Mother	– Charlotte Minneau
Her Brother	– Type like David Butler

Open up in bedroom of Finlayson's home, Finlayson asleep. Stan enters, pulls up the shades and lets in the sunlight. He has a tray with a block of ice on it. He wakes Finlayson up and we get over that Finlayson had a wild night. We see Finlayson's head pulsating; he grabs the cake of ice and puts it on his bald head and gets over that he feels better.

Stan speaks title, "Will you have your breakfast in bed, sir, or with your wife?" Finlayson gives him a double-takem and asks, "What do you mean?" Stan says, "You were married last night, sir." Finlayson can't remember. He asks Stan, "What does she look like?" Stan goes through a little pantomime describing the new wife. Finlayson starts to dress.

Cut downstairs and introduce the wife, her brother and mother, who have just moved in and taken possession. The brother is a type which makes himself at home any place.

Bring Finlayson downstairs and he gets over that it is a frame-up. The mother and brother tell him that he married this girl and that he will have to do right by her. During this sequence we show an enmity between the wife's relation and Stan and Babe. We may use a nice looking maid.

Finlayson decides to pack up his stuff and go to the beach to get away from it all of which Babe and Stan are very much in favor. They sneak out without the wife or relatives knowing it. FADE OUT.

FADE IN at the beach. Finlayson is riding in a Rolls-Royce, open car with top down; Babe is driving the car with Stan sitting beside him. There is a line of automobiles and where Finlayson's car accidentally gets in line we show a bathing beauty parade. At the place where the girls get into automobiles a man places a number on each car. Finlayson's car comes to this spot and is numbered; a bunch of swell looking girls get into the car. Finlayson sees the girls, forgets all about home and gets very familiar with them. The car drives on in the parade.

In another setup at the Judge's stand a few cars stop and are given some kind of prize. Finlayson's car appears on the scene and makes a big hit with the Judge. The Judge comes over to Finlayson and shakes his hand, which denotes that Finlayson has won the first prize. All the girls gather around Finlayson and the Judge. A few newspaper photographers and news weekly cameramen snap pictures, unknown to Finlayson, then quickly disappear. Finlayson by this time is having a time of his life and his making dates with all the girls. Play some gag or something for a laugh here as we FADE OUT.

FADE IN next morning at Finlayson's home. The brother, mother and wife are wondering what became of Finlayson. They pick up a newspaper and we show insert of the picture with Finlayson and all the girls, with writing to the effect that his girls won the beauty contest, etc. At this the wife starts crying. The mother and brother go into a rage and decide to go after him.

(We may use the gag where the wife calls an ambulance, it arrives at the house, they get in it and drive to the beach.)

Cut to a suite of rooms at a beach hotel and show Stan waking Finlayson, with the usual tray of ice. Finlayson gets over he has had another tough night. Stan hands him the paper and Finlayson sees the picture and takes it big. He calls Stan and Babe to him, says "I'm in for it now," and starts to bawl Babe out for getting the car into the parade.

At this point the phone rings and we show one of the girls on the other end of the line asking Finlayson for bracelets, diamonds, etc., that he had promised her. Finlayson gets over, "As soon as my head clears I'll give them to you – don't worry." He hangs up.

Cut to exterior of the hotel; the ambulance drives up. The wife, brother and mother get out and dash into the hotel. They stop at the desk. The mother takes the phone.

Stan answers the phone and by the way she hollers over it Stan gets over it almost broke his ear drum. He goes to Finlayson and says, "Your wife and family are downstairs, and by the way she talked it sounds like they mean business." Finlayson goes into a panic.

They finally get a bright idea to disguise themselves and get out before the family comes up. They go through a little routine which finally puts Finlayson in a stooping position; Stan gets on Finlayson's back and they put on a large cape and a hat with bits of blonde hair attached to it. Babe also disguises himself. As they are almost ready, we cut to the wife and family just coming out of the elevator.

As the family gets out of the elevator they see Stan, Babe and Jim coming toward them, but have not seen which door they came from. The three pass the family, who by this time are all wild. Stan and Babe feel very foolish and give the family silly grins. They get into the elevator with difficulty and go down. The wife and family discover who it was and start after them.

Play this routine through the lobby, from where they go the rounds of concessions, the wife and family following, possibly bring a cop into it. Finally the menace gets so close they have to duck into a dance hall. Play this routine here for what it is worth, with the menace following them through the dance hall. They come out and finally duck into the fun house, where we play another routine for what it is worth.

They come out and duck into a concession called "Over the Waves," and hide in a small compartment. At the exit of "over the Waves," we show the wife and family, who have apparently lost them and are looking around for them in a crowd of people.

Cut to the inside; the attendant pulls a lever and they fall onto the waves. This separates them, throwing all three out onto the sidewalk in front of the crowd and wife and family.

From here we go into a "wow" finish and FADE OUT.

THE SECOND 100 YEARS

Production history: Production S-2. Script finished June 10, 1927. Filmed Saturday, June 11 through Saturday, June 18 (including filming on Sunday, June 12). Copyrighted September 21, 1927, by MGM (LP 24437). Released October 8. Two reels; black and white with tinted sequences.

Produced by Hal Roach. Directed by Fred L. Guiol. Photographed by George Stevens. Edited by Richard Currier. Titles by H.M. Walker.

With Stan Laurel (Little Goofy), Oliver Hardy (Big Goofy), James Finlayson (Governor Browne Van Dyke), Frank Brownlee (Prison Warden), Tiny Sandford (Guard), Budd Fine (Suspicious Policeman), Edgar Dearing (Officer), Alfred Fisher (Elderly Officer), Ellinor Vanderveer (Countess de Cognac), Eugene Pallette (French guest at dinner), Otto Fries (Lecoque), Bob O'Connor (Voitrex), Dorothy Coburn (Flapper girl painted by Stan), Jack Herrick (Convict who takes letter), Charlie Hall (Convict), Rosemary Theby (Dinner guest).

Prison cellmates Stan and Ollie attempt to tunnel their way out of prison but succeed only in breaking into the warden's office. They also break a water main and cause a flood. Later, they escape by turning their prison garb inside out and disguising themselves as painters. They attempt to ward off a suspicious policeman by painting everything in sight. A passing limousine provides a means of escape. The convicts steal the clothes of the two occupants – a couple of visiting French prison officials – and forcibly eject them. The limousine drops off the now tuxedo-clad jailbirds at the home of the Governor, where they are given a banquet in "their" honor. A special after-dinner treat is a visit to the prison – where old convict pals instantly recognize the faux Frenchmen, and the two real dignitaries are found in a cell, complaining about having been arrested for running around in their underwear.

The Second 100 Years, like the other Hal Roach films now being distributed by MGM, was promoted with a "Press Sheet." This was sent to theater managers and newspaper editors and contained photographs, reviews, news tidbits and other items to help promote the movie. The front page proclaimed, "New starring team uncorks riotous performance in first picture as comedy duo," but called that team Oliver Hardy and Stan Laurel. One article proclaimed the "famous comedy trio" as Finlayson, Hardy and Laurel. The main titles of the film eschewed the issue by simply stating, "Hal Roach presents THE SECOND 100 YEARS" – note that the title had numerals. The next title gave the cast – Stan Laurel, Oliver Hardy, James Finlayson, Stanley J. Sandford (spelled correctly!).

It's ironic that one promotional article should include Finlayson as part of the team because Laurel and Hardy are clearly the stars of this movie, with Finlayson only having a few scenes in support. Two films later, Stan Laurel and Oliver Hardy would

Ellinor Vanderveer, as the Countess de Cognac, seems unimpressed by the two French prison officials.

share a credit before the *Putting Pants on Philip* title flashed onto the screen, and this "name above the title" billing seems to be the reason why the comedians considered this to be the first "official" Laurel and Hardy movie, despite its highly unusual characters and plotline.

The script for *The Second 100 Years* consisted of four legal-sized pages, and again the writers were definitely counting on Stan and Babe's skill at improvising comedy to carry some of the sequences. The script proposes an elaborate opening routine involving a dummy (substituting for Stan) and a prison guard, presumably the character played by Tiny Sandford. This was replaced in the film by a cute scene in which the boys attempt to share their one cigarette, but are thwarted because neither one has a match.

"Frank Brownley" in the script is Frank Brownlee, born in Dallas in 1874; he appeared in over 100 films through 1943 and passed away at 73 in Los Angeles on February 10, 1948. Most of his films were Westerns, but he was active in Roach comedies in 1927, appearing in With *Love and Hisses, Sailors, Beware!, Do Detectives Think?* and *Call of the Cuckoo*; later he would return to the L&H fold in *Pack Up Your Troubles* (as the drill instructor who barks, "Yoooouu LUNKHEADS!") and as the harried police chief in *The Midnight Patrol*.

In the film, when Governor Finlayson is meeting with Warden Brownlee, he comments on the imminent arrival of the French prison officials with, "They're studying my prison ideas – So they can adopt some other system." Beanie Walker's witty titles add a lot of humor to this film and other Roach comedies of the time.

Tiny Sandford gets his first lengthy scenes with Laurel and Hardy in this film. After Warden Brownlee has spent a significant amount of time yelling at Laurel and Hardy for digging up the floor of his office (and choking Stan in a fit of pique), he has Sandford put a row of convicts through their exercises. The script barely hints at this, but in the film it develops into a substantial routine wherein the prisoners line up and do deep knee bends, with Stan continually being out of synch. (In later films such as

Stanley John "Tiny" Sandford, as a glowering prison guard, gets his first significant scene with Laurel and Hardy in this film.

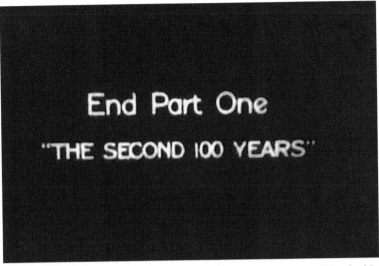

A frame from an original print proves that the title was given as "100," not "Hundred," despite some publicity articles. *Courtesy of Ed Watz.*

Second Hundred Years Funnier Than First

The intriguing theme as to how one might spend his time if only a given year in which to live, has been exploited in drama and fiction, but it remained for that famous producer of original comedies, Hal Roach, to present an ingenious twist to the opposite angle of the subject. "The Second Hundred Years," latest Hal Roach M-G-M offering, which has been booked by the .... theater starting ...., is a lighthearted treatment of one way of spending the last hundred years of a two-century lease on life.

Although in modern, not bibical times, Oliver Hardy and Stan Laurel find themselves faced with the problem of how to while away the remaining hundred years, after the first century had expired. How they get this way is the result of many ludicrous situations into which they fall in the course of an extremely amusing plot. Jimmy Finlayson, the third member of Roach's effervescent

Scene from the HAL ROACH *comedy* "THE SECOND ONE HUNDRED YEARS"

SCENE CUT NO. B

trio, contributes to the merriment as the governor. Supporting the all-star cast are other sterling players, directed by Fred Guiol.

A ready-made review from the Press Sheet.

You're Darn Tootin', Ollie would join him.)

The "century plant" gag has Stan and Ollie trying to escape their captors by backing away from the line of marching prisoners; Ollie backs into the pointy end of the plant and, thinking that a guard is behind him, tells Stan, "This one's got a bayonet!"

"Painting different things as they go along" in the script develops into an elaborate routine, filmed on the Roach backlot, where the boys whitewash everything in sight to prove to a suspicious cop that they are indeed painters. A parked car gets special

Stan's Haircut

WHEN Stan Laurel, Hal Roach featured comedian in Pathe comedies, sails for London the latter part of this month, to visit his father for the first time in eighteen years, he will be forced, by the cruel vagaries of fate, to appear in the parental home with his head shaved. Such is the life of a screen player.

Laurel and Oliver Hardy, well known for their comedy team work, are to appear as convicts in their next production at the Hal Roach Studios, starting immediately. Their locks will be shorn within a day or two. Then, immediately after the completion of this comedy, Laurel will sail, hair or no hair.

When *Motion Picture News* published this story on July 8, 1927, the film had already been shot – but Stan's shaved head would eventually result in his lasting "fright wig" hairdo.

James Finlayson may get credit on this lobby card, but it's Frank Brownlee scowling at the boys.

HAL ROACH
presents
THE ALL STAR COMEDY

THE SECOND 100 YEARS

with
STAN LAUREL·
OLIVER·HARDY
JIMMY
FINLAYSON

A
Metro-
Goldwyn-
Mayer
PICTURE

treatment on its fenders, headlights and windshield – and Stan makes sure it's well painted under the hood. The boys also paint the windows of shops belonging to Hot Dog Kelly and Ice Cream Cohen before Stan, painting a lamppost, fails to notice the sudden arrival of flapper Dorothy Coburn and accidentally paints her derriere.

A recently discovered, more complete print of the film reveals that the painting sequence originally ended with a title, "Four hours later," and a scene of the cop running after the boys in the dark. Stan drops his can of paint, causing the cop to trip over it and splatter himself with the gooey whitewash.

I have no idea precisely what a "Brandenburg takem" is, but surely it refers to actor, prop man, assistant director and general man of all work around the Roach lot Chet Brandenberg (with an e), whose appearances in front of the camera were few but which must have contained some impressive reactions.

During the dinner party sequence, the film has no routine of Stan stealing silverware as suggested by the script. However, "several gags of etiquette and conversation" develops into a bit where Ollie tries to keep Stan from eating with his knife; later, Stan is bedeviled by the cherry on top of a fruit cocktail, which he chases from his own plate onto that of other guests, including Finlayson. This routine would reach full, ah, fruition with Anita Garvin's unforgettable performance in *From Soup to Nuts*.

June 10, 27

Open longshot JAIL CORRIDOR.

After getting over the different types in each cell cut to Babe and Stan. Introduce them arguing – Babe blaming Stan for being there. The guard hollers at them. Babe and Stan smile at him.

Babe then gets over that Stan had better continue to dig the tunnel which they have been working on for several days. He slips Stan a foney looking map. Stan takes his hat and coat off, takes a pillow off the bed, puts the coat around the pillow and puts hat on top, and places it in the position with its back toward the door. He quickly gets under a small table, pulls out a loose tile and exits down a hole.

Babe starts holding conversation with the dummy. The guard at intervals walks past the gate. The guard finally stops and looks in and gets over his interest in Babe's conversation. He stays there long enough to get Babe upset. At that point Stan comes up from under the table, speaks title to Babe "We're nearly through." Stan sees the guard, takes a double takem. The guard gets sore, sees that he is being fooled with the dummy, enters the cell and takes the hat and coat off the dummy and throws the pillow on the bed. He grabs Stan, drags him out of there and places him in the next cell to Babe.

As he locks the door he places a big key on a hook on his belt. He starts marching up and down the corridor again, passing Stan and Babe's cells. As he passes Babe's cell Babe reaches out and takes the key off the hook, unlocks his door, and as the guard turns and passes Babe's cell again Babe hangs the key on the end of the guard's gun. The guard unaware of this passes Stan's cell, Stan takes the key, unlocks his door. As the guard turns and passes Stan's cell again Stan follows behind him and gets back into Babe's cell again. The guard then turns and passes Babe's cell, Babe hangs the key back on the hook. As the guard gets to Stan's cell he sees it empty, he takes it, starts getting all excited. He runs to Babe's cell and does a bigger takem when he sees Stan back in Babe's cell. He warns Stan to cut out this monkey business.

We cut to the Warden's Office. Introduce Frank Brownley as the Warden and Jimmy Finlayson as the Governor of the jail. Jimmy gets over to Brownley in title to the effect that Jimmy is giving a banquet at his home that night in honor of a couple of French Criminal Experts who are visiting this country and making a tour of inspection of the jails.

Cut back to Stan and Babe's cell. Stan and Babe get over that the guard has left the corridor and now is their chance to make their getaway. They quickly enter down the hole under the table.

We cut to an underground shot of a roughly cut tunnel. We see a small pick, a piece of candle, couple of matches, and a small shovel. Stan and Babe crawl in on their hands and knees, Babe gives Stan the candle, strikes a match and lights it. They then look at the rough map, Babe gets over that they are going in the right direction – everything is okey. Babe takes the shovel and starts digging. Stan places the candle in back of him, picks up the small pick and starts to pick. Stan's fanny gets too close to the flame of the candle and starts burning him. He doesn't take it at first. Finally the heat becomes too intense and he takes it. As he does he excitedly sticks Babe in the fanny with the pick. Babe bawls him out and Stan starts to cry.

Babe takes the pick from him and tells him to hold the candle and the map. Babe then takes the pick and starts picking. Stan watches Babe and accidentally holds the paper over the candle and burns the map. Stan is worried and doesn't want to let Babe know it. Babe turns to Stan and asks "Which way now?" Stan gives him a silly grin and points to the burned paper. Babe gets sore and gets over that he figures it is about time to dig upward. He makes a strike with the pick. As he does so the end of the pick hits a water pipe. The water starts squirting out. They both try to stop the flow. Finally Stan sticks his finger in the hole. The water stopped, Babe continues to pick upward with the pick.

We cut to the Warden's Office – the warden seated at his desk. In front of the desk we see the carpet moving up and down. The warden takes this and decides to watch. Finally the pick comes thru, making a hole in the carpet. Babe's hand reaches up, starts feeling around, he finally tars the carpet and quickly comes up out of the hole with his back to the warden. Not realizing for a minute where he is, and without looking around, he gets on his hands and knees and reaches down into the hole and pulls Stan up. They both take it when they see where they are. Babe gives Stan a dirty look and starts to bawl him out for burning the map. They both turn simultaneously and see the warden. They make one wild dash out of the office into the corridor followed by the warden.

We cut to the corridor. The guard is lining up all the prisoners. Stan and Babe run in followed by the warden. They get all mixed up with the other prisoners. The warden roughhouses Stan and Babe, then bawls out the guard for not watching them more closely.

During this we cut to a shot in the tunnel. The water is by this time just pouring out of the water pipe. The tunnel is half-flooded.

We cut back to the corridor. The prisoners are finally all lined up. The guard gives them an order, they all start to lockstep and make an exit, leaving the warden blustering and yelling at them. He is sore.

We cut to the exterior. The prisoners and the guard exit from the jail into the prison yard. The guards start to put the prisoners thru their exercises.

Cut back to the corridor. Show the warden pacing up and down, still in a rage. He finally exits.

We cut to warden's office which by this time is all flooded. His desk, chairs, etc. are all floating around. The warden enters looking backwards still raving. He makes a big step into his office and falls into the water out of sight. He finally comes up and takes it big.

Cut back to the prison yard. Prisoners still exercising.

Cut to a shot and show the prison cook hitting a gong which is the signal for lunch.

The guards hearing the gong, line up the prisoners, and they start a lockstep towards the jail. Stan and Babe on the end of the line. We do the gags of Stan and Babe leaving the line and doing the lockstep backwards, each time bumping into different guards. They finally join the line again, after gag with the century plant. They pass a couple of painters. Babe gets an idea.

The painters put down their buckets and brushes and exit for lunch. Stan and Babe get away from the line and exit backwards around corner.

We cut to the corridor. Prisoners are all lined up. The guard starts counting them.

We cut back to Babe and Stan. We see them just turning their coats inside out. They have already turned their pants the same way, and when they get them on they are both dressed similar to the painters. They pick up the buckets and the brushes and start painting their way towards the gate.

We show a couple of guards walking around passing them etc. and paying no attention to them, not realizing who they are. Stan and Babe finally paint their way out of the jail.

We cut to extra set up. Stan and Babe enter from around the corner and are all tickled to death that they have gotten out. A cop enters the scene. Stan and Babe take it and get all flustered and start painting promiscuously. The cop gets suspicious of their actions and starts to follow them.

We go into a walking chase – Stan and Babe painting different things as they go along, out of embarrassment.

It ends up with Stan accidentally painting a girl's fanny and the girl getting sore. Stan and Babe start to run with the cop after them. We run them thru a couple of sets.

Cut to a hotel setup. Big limousine standing in front of hotel. We introduce the two Frenchmen. They tell the chauffeur to drive them to the Governor's house. As they step into the limousine Stan and Babe enter on the run around the corner and seeing the open door of the car they jump in and the door closes on the car as it pulls out. The cop enters around the corner on the run, stops, looks around, and does a "Brandenburg" takem.

Cut to a shot of the car going along the boulevard away from the camera. Out of each window we throw two dummies dressed in underwear. As they land we cut to the two Frenchmen. They get up and start running in different directions.

Cut to Finlayson's home. The guests are all awaiting the arrival of the two Frenchmen. General excitement. Finlayson is there pinning it on for the folks.

Cut to the exterior of the home. Car pulls into driveway and as it stops in front of the house two policemen step forward – one opens the door of the car, and out steps Babe and Stan dressed in the Frenchmen's clothes. They take it as they see the cops. The cops salute them, Stan and Babe start to make an exit and the cops show them to the front door.

Cut inside of house. Butler enters and announces the two Frenchmen. Stan and Babe step in. The guests all bow and Stan and Babe bow to them. Stan then turns to the butler and bows to him. Babe stops him. Babe then crushes his opera hat and gives it to the butler. Stan sees this and crushes his silk hat, mashing it all up, and hands it to the butler. The guests all laugh. Babe gets over to them that Stan will have his little joke, then gives Stan a dirty look and maybe a kick in the pants. Jimmy comes over, shakes hands with them. As he does so Gene Pallette, a French type, comes over very excitedly and kisses Babe and Stan on the cheeks. They take this not knowing what to do. Pallette then says something in French to Babe. Babe takes it, then recovers his dignity and replies in bum French, just getting by. Stan gets clever and he makes a French crack. The people all laugh and Babe laughs and he kicks Stan again.

We cut to a shot of the butler, he is hitting a big gong for the signal for dinner.

Stan and Babe take it and start doing the lockstep. As the guests all kind of look surprised at this Stan and Babe suddenly recover themselves and to alibi their actions they do a little dance, Babe finishing up with a title "An old custom in France." They all exit to the dining room.

As they are walking around the table looking for their places, Stan starts lifting the silverware and putting it in his pocket. Babe takes it away from him and reprimands him. Stan then pulls out a big silver platter from under his vest. They finally get seated. The butlers start serving soup. One butler calls to another by number, saying "Number Five." Stan gets to his feet and says "yes sir." We get over before this that that was Stan's jail number. Babe pushes him back in the chair. We then go for several gags of etiquette and conversation. Butler comes into room, goes to Finlayson and tells him he is wanted in the other room. Finlayson excuses himself and makes an exit. We see thru the arch there the warden. Jimmy enters to him. He gets over very excitedly regarding Stan and Babe's escape. Jimmy gives him orders to scour the country for them. Babe looks over and sees the warden, maybe spills some coffee over some fellow opposite him. Jimmy returns to the table, tells the guests bout the two convicts who have escaped. We go for a gag with Babe and Stan.

We fade in, it is after dinner, guests are seated in another room holding general conversation. Jimmy gets over to one of the guests that he will give them a little surprise by taking them for a visit around the jail. He then gets over to the company that they have a little surprise for them and all are to follow him. They all exit thru door.

We cut to the corridor of the jail. They all enter around the corner. When Stan and Babe enter they take it big. Nearby Babe is a reward poster with the pictures of Stan and Babe on it. Underneath this poster is a table with a big stack of the same posters. Babe quickly tears the poster off the wall, gets over to Jimmy that he would like to keep it as a remembrance. Stan picks up stack of them, puts them under his arm, says he would like to do the same as Babe. Jimmy takes it. Jimmy then starts leading the company to the different cells, and as they look in there we see the different tough characters.

As Babe and Stan look in each cell the prisoners recognize them, saying "Hello Babe, Hello Stan." Stan and Babe get over for them to keep quiet. They finally come to the last cell and in there we see the two Frenchmen in their underwear. As Stan and Babe look in the two

Frenchmen recognize them, start excitedly jabbering, jumping and tearing their hair and almost going into hysterics. Pallette understands what they are saying and quickly tells Jimmy the situation. The guests hear it and they all take one look at Babe and Stan and scatter in all directions.

We go for a gag where Stan and Babe are put back in the cell and FADE OUT –

the end.

THEIR PURPLE MOMENT

Production history: Production S-10. Written early February 1928. "Midgets rehearse" Saturday, February 11 and Tuesday, February 14. Shooting started Wednesday, February 15. Filming on February 16 at "28th and Congress" but on a Roach studio stage all other days; finished on Friday, February 24. Retakes were shot Wednesday, March 7. Copyrighted May 19, 1928, by MGM (LP 25254). Released May 19. Two reels.

Produced by Hal Roach. Directed by James Parrott. Supervising Director, Leo McCarey. Assistant Director, Lloyd French. Art Direction and Props, Theodore Driscoll and Harry Hopkins. Photographed by George Stevens. Assistant Cameramen, Jack Roach and E.L. White. Gowns by [William] Lambert. Edited by Richard Currier. Titles by H.M. Walker.

With Stan Laurel (Stan Pincher), Oliver Hardy (Himself), Anita Garvin (Ollie's girlfriend), Kay Deslys (Stan's girlfriend), Fay Holderness (Mrs. Pincher), Lyle Tayo (Mrs. Hardy), Tiny Sandford (Maitre d' at the Pink Pup), Leo Willis (Cab driver), Jack V. Lloyd (Chef), Dorothea Wolbert (Gossip), Clara Guiol (Cigarette girl), Jack Hill (Doorman/Pink Pup patron), Gene Morgan, Sam Lufkin, Chet Brandenburg (Waiters), Ed Brandenburg (Pink Pup patron), Dorothy Coburn (Hat check girl), Harry Earles (Midget performer), The Erwings' Band (Orchestra), Frederick Sullivan (Distinguished gentleman in portrait photo).

Stan's wife is such a penny-pincher that, in order to have any of his pay for himself, he has created a secret compartment. Prominent in his home is a framed portrait of a gentleman wearing a cutaway coat; Stan is able to open this "coat" and insert a few dollars each week in the "pocket." Ollie and his equally fearsome wife come to visit. The boys are eager to get away by themselves, and tell the wives they're going bowling. They unintentionally wind up outside a swanky cafe, where two good-time girls are in trouble because they can't pay their bill. Since Stan has brought the bankroll that he has so carefully stashed away, he and Ollie magnanimously decide to stake the girls to another lavish meal, and eventually invite a cab driver to join them. As they're enjoying this sumptuous feast, Stan opens his wallet to discover that his wife has replaced his money with cigar coupons. The boys attempt to beat a hasty retreat, but are prevented when their wives show up, having been alerted by the neighborhood gossip. Eventually, all parties wind up in the restaurant's kitchen, where a pie-throwing battle ensues.

Significant changes mark the journey that *Their Purple Moment* took from script to screen. The script does a better job of using every element, making sure that there's a comedy payoff for everything that's introduced. The film, however, brings in bits of business that don't come to full resolution and seem arbitrary.

This script barely made it to five legal-sized, single spaced pages. The first three pages describe the action pretty much as it was filmed. The only differences are that instead of Stan bringing home a phonograph record of "Three o'Clock in the Morning," he's brought home a record of Asian music with exotic characters adorning

In a gag cut from the film, Ollie's attempt to wind up Stan's Victrola does not have the intended result.

A deleted gag; headwaiter Tiny Sandford and wives Lyle Tayo and Fay Holderness suspect something's afoot.

Although the Al G. Barnes circus troupe seems to be saying "J'accuse!" in this deleted scene, they actually help Stan and Ollie escape.

the label. Originally, the record would have had more of a reason for being in the film. The script details a gag in which Babe attempts to wind up the Laurels' Victrola, with unfortunate results. This was filmed but for some reason was cut. The gag was repeated and retained in the team's next film, *Should Married Men Go Home?*

Their Purple Moment is the first L&H film directed by James Gibbons Parrott (1897-1939), who was starring in Hal Roach comedies as "Paul Parrott" in 1920, a few years before his older brother, known professionally as Charley Chase, came to the studio. He would ultimately direct 21 of the domestically-released Laurel and Hardy movies, along with 12 of their foreign-language editions.

The script makes no suggestions for the casting, but the film is populated with some formidable females. Fay Holderness (1881-1953) here plays Stan's wife, and is not fond of Asian music. She evidently would be two years later in *Hog Wild*, now playing the spouse of Ollie, who thoughtfully puts up a radio aerial because "Mrs. Hardy wants to hear Japan!" In *Their Purple Moment*, Mrs. Hardy is played by Lyle (pronounced "Lily") Tayo (1889-1971), who would later play the prospective Christmas tree customer in *Big Business* who has no husband, and the mother of Chubby in the Our Gang comedy *Shivering Shakespeare*, who attends the school play about ancient Rome and scolds her son every time he lifts up his toga to see what his

In another discarded gag, Fay and Lyle seem to recognize those two Floradora Girls.

next line is. Anita Garvin (1906-1994) had already given her wonderful performance as noveau-riche Mrs. Culpepper in *From Soup to Nuts*, and would later have memorable turns in *Blotto, Be Big, Swiss Miss* and *A Chump at Oxford*; here's she's at her most malevolent as the good-time girl who carries a stiletto. Her companion is just as lethal; she's got a Saturday Night Special in her handbag. She's played by Kay Deslys (pronounced "De-lease," 1899-1954), and she would appear prominently in *Should Married Men Go Home?, We Faw Down, Perfect Day* and *Below Zero*. The town gossip is played by Dorothea Wolbert (1874-1958), who had been in dozens of Hal Roach shorts and her own series of one-reel comedies; in a 1955 episode of *I Love Lucy*, she would play a character conveniently named Dorothea Wolbert.

The cab driver who is magnanimously invited to a steak dinner by Ollie is portrayed by Leo Willis (1890-1952), who would also have prominent roles in *The Hoose-Gow* (as the "gentleman over there" who tries to help the boys escape from prison) and in *Below Zero*, as the thug who tries to purloin Stan and Ollie's newly-found wallet full of cash. Frequent L&H co-star Stanley J. "Tiny" Sandford (1894-1961) is the headwaiter who suspects that the boys can't pay their ever-mounting bill, and a temperamental chef, not mentioned in the script, is played by Jack V. Lloyd (1885-?), who had appeared as Stan's rival in the first film to feature Laurel and Hardy in its cast, the 1921 pilot film *The Lucky Dog*.

The actor who is depicted in the prominent photograph adorning Stan's living room is Frederic Richard Sullivan (1872-1937). A nephew of composer Sir Arthur Sullivan, he was a film director and actor who can be seen in livelier fashion in the Marx Brothers' *Duck Soup* and W. C. Fields' *You're Telling Me*. Another portrait of him is visible in Ebeneezer Laurel's mansion in *The Laurel-Hardy Murder Case*.

Which brings us to the midgets, or "little people," performers from the Al G. Barnes circus who were spending the winter in Los Angeles. They were collectively paid $50.00 per day for six days' work, most of which wound up on the cutting-room floor. The script is entirely different from the film for its last page and a half, detailing a remarkable sequence that now exists only in its pages and a few photographs.

Sometimes deviations from the script came during the filming, sometimes at sneak preview screenings for full, unsuspecting audiences. The changes in *Their Purple Moment* evidently came about somewhere in between. Hal Roach told historian Richard W. Bann in 1981, "The routine with the midgets – escaping as midgets – did not pay off in the screening room. Otherwise we would have kept it." One wishes that the footage still survived, as the script and photos suggest a memorable and funny scene.

This sequence was replaced with a scene in which Stan, Ollie, the waiter, the wives

The new finale to the movie involved Fay Holderness, Stan, Tiny Sandford, Jack V. Lloyd, Babe and Lyle Tayo in a pie fight – along with an unknown waiter who keeps taking unintended dives into mashed potatoes.

DOROTHEA WOLBERT   FAY HOLDERNESS
Gossip   *Mrs. Pincher*

and the ornery chef battle it out in the nightclub's kitchen, using pies as the chief artillery. The matter of the unpaid bill is never resolved; moreover, this skirmish with only six combatants seems pretty scrawny after we've seen the huge pie fight in *The Battle of the Century*. The film doesn't come to a satisfying conclusion, it just stops.

Nevertheless, as Mr. Roach told Richard Bann, "The business with the pies may not have been great, but that always worked with audiences. We didn't have time for anything better. Run your print with an audience then come back and tell me if we did the right thing changing it."

If we can't see the tantalizing original finale, at least the script gives us the opportunity to read it.

S-10 - Laurel-Hardy

Open on title, "Saturday afternoon, when all good husbands bring their pay checks home."

Fade in on interior of Stan's home, his wife counting cigar coupons with a premium catalog nearby. She hears the bell, goes to the door and admits Stan.

Stan enters and kisses his wife on the cheek. She immediately starts pantomiming for his paycheck. He hands it to her and she counts it quickly, then gets over that there is money missing. Stan hands her a phonograph record and pantomimes it cost $3.00. She looks at the record and discovers that it is "Three o'clock in the Morning." She gets over that she doubts very much that the record cost that much. Stan gets over a suggestion of guilt, gives her a winning smile and exits.

Stan enters hall and comes to a picture of his grandfather, looks all around to see that he is not being watched. The wife appears from a door upstage, unbeknownst to Stan, and sees him take a dollar from under his collar. He opens grandpa's coat, takes out a wallet, puts the dollar in it and replaces the wallet, then exits back to living room.

The wife makes a hurried entrance back to the living room and Stan wonders whether she saw him or not.

The doorbell rings and Stan admits Babe and his wife. He brings them into the living room and misses his wife.

Cut to Stan's wife substituting the coupons for Stan's money, which she puts into her apron pocket. She returns and nods to Babe's wife pleasantly and also to Babe. She also nods to Stan, but it is a menacing nod. Stan starts to acknowledge it, then wonders what's wrong. The two wives engage in conversation and the two boys ease over to one side.

Babe tells Stan that his wife caught him holding money out. Stan gets over that he was too slick for his wife, takes Babe into the hall and pulls out the wallet, taps it knowingly and puts it in his pocket. Stan speaks whispered title to Babe, "How are we going to get out?" Babe gets over he will tend to it.

They come back to the other room and Babe asks the women if they can go and see the new Ford. Stan's wife tells them they can go, but for him not to buy any more records. This reminds Stan of the record he bought, so he puts it on. As Babe returns with their hats, he sees Stan having trouble with the Victrola – the crank keeps coming out. Babe tells Stan to step aside and he will show him. Babe steps up to the Victrola and tells Stan it's all in the wrist. He proceeds to wind the Victrola and the spring breaks and comes flying out. Stan gets over to Babe, "It's all in the wrist." They then turn to the wives and make an awkward exit together.

As Stan and Babe start out of the house they meet a gossip friend of their wives. She looks them over and says, "This is a nice day for chasing." She gives them a dirty look and starts in. Stan gives her a razzberry and as she turns again she finds him blowing his nose. The door opens and the wives greet her and start talking very fast as the door closes. FADE OUT.

FADE IN, exterior of cafe. Stan and Babe look over the advertised entertainment and decide to go in. As they start in, two fellows come running out and down the street. The boys wonder what's the matter. Then two girls come out with a waiter. The waiter tells the girls, "Somebody will have to pay your check!" The girls get over their distress, look off and see Stan and Babe and give them a wistful look.

The two boys look at each other, return the girls' look and exit to help them. They volunteer to help the girls and the girls thank them.

A taxi driver steps up and asks the girls if they want him to wait. The girls tell Stan to tell him to wait. Stan tells him to wait. Babe gives Stan a reproving look and says to the driver, "Wait." The taxi driver starts back to his cab.

Babe gallantly takes his girl's arm and starts into the cafe. Stan tries to imitate Babe's action and falls down with his girl. While he is sprawled on the ground with his girl, the gossip enters and sees this. She turns and hurries away to tell their wives.

Cut to interior of cafe. The boys sit at a table with the girls and a waiter takes their order for four dinners. Babe's girl tells him that she will take care of the fellow who ran out on her. Stan turns inquiringly to his girl and she shows him a stiletto. Stan takes this and then motions for everyone to look at the midgets dance.

Show a little bit of the midgets dance. When they finish Babe invites them over to their table and buys them candy and cigars, and the midgets leave, thanking them. Stan reaches for his wallet to pay for these and discovers the coupons. He tells the cigarette and candy girls to put it on the check.

Stan starts to suffer. He looks at Babe, sees him having a great time. The waiter returns with the four dinners. As he starts to serve them, the taxi driver, enters with the meter. Babe greets him jovially and says, "Another dinner!" Stan continues to suffer. Babe starts to eat and notices Stan sitting there. He asks Stan if he is sick. Stan shows him the wallet and passes it under the table to him.

Babe reaches under the table and opens the wallet. Without raising his head he does a lot of heavy thinking. He raises his eyes enough to see the waiter put a steak in front of the taxi driver, then comes up facing the lens with a woebegone look. He looks at Stan and whispers, "What'll we do?" Stan gets over, "I don't know."

While they are wondering, the lights go out and the midgets start a new number. Stan and Babe slide down under the table and start sneaking. We show an insert of them crawling along, and a waiter enters, trips over them and falls with his face in the mashed potatoes. Stan and Babe quickly jump back to their table. The waiter looks around trying to figure out who caused him to fall. Stan and Babe look at him innocently. A mean looking fellow pulls out his watch and tells the waiter to hurry, he has to catch a train. The waiter bows to him and exits, still looking for the person who tripped him.

Cut to the gossip coming to Stan's home. She enters the house. There is a pause and she comes out with the two wives. Show walking shot of the three of them going down the street, the gossip falling a little in the rear.

Cut back to Stan and Babe and everyone is finished eating. The waiter puts the check down. The two of them look at each other and at the food and at the meter, and the lights go out again.

They duck down under the table and start to sneak away. The waiter enters – more mashed potatoes! The boys jump back quickly to their table and we repeat the action of the waiter getting up wondering who spilled him, and the man again calls the waiter's attention to his train.

Stan and Babe look at each other, look at the meter and it goes up again.

We then cut to the wives and the gossip walking along, and cut to insert of their feet. In the insert they cross a mud hole. The two wives jump it and the gossip goes in on her face.

Back to Stan and Babe. The girls are now primping up preparatory to leaving. Babe looks and sees his girl's gun' Stan looks and sees the stiletto. They then look at each other and something attracts Stan's attention and he looks past Babe.

Cut to the two wives entering the cafe.

Stan looks back at Babe, and Babe speaks title, "What could be worse?" Stan points off to the wives. Babe looks off and sees them.

The two boys suffer, and to make matters worse the two girls get up to leave. Stan and Babe rise awkwardly and the waiter hands them the check. They start fumbling in their pockets and get over the hopelessness of the situation.

A thought dawns on the waiter and he speaks title, "I don't think you fellows have any money." Babe indignantly pulls out the wallet, hands it to Stan and says, "Pay the man." They then do an "Alphonse and Gaston," passing the wallet back and forth to each other. The waiter puts a stop to it by grabbing the wallet himself. He looks in and sees the coupons.

Stan and Babe start to make an embarrassed exit, the waiter after them. They quickly get through a door and the waiter starts in after them. Show them coming in and out of several doors. They open a door and the waiter is standing with his back to them. The waiter looks into a mirror which he thinks is a door, sees Stan and Babe and runs at them, crashing into the mirror.

They finally reach their wives' table, see the wives and duck under the table. The waiter comes in and the wives turn to him. The two boys start to crawl out. The other waiter comes in, trips over them and again falls in the mashed potatoes.

During this confusion the boys run out and come into the midgets' dressing room, run over to the window and see that it is barred. They come back to the midgets and tell them they are in trouble, and the midgets volunteer to help them.

The waiter opens the door quickly and Stan and Babe duck under the dressing table. The waiter runs over to the barred window, gets over they couldn't have got out there, looks back at the door and figures they must be in this room. He looks under the table and they are not there. Flash of a couple of midgets looking innocently at him. He goes back and takes his place by the door.

The music strikes up the "Floradora Sextette" and the midgets come out and go into their dance, and we see that Stan and Babe are two of the Floradora girls.

We then play the dance through, and one by one the waiter, taxi driver, the two girls and the wives recognize them. They all come down and form a group together. The dance is about over now and the two boys see all their menaces lined up together and start getting bawled up in their dance. Their predicament is so hopeless that they start laughing at the silliness of it all, and hurriedly make a very embarrassed exit.

The wives pay off the waiter and taxi driver, then turn and

menacingly start for their husbands.

The wives come into a room and see the boys going out a window, and start out in another direction.

The taxi driver in counting his money drops one of the bills. As he bends to pick it up, the waiter trips over him and falls in the mashed potatoes.

Cut to the street; Stan and Babe as midgets come up to a cop. The cop picks Stan up, tickles him under the chin, and Stan pulls the cop's mustache. The cop sets Stan down and bows very politely as they exit.

As Stan and Babe go around a corner they see their wives coming out the entrance of the cafe. The wives see them. The boys are standing over a sidewalk ventilator and their dresses fly up in the air. Several people watching this take it big.

The boys now stand up and exit around the corner, the wives following. They pass the cop and he takes it big.

The two boys continue down the street with their wives after them. The wives finally catch them and Stan and Babe start laughing. The wives tell them, "Come on home and we'll give you something to laugh at."

They start down the street, the boys a little ahead. Stan and Babe look back, miss the wives and wonder what has become of them. Cut to the wives just coming up out of the mud hole. FADE OUT.

EARLY TO BED

Production history: Production L-12. Written early May 1928. Filmed Monday, May 21 through Tuesday, May 29. Retakes and added scenes directed by Leo McCarey on Monday June 18, Tuesday June 19 (Hardy only), and Monday June 25 (Laurel only). Copyrighted Oct. 6, 1928, by MGM (LP 25719). Released Oct. 6. Two reels.

Produced by Hal Roach. Directed by Emmett J. Flynn. Supervising director, Leo McCarey. Assistant Director, Lloyd French. Uncredited Assistant Director on retakes and added scenes, Jean Yarbrough. Set Decorations and props, Harry Black and Harry Hopkins. Photographed by George Stevens and Len Powers. Assistant cameramen, John MacBurnie, Walter Williams, Jack Roach, and E.L. White. Edited by Richard Currier. Titles by H.M. Walker.

Starring Stan Laurel (Himself), Oliver Hardy (Himself), Buster (Their dog).

Stan and Ollie are sitting on a park bench with their faithful little dog, Buster. Ollie reads a letter informing him that he has inherited a fortune. Mr. Hardy displays his newfound wealth with a lavishly decorated mansion; he thanks Stan for his friendship by making him the butler. After a wild night on the town, Ollie returns home in an inebriated state and plays a number of "jokes" on his servant; Stan finally has enough, announces that he's leaving, and begins breaking some precious bric-a-brac to prove it. When he sees how shocked Ollie is at this rebellion, Stan prompts a chase by running through the house and demolishing many of the furnishings. The pursuit ends at a decorative fountain, which displays many gargoyle heads that look just like Ollie. Mr. Hardy replaces one of the heads with his own; when he can't spout water as continuously as his marble lookalikes, Stan hits this defective head with a shovel until Ollie reveals his ruse and says, "Let's forgive and forget and be pals again."

One of the few misfires in the Laurel and Hardy canon, *Early to Bed* suffers because the wrong man is given the inheritance. Ollie always thinks of himself as being superior to Stan, so to see him gleefully abusing his underdog partner is not terribly funny. If Stan had received the inheritance and made Ollie his servant, it would have undermined Ollie's pomposity and might have been a welcome example of Mr. Hardy getting his just desserts. (This idea was fulfilled with the "Lord Paddington" scenes in the team's 1940 feature *A Chump at Oxford*.)

The film was directed by Emmett J. Flynn, who had piloted several feature-length Westerns and costume dramas, primarily for Fox. This was his only short comedy, his only film for Hal Roach, and his last silent production. He made three talking feature films in 1929 and then left filmmaking, for all intents and purposes, at 38. After that, he went into a personal and professional tailspin that included a stretch in San Quentin. He died from chronic alcoholism on June 4, 1937, only 44 years old.

Flynn spent eight days making this short, curiously using an entirely different crew (Stevens, Roach and White) on the last two. Three weeks after he finished, Leo

McCarey directed three days' worth of retakes, and I suspect that much of the footage in the finished picture was his work.

McCarey added the opening scene in which Ollie reads the letter informing him that he's now rich. (He gives the envelope to Stan, who gives it to Buster, who deposits it in a trash can.) Incidentally, *Early to Bed* and *Brats* are the two films which have Laurel and Hardy as the only human cast members. In *Early to Bed*, they are accompanied only by their adorable little dog, while *Brats* shows us the household's cat for about three seconds. (*Brats* also has a mouse among the cast members, but since it's an animated cartoon that doesn't count.)

The script for *Early to Bed* obeys the spirit of the film if not always the letter. In the script, Ollie very jealously guards a watch given to him by "the boys at the Masquers' Club." This was a fraternal organization whose members were mostly comedians. Stan and Babe were members; Charley Chase was its president at one time. The members met in a large house at 1765 Sycamore Street in Hollywood for over 60 years; the club still has a presence on the Internet. In any event, Ollie's watch is not noted in the film. Likewise, the scripted ideas of Stan bringing Ollie's mattress downstairs, and Ollie giving Stan a check signed by Santa Claus, didn't make it into the movie.

The most striking difference comes at the end of the script, which suggests that

The entire cast of *Early to Bed* (Buster's the one at left), moments before fortune smiles upon Mr. Hardy.

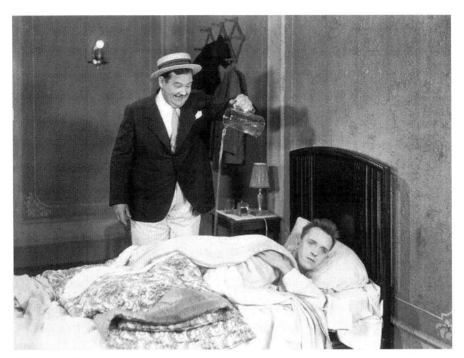

Ollie's "jokes" aren't much more amusing to us than they are to Stan.

Stan's stumble into the birthday cake he made for Ollie causes Mr. Hardy to think that his butler is frothing at the mouth.

A gag not in the film has Ollie's atomizer hitting more than its intended target.

Stan and Ollie fall out of a window as the wrap-up gag. This does nothing to resolve the story, and doubtless Leo McCarey created the film's final scene, wherein Ollie finally reveals himself as one of the fountain's gargoyles, and says to Stan, "Let's forgive and forget and be pals again." While one isn't quite convinced that Ollie has entirely seen the error of his ways, this is certainly a much more satisfying finish.

S-12   Laurel-Hardy

Open with title to the effect: "Three o'clock in the morning –
his master's birthday."

1. Fade in on Stan asleep in a chair, beside a table on which there
is a birthday cake, the candles partly burned down.

2. Stan is awakened by the dog, Buster. He tells the dog to go to
bed, and the dog starts. Stan looks at the cake and picks up a card
which he has placed beside it. Insert card reading: "Dear master: I
baked this out of my own head especially for you."

3. Disconsolate, Stan puts down the card and starts pinching out
the candles, burning his fingers. The dog returns, and Stan tells him
to go back to bed. The dog refuses, so Stan picks him up, carries him
into a living room and puts him in a little bed with Buster's name on
it.

4. Stan sees that the water container is empty, takes it and goes
to the conservatory.

5. Stan comes in to fountain, starts to fill container with water,
and it stops running. He tapes it on the head a couple of times. A
pebble falls out of the mouth, and the water starts running again. Stan
fills the container, puts it by the dog's bed, and exits to hall. Insert of
clock in hall, time 3:05. Stan gets over the master is late getting
home.

6. Cut to Babe coming up to front door and ringing bell in jovial
mood.

7. Cut to Stan. He hears doorbell, gets over that it is Babe, runs
into dining room and lights the candles on the cake. He then goes
back, opens the door, and looks out. In the meantime, babe has hidden
behind some shrubs. Stan closes the door, disappointed, goes back and
pinches out the candles again.

8. Cut to Babe, listening at the door.

9. As Stan finishes putting out the candles and comes back to hall, the doorbell rings again. Stan goes all the way out on the porch, and as he does so Babe sneaks into the house and closes the door. Stan comes back to door on exterior. The peekhole on door opens, and Babe teases Stan. Stan knocks on the door, but Babe won't let him in. Stan finally gives the door a big slap just as Babe opens it, and Stan falls to the interior.

10. Stan picks himself up, a little big disgusted, while Babe stands there enjoying it immensely. Babe takes off his opera cloak, hands it to Stan, then his hat and cane. Babe takes his glove off his left hand and throws it into the hat. He goes to take the other glove off, gets a little confused, and tries to take it off the bare hand. Stan gives him a little disgusted look and shows him what to do, and Babe finally gets the glove off.

11. Babe pulls out a watch, shows it to Stan and says, "See that? A present from the boys at the Masquers' Club."

12. Babe gets over he feels pretty spry, and speaks title to Stan: "Have my guests arrived yet?" Stan says, "I sent them home. You've got to catch a train at seven in the morning." Stan tries to tell Babe it's time to go to bed, but Babe doesn't want to go to bed, and starts dancing around. Stan tries to quiet him, telling him that the dog is asleep. Babe smiles and starts clapping his hands and calls Buster.

13. Cut to the dog, asleep in a funny position. He takes it, scrambles up and out of the scene.

14. The dog comes in with a mad rush through the hallway and jumps up on Babe's chest, knocking him over. Babe sits up with a worried look and immediately feels for his watch. He pulls it out, much relieved to see it intact, and speaks title to Stan, "I wouldn't break that watch for a million dollars."

15. Business of Babe calling the dog and Stan trying to put the dog back to bed. Stan finally gets the dog back to bed, then comes back to the hall and sees Babe moving the hands of the clock back. Stan gets very annoyed and sets the clock right, then takes Babe by the arm and says, "You're going to bed." Babe protests, and Stan tries to push him up the stairs.

16. A little struggle ensues, and Babe suggests that they race up the stairs. Stan is disgusted, but gets over that he will do anything to get Babe to bed. They get on their marks, and Babe says "Go!" They run, and as Babe gets to the bottom of the stairs, he stops and marks "Time." Stan continues upstairs, stops and sees Babe at the bottom. Babe gets over he is having a lot of fun. Stan pantomimes for Babe to come on up to bed. Babe gets an idea, and says "Bring my bed down here." Stan gives a helpless look, and starts for the bedroom.

17. Stan goes to the bed, pulls the mattress off, exits with it over his head. As he gets halfway down the stairs, Babe passes him on the way up. Stan gets to the bottom, puts the mattress down, looks around for Babe and sees him at the top of the stairs. Stan gets a big sore now, picks up the mattress and starts running up the stairs. Babe tries to pass him again, but Stan sees him, and Babe, caught in the act, has to go back.

18. Babe and Stan enter bedroom. Stan throws the mattress on the bed and starts to undress Babe. He gets the coat off and then starts on the vest. Babe gets ticklish and starts running around the room. Stan gets mad and leaps on Babe, and they go into a struggle, which ends up with Stan being all disheveled.

19. Stan completely breaks down and starts crying. Babe gets over he is sorry, and tells Stan that he will go to bed. This pleases Stan. Babe exits to the closet while Stan straightens up the bed. As Stan gets the bed all fixed, the door starts to open. Stan takes it as the door slowly opens and discloses the dog standing there. Stan goes over to pick the dog up, and as he does the closet door opens and out walks Babe in a summer outfit. Stan takes it, throws the dog out the door, then looks at Babe and starts to cry and says, "I'm going to bed. I hope you miss your train." He exits, slamming the door, leaving Babe giggling.

20. Cut to Stan's room. He enters, throws his coat down, and starts to undress.

21. Cut to Babe sneaking downstairs.

22. Back to Stan in his nightdress and stockings. He winds the clock, throws the sheet back to get into bed and discovers Buster

looking up at him. He opens the door and puts the dog out.

23. Cut downstairs to Babe. He enters the dining room and notices the birthday cake. He comes over to it, sits down, reads the card and becomes remorseful. He decides to make it up with Stan and exits.

24. Cut to bedroom, Stan in bed. Babe enters and walks over to the bed. Stan's head is covered and his back is toward Babe. On the table by the bed is a pitcher of water and a glass, a small bed lamp and Stan's clock. Babe gently picks up the sheet, peeks in and giggles. Stan turns and looks at him disgustedly, and then turns away again.

25. Babe goes to the foot of the bed and tickles Stan's feet. Stan gets peeved and doesn't want to make up at all. Babe tries several ways to get Stan into a good humor, with no success. He finally sees the water pitcher, takes it, but gets over to Stan, "Are you going to get up?" Stan says, "No," not knowing that the pitcher of water is over him. Babe starts pouring. Stan takes it, doesn't know what it is, finally turns and discovers Babe with the pitcher.

26. Stan finally gets up and tells Babe, "I'm through! I'm leaving in the morning!" Babe gets a little sore and says, "All right, if you can't be a regular fellow, you can leave right now." Stan says, "Give me my money," and Babe tells him he will pay him as soon as he is ready to go. Babe exits to his room, and Stan starts to dress.

27. Babe enters his room, and slams the door so hard that it bounces back and hits him, knocking him down. He thinks of his watch, pulls it out, sees it is okay, and with a sigh of relief places it on the dresser.

28. The door opens and Stan comes in, the dog standing behind him. Stan says, "I want my money." Babe says, "How much you getting?" Stan takes it and answers, "I don't know, you've never paid me." Babe says, "I'll pay you what you're worth," and quickly writes a check. Stan tears the check out of Babe's hand and walks to the door.

29. As Stan gets to the door, he looks at the check and discovers it is signed, "Santa Claus." He turns to Babe, sore, and says, "I want my money." Babe says, "You won't get a cent." Angry at this, Stan

starts pacing the room and kicking at things. He kicks two or three articles, and turns and looks at Babe. Babe is taking it big. This gives Stan the idea to get even, and he starts breaking things in earnest, topping it with spotting the watch on the dresser, picking up a shoe and smashing the watch. Stan exits, leaving Babe dumbfounded.

30. In hallway, a big vase crashes. Babe, in his room, takes it and starts to exit.

31. Stan enters to stairway landing and tears down the portieres. Babe sees this from hall. Stan then kicks open a window. Shot outside showing Stan as he kicks the window through to show height.

32. Stan then picks up the portieres and throws them out the window, then exits down the stairs. Babe sees all this, and comes to top of stairway. Stan breaks a clock, and with a defiant look at Babe exits into living room. Babe follows and comes into living room archway.

33. Stan picks up a wicked looking dagger, one of Babe's trophies, and slashes the beautiful painting of "Blue Boy." Right next to him is a beautiful cabinet filled with priceless articles, which he crashes. This burns Babe up. Stan starts looking for something big to break, and he and Babe both see a beautiful vase at the same time. Babe beats Stan to it, and protects it with his arms. Stan throws a knife, smashing the article in Babe's arms.

34. Without giving Babe a chance to recuperate from the shock, Stan kicks the leg off the grand piano, picks up the leg, and uses it as a lever to pry out the insides of the piano. This is more than Babe can stand. He takes off his coat, throws it down, and starts for Stan.

35. Stan exits to dining room, knocking things over on his way, such as articles on top of the buffet, etc. He throws some article at Babe. Babe catches it, and throws it back at Stan. Stan ducks and the article goes through a beautiful stained glass window in rear of a dining room. This infuriates Babe, and he chases Stan in earnest.

36. In the chase, Stan has pulled the tablecloth off the table, upsetting the cake on the floor, so when Babe is chasing him Stan slips and falls into the cake. He comes up with the appearance of a

mad dog frothing at the mouth. Stan plays a big "going crazy" scene, with titles telling Babe he is nuts, and that Babe has driven him insane. Stan goes for guns, knives and things on the wall. By this time, Babe is thoroughly frightened.

37. Make cuts of the dog taking it big all through this.

38. Stan finally gets a wicked looking tomahawk and starts after Babe. Babe runs to the other room and dives into the fountain. Stan enters conservatory and looks all around for Babe, enters to the fountain and sees a little bubble come up. He makes a swipe at it. From another part of the pool, larger bubbles come up and Stan makes a swipe at them.

39. Stan finally sits on the edge of the fountain, and a big bubble comes up and hits his fanny. While Stan's back is turned, Babe takes the place of one of the heads around the fountain, getting his mouth full of water quickly, and starts spouting water the same as the other heads. Also show cut of the dog, with his head in the fountain like Babe's.

40. This action ad-libs to a point where Stan finally knocks Babe unconscious with the tomahawk.

41. Quick dissolve to foot of staircase, Stan starting to drag Babe upstairs. Stan is tired and sleepy. Halfway up the stairs, Babe comes to, and shows the audience that he is stalling, letting Stan do all the work. This scene plays to top of stairway.

42. Stan does not realize that he is at the top, and keeps on going to a footstool, cedar chest and window, making three extra steps to the open window. He is just about to pull Babe up the last step when Babe comes to and suddenly realizes they are both going out the window, but it is too late. He screams, and as they both fall out the window we fade out.

PERFECT DAY

Production history: Production L-26. Written late May-early June 1929. Filmed Monday, June 3 through Saturday, June 8. Released August 10. Copyrighted Aug. 12, 1929, by MGM (LP 589). Two reels.

Produced by Hal Roach. Directed by James Parrott. Assistant Director, Lloyd French. Photography by George Stevens. Edited by Richard Currier. Sound by Elmer Raguse. Story Editor, H.M. Walker.

With Stan Laurel (Himself), Oliver Hardy (Himself), Edgar Kennedy (Uncle Edgar), Isabelle Keith (Mrs. Laurel), Kay Deslys (Mrs. Hardy), Baldwin Cooke (Next-door neighbor), Lyle Tayo (Cooke's wife), Harry Bernard, Grace Woods (Friendly neighbors across the street), Charlie Rogers (Parson), Buddy (Dog), Charles Reynolds, Buddy Moore, Robert Mallon, Marie LaVerne, Pete Gordon, Cy Slocum (Neighbors). Part cut from final release print: Sammy Brooks (Neighbor).

Stan and Ollie are planning to spend a lovely Sunday afternoon away from home on a picnic with their wives – and with their grouchy Uncle Edgar, whose severe case of the gout has caused his left foot to be wrapped in a large bandage. An argument between the boys almost ruins the day's supply of sandwiches, but eventually order is restored. The family's intended mode of transport is a 1923 Ford Model T touring car, which turns out to be not quite as sturdy as its reputation suggests. A flat tire, an exploding engine, a brick-throwing skirmish with a neighbor and other obstacles prevent the group from leaving the curbside by their home. Finally, all seems to be repaired. The car starts, the picnickers happily drive around the corner, and immediately plunge into a huge, muddy sinkhole.

One is struck by some major differences between the *Perfect Day* script and the film right from the start. "Uncle Jimmie" was obviously going to be James Finlayson, the part played in the film by Edgar Kennedy. Finlayson's stock in trade was expressing his frustration and annoyance, while Kennedy's was in trying to suppress it. The film would likely have been very different if Finlayson, with his more explosive style, had played the gout-ridden uncle.

There are very few lines of dialogue in the script. "Remember, this is the Sabbath" shows up, although in the script it's spoken by Mrs. Hardy during the brick-tossing battle with the next door neighbor; in the film, Mrs. Laurel says it to both boys after they've been throwing sandwiches at each other. The entire opening scene, running almost five minutes, is not in the script, and it's a very important one as it establishes the personalities of the wives and Uncle Edgar (not to mention Buddy, the mischievous dog).

Babe's suggestion to "throw out the clutch," which Stan takes too literally, is also in the script, but there's no mention of the clanging bell sound effect when Ollie hits him

On location at Vera Avenue in Los Angeles, the boys are joined by Stan's eighteen-month-old daughter, Lois.

on the head with it – something which was thought of as a revolutionary innovation in sound films at the time.

Much of the comedy in *Perfect Day* comes from accidental abuse to Uncle Edgar's bandaged gouty foot. Buddy chews on it in the opening scene, and later Stan steps on it, sits on it, closes the car door on it, and drops a car jack on it. The coup de grace, or maybe in this case the coup de pied, is when Stan is trying to change a tire and, at Edgar's insistence, pulls the jack out from under the wheel – which sends it, and the car, crashing down on Edgar's tootsies. All of this was improvised, as the script merely suggests, "Gags of Stan and Babe stepping on the Uncle's gouty foot, etc."

The script suggests a finale in which a leaky radiator is plugged up with corn meal. It soon erupts with volleys of mush, prompting a messy battle involving the neighbors and a cop. This gag had been suggested for the silent *Bacon Grabbers*, but didn't make the final cut there, either. It would find its proper place in *The Hoose-Gow*, two films after this one. The script also directs that the car finally "back out of the driveway" and into the mud hole, but of course it was much funnier to see the family, thinking that they're finally on their way, rounding a corner and directly plunging into the watery abyss.

Aside from Finlayson, the script doesn't suggest anyone for the cast. Edgar

Which is the flat? Which is the spare? The boys will soon find out, to their frustration.

Grace Woods, Harry Bernard and Marie LaVerne attend the boys' little battle – and so does the ominous boom microphone.

Kennedy, Kay Deslys and Lyle Tayo had appeared in several L&H comedies at this point. Harry Bernard (1878-1940) was an Englishman who made his name in San Francisco-based vaudeville (literally, since his real name was Frederick Owen Salmon). He had worked in the movies since 1915 and debuted with Stan and Ollie as an

STOP RUINING A GOOD SHOW WITH INFERIOR SHORTS!

AMATEURISH talking comedies and mediocre Talking Acts are running wild in this industry today! They are dragging down good shows and cheapening theatres. Lay off them before they ruin you! There's a new type of talking short now that has kept pace with the intelligent progress of talking feature pictures. Metro-Goldwyn-Mayer, who sounded the death-knell of experimental, laboratory full-length talkies to give the industry the New Era, Road-show-size talkies, now assures exhibitors that they need no longer book old-fashioned, childish talking shorts into their theatres. The day of M-G-M's New Era, Road-show Quality Talking Shorts is here!

WHEN THE SHOW IS PERFECT
You'll find that M-G-M's New Era Shorts help to make it so!

HAL ROACH TALKING COMEDIES

These are the class talking comedies that play the big Capitol Theatre, N.Y., and similar de luxe houses everywhere. Hal Roach gives to his talking comedies talent, care and resources comparable to that which goes into the making of feature pictures.

3 OUR GANG
There's nothing in the comedy field to compare with the charm and delight of the Gang talking! They have won a new fame and following in talking comedies.
2 OUR GANG (Synchronized)

3 LAUREL-HARDY
Their talking comedies, "A Perfect Day," booked into the Capitol, N.Y., and other de luxe houses is the first of their class talking comedy of the new season.
2 LAUREL-HARDY (Synchronized)

3 CHARLIE CHASE
Charlie Chase brings to the talking screen talents of song, dance and mimicry that make his personality more winning than ever. "Leaping Love" is just a sample!

3 HARRY LANGDON
Langdon is to be the surprise talkie star. His first dialog comedy reveals a comic manner of speech that is irresistibly funny. Credit Hal Roach with another money hunch!

26 METRO MOVIETONE ACTS

Only the Biggest Names with established drawing power in Metro Movietone Acts. Theatres have learned that M-G-M class and quality differentiates these Acts from all others.

AMONG THE HEADLINERS IN METRO MOVIETONE ACTS
Van & Schenck   Ukelele Ike   Raymond Hitchcock
Irving Aaronson & Commanders   Phil Spitalny   Happiness Boys
Titta Ruffo   Yvette Rugel   Gus Edwards, etc.

12 M-G-M COLORTONE REVUES

These tabloid musical and dancing entertainments put your theatre in the Broadway de luxe class. Only M-G-M gives you revues of this kind with names like Charles King featured, and with dance experts like Sammy Lee and creators like Gus Edwards. Gems of beauty entirely in color and all-talking, singing, dancing.

SAMMY LEE   CHARLES KING   GUS EDWARDS

52 HEARST METROTONE NEWS

The world's greatest publisher has placed his world-wide resources behind the creation of a Super-Sound News. Once a week starting September 28th, on disc or film. The only sound newsreel produced by a news-gathering organization.

104 M-G-M INTERNATIONAL NEWSREEL

News and International Newsreel as represented in the M-G-M International Newsreel means that no other outfit can begin to compete in world news coverage. Twice Weekly starting July 31st.

The combined staffs and resources of M-G-M

Everybody's happy when you've got—

As this MGM advertisement from the July 1929 *Motion Picture News* indicates, there's nothing more embarrassing than inferior shorts.

Uncle Edgar's gouty foot seems to be a continual target for the car door.

obstreperous truck driver in 1928's *Two Tars*. Here, he is a remarkably friendly neighbor across the street who continually wishes the boys a pleasant journey. He's outdone, however, by his wife, who happily shrieks "Good-byyyyyyyyyyye!" over and over again. She is played by Missouri native Grace Woods (1885-1952), who had appeared in many Roach silent shorts (including *Two Tars*, where she's sprayed with a faceful of dirty motor oil). She worked in many comedies and Westerns and was later a seamstress in the wardrobe departments of several studios.

In 2011, a ten-DVD set of Laurel and Hardy-Hal Roach sound films, released by Universal-Vivendi, made *Perfect Day* available with its original 1929 soundtrack for the first time since – well, 1929. This does not contain the sprightly Leroy Shield and Marvin Hatley music cues which have enhanced the film since its 1937 reissue. However, the absence of music does lend a certain gritty documentary feel to the film, and one can more clearly hear much of the improvised background dialogue, especially from the wives, who are incessantly chatty.

Perfect Day is one of the best L&H talkies, and happily the three houses which figure prominently in the film are still well-maintained and instantly recognizable on Vera Avenue in Los Angeles. Presumably, the residents have long since become accustomed to Laurel and Hardy devotees making pilgrimages, and then departing with loud and lengthy cries of "Good-byyyyyyyyyyye!"

L-26 Laurel – Hardy

The story is about Stan and Babe who are going to take their wives and Uncle Jimmie to a Sunday picnic in their new second-hand car.

FADE IN on the driveway at back of a bungalow, garage in background, kitchen door in foreground. A Ford touring car is standing in the driveway. Stan and Babe and their wives enter from the kitchen door, helping Uncle Jimmie. Jim has one foot all bandaged up, suffering from gout.

They put Jimmie and the wives into the back seat. Stan and Babe are all pleased. A neighbor enters and talks to Babe over the fence, getting over it is a beautiful morning, etc., and Babe tells him of the wonderful trip they re going to have. Babe starts up the car, wishing good-bye to the neighbor, and starts to back out.

Show insert of tack as the rear tire rolls over it. There is a loud "pop" and Babe stops the car. He and Stan get out to see what the trouble is and discover it is the flat tire. They get the wives and Jimmie out of the car so they can get the jack out of the back seat. Gags of Stan and Babe stepping on the Uncle's gouty foot, etc., and business of jacking the car up. They finally get it set and come around to fix the tire. Insert the jack slipping down, and the wheel drops onto Jim's foot. He takes it, and Babe suggests it would be better if they stay in the car, so the three pile in again.

Babe fixes the jack again. Stan takes off the spare tire and leans it against the car. Babe takes the rear tire off and leans it against the spare. Babe exits to the garage to get something, and Stan thinking he has the bum tire puts the spare back on the rack. Babe returns and puts the bum tire on the wheel, thinking it is the spare.

They get over the job is well done and climb back into the car. Babe again wishes the neighbor good-bye, starts the motor and the rear wheel spins around. They can't figure why they are not moving.

Babe stops the motor, gets out and discovers that the car is still on the jack. He makes Stan remove the jack. Stan has the two wives and Jimmie get out of the car again while he puts the jack under the seat, then helps them back into the car.

Babe again wishes the neighbor good-bye, starts up the motor and starts to back up. He gets over there is something wrong, stops again, looks over the side and discovers the tire is still flat. They have the folks get out again, take the jack and jack up the car, take the tire off quickly, pull out the tube and Stan exits to the garage to patch it.

While talking to the neighbor, Babe strikes a match and throws it out of the scene. The lighted match goes into a spot of oil on the driveway under the motor. A lot of smoke starts coming from the motor. Babe takes it, opens the hood and looks in, then looks underneath and sees that it is the oil burning. He puts it out and crawls under the car to see if any damage was done.

As Babe crawls under the car there is still some smoke coming from the motor. Stan enters from the garage, takes it, thinking the motor is on fire, grabs a pail of water and pours it over the motor. Babe comes up sopping wet and bawls Stan out. They quickly put the tire back on.

Babe makes the others get out of the car again so he can get the pump. He gets the pump and this time they all stand around waiting. Babe starts pumping, grunting and sweating. Stan tries to help him.

Cut to the tire and show a balloon swelling on the side of it. Babe continues pumping and the balloon gets bigger. It finally explodes and everybody takes it. Somebody steps on Jim's foot and he lets out a howl. Babe then gives up in despair and says, "Well, that's it."

One of the wives says, "What's the matter with this spare," patting it with her hand and getting over it is solid. Babe takes it, gives Stan a dirty look, puts the pump back into the car and helps the folks in while Stan is starting to change the tire.

They get the tire on and by this time Babe is sore. They get into the car and a little half-heartedly Babe says good-bye to the neighbor again. Babe starts the motor and again the rear wheel spins with the jack underneath it. Babe takes it, they get out again and discover the jack. Babe takes it out quickly and throws it at Stan. Stan ducks and it goes through the neighbor's window. The neighbor takes it big, picks up a brick and throws it through the windshield. Babe and Stan both pick up bricks and Babe's wife says, "Oliver! Remember this is the Sabbath!" This stops Babe and Stan and they both throw their bricks away. We hear a crash and show that the bricks have gone through a window in their kitchen.

Stan and Babe turn down the windshield and push the top back. Do a routine of business with the top, involving Jimmie and the wives.

Babe tries to start the motor again but it won't work. Stan and Babe get out of the car and make the others get out so they can get the crank out of the back seat. He gets the crank and one of the wives says, "We're going in the house – let us know when you get this thing fixed." The three exit into the house.

Babe starts to crank the car and it gives a little leap toward him. He takes it and tells Stan, "Why don't you do something to help me?" Stan asks "What can I do?" Babe says "Throw out the clutch!" Stan quickly pulls the clutch out and throws it out of the car. The neighbor laughs and Babe walks over and picks up the clutch, and with murder in his eyes walks over to Stan, takes off Stan's hat and clunks him with the clutch.

Babe puts the clutch back in, starts toward the front to crank the car and the motor suddenly starts running. Babe quickly throws the crank into the back seat, yells to the wives and Jim, they all come running out and get into the car. They say good-bye again to the neighbor and are about to start out when Stan pulls the throttle down and the car leaps forward, bumping into the garage and puncturing the radiator. Babe sees it and says, "Well, that's it." The wives and Jimmie get out of the car again disgusted and go back into the house.

The neighbor says, "I wouldn't let a little thing like that worry you – you can stop that leak in a minute." He suggests the corn meal and Stan or Babe gets it to put into the radiator.

The neighbor tells them to start the motor and get it warmed up. They do so and the leak stops. The car is now running perfectly and they again call the wives and Jimmie. All get into the car and say good-bye again. They are just about to back out when the corn meal blows the radiator cap off and starts spraying a veritable snow storm all over them. They go into a much throwing routine, ending up with a cop stopping activities.

The cop tells them to go on to their picnic. They back out of the driveway and as they come onto the road we see that the road has been torn up. The car backs into a big mud hole and sinks out of sight. FADE OUT.

THE HOOSE-GOW

Production history: Production L-28. Script written late August 1929, finished August 29. Filmed Friday, August 30 through Tuesday, September 10. No filming on Monday, September 2 (Labor Day). However, the L&H unit was working on Sunday, September 8. Copyrighted November 11, 1929, by MGM (LP 840). Released November 16. Two reels.

Produced by Hal Roach. Directed by James Parrott. Assistant Director, Lloyd French. Photographed by George Stevens, Len Powers, and Glenn Robert Kershner. Edited by Richard Currier. Sound by Elmer Raguse. Story Editor, H.M. Walker.

With Stan Laurel (Himself), Oliver Hardy (Himself), Tiny Sandford (Warden), James Finlayson (The Governor), Dick Sutherland (Prison cook), Leo Willis (Leo, prisoner with apples), Ellinor Vanderveer, Retta Palmer (Snooty ladies in Governor's party), Charlie Hall (Prisoner and officer in lookout tower), Blackie Whiteford (Prisoner who directs Ollie to his table), Eddie Dunn, Baldwin Cooke, Chet Brandenburg, Ed Brandenburg, Charles Dorety, Ham Kinsey, Tiny Ward (Prisoners), Sam Lufkin, Leo Sulky (Prison guards).

Stan and Ollie are transported to prison in a paddy wagon, despite their protests to a warden that they "were only watching a raid." They are put to work on a labor camp with fellow prisoners digging a road. Stan's lack of prowess with a pickaxe results in torn clothing for Ollie – and in a leaking radiator belonging to the car of the Governor, who has come to inspect the camp. A helpful convict tells the boys to plug the leak by getting some rice from the cook tent. This seems to work, until the radiator suddenly and violently overflows. Naturally, this gusher prompts a melee in which the Governor, the elegant ladies in his party, the warden and all of the roadside gang are covered with gooey rice.

The script for *The Hoose-Gow* suggests James Finlayson for the part of the Governor. We're pretty familiar with him, but the suggestion of "a rough looking character on the Jack Herrick type" is a puzzler. It turns out that Mr. Herrick was a former boxer (as were many employees on the Roach lot), born in Hungary in 1891; he appeared in about 50 movies between 1923 and 1949, mostly uncredited bits. However, he did manage to appear in Chaplin's *The Gold Rush*, Harold Lloyd's *For Heaven's Sake* and Laurel and Hardy's *Pardon Us*. His part in the film was instead essayed by Leo Willis (1890-1952), who had played the cab driver in *Their Purple Moment*. A widowed father of two young daughters, Leo specialized in playing robbers and thugs in more than 100 films between 1916 and 1938. He had small roles in films starring Harold Lloyd, Eddie Cantor and the Marx Brothers, but was seen to good advantage in eight films with Stan and Babe.

Also prominent in the film as a snooty society lady in the Governor's party is Ellinor Vanderveer (1887-1976), who had also encountered Stan and Ollie as convicts in *The Second 100 Years*. She, too, was a single parent, supporting her daughter Barbara with frequent work as a "dress extra," almost always as a society lady, often providing her own elegant wardrobe. She can be seen in *Frankenstein, Casablanca* and many classic films; her shining moment is in the 1934 Our Gang comedy *Washee Ironee*, where she plays the distant mother of young Wally Albright. She was the target of a pie in Laurel and Hardy's *The Battle of the Century* and sat on some ice cream cones in the classic Roach comedy *A Pair of Tights*. As for *The Hoose-Gow*, she told her friend Robert B. Satterfield in 1976, "That was a lot of fun making this picture, but it took two weeks to get the rice out of my hair and my clothes. That rice really was cooked, right onto my lovely clothes. Working with Laurel and Hardy was very pleasant.... You never knew what they were going to do next. That was what made it so exciting working with them."

Ah, the rice. The "plugging the radiator" idea had been suggested for Laurel and Hardy's silent *Bacon Grabbers*, where the adhesive element was going to be Cream of Wheat. In *Perfect Day*, it was to be corn meal. But the gag finally gets its moment on film in *The Hoose-Gow*, with rice as the main ingredient.

The script notes that the opening should be filmed at the "gates to the County

Working with frequent director James Parrott sometimes led to hijinks on the set, or at least hijinks posed for Stax Graves' camera.

In the paddy wagon after "watching a raid"; the gentleman at left is Leo Willis.

Hospital," and indeed this was shot at the Los Angeles County Hospital at 1651 Marengo Street; this was the same location as the "prison gate" in *The Second 100 Years*. The script also notes that the rest of the opening scene should be filmed at the "interior of the real county jail yard," so the crew journeyed two miles north to the Los Angeles East Side Division Jail (also known as the Lincoln Heights jail) at 419 North Avenue 19.

The script's suggestion, "Babe pinches Stan's arm," develops into a more involved routine in which Ollie and Stan kick each other near the parked patrol wagon and accidentally kick prison guard Tiny Sandford in his derriere. The idea that hammers and saws should be thrown over the prison wall to help Stan and Ollie escape was made more direct by the simple yet dramatic gesture of throwing a rope ladder.

Stan and Ollie return to prison after Tiny Sandford's well-aimed warning; meanwhile, Stax Graves and his camera make a surprise appearance at left.

Ollie's jacket and derby are ventilated by Stan's pickaxe, an on-location inspiration.

Ollie thought he was chopping a tree, not a lookout tower; the cook tent is the unfortunate target in this unscripted scene.

Stan and Babe take a coffee break from the rice-throwing melee.

Original 1929 promotional artwork.

During the lunchtime scene, the script's suggestion that the convicts bang on the table with knives and forks, and the notation "(See Coffee Dan)," refers to a popular San Francisco speakeasy in which patrons would get the attention of waiters by rapping on the table with a small mallet or a dish. (The Coffee Dan's nightclub was immortalized with a scene in the 1927 Al Jolson film *The Jazz Singer*.)

The suggested gag of Babe having soup poured into his upturned derby is not in the film. Nor is the elaborate sequence of the cocoanut cake and the bee, although this was later worked into Laurel and Hardy's guest appearance in MGM's 1930 Technicolor musical *The Rogue Song*, now a mostly-lost film. The scene was replaced in the film with a repeat of the salt-and-pepper gag used earlier in *You're Darn Tootin'* (1928), in which Stan unscrews the top of the shakers, causing Ollie to unwittingly dump the entire contents into his soup. (Here, the gag is topped when Ollie growls at Stan, "I oughta make you eat that," and then unknowingly pours the soup onto Tiny Sandford's shoes.)

During the road camp scenes, Stan manages to plunge his pickaxe into Ollie's coat and derby several times, evidently an inspiration that came during the filming. The great scene where the boys decide to chop wood in exchange for food, and accidentally topple a lookout tower, is not in the script. However, the script suggests another gag in which Governor Finlayson falls into a ditch, and this is not in the movie.

The film's ending differs from the script's; instead of Stan and Ollie finding themselves all alone and running away, they seem to disappear during the rice-throwing battle. Governor Finlayson vows to "get the militia" and he and Sandford jump into a car which backs into a truck, on which is perched some barrels of whitewash. These tumble into the back seat of the car, and Stan and Ollie emerge, white as the driven snow.

L-28 (Revised)

Fade in on long shot showing gates to the County Hospital and have sign reading "County Jail." Police patrol wagon pulls into the picture, the warden opens the gates and the car comes on through out of scene at a fast rate of speed.

Cut to interior of the real county jail yard. The patrol wagon stops and a cop gets out and herds about ten bums out of the wagon. As the last one gets out, the cop starts counting them, then looks back in the wagon and yells, "Come on, you guys!" Babe and Stan step out and Babe says "We had nothing whatever to do with this – we were merely watching the raid." The Warden gets over, "It's too late now; why didn't you tell that to the Judge?" Stan says, "We did, but he wouldn't believe us." The warden gives Stan a dirty look. Stan resents it and says, "You can't keep us here!" Babe pinches Stan's arm and tells him to shut up.

Babe produces two apples from his pocket and tells Stan they are the means of escape, and pointing to one of the convicts in front of the line he tells Stan that that fellow gave them to him. Stan looks toward the convict.

Go to closeup of the convict, a rough looking character on the Jack Herrick type. He turns and gives Stan a wink and nods his head.

Back to the two boys. Stan takes one of the apples to examine it, and as he is doing so the guard turns and nearly catches him. Babe hides his apple and Stan quickly puts his behind his back. The guard walks over and demands the apple from Babe, which Babe gives to him. Stan realizes what is happening and puts his apple in his mouth. The guard demands the apple from Stan, who shows him both hands, telling him that he has no apple. Babe looks at Stan and in pantomime asks him what he did with the apple. Stan opens his mouth, showing Babe the apple. The guard turns and sees the apple and demands it from Stan. Stan tries to get the apple out of his mouth but realizes it is stuck. After a little routine of trying to remove the apple from Stan's mouth, the guard loses patience and gives Stan a swift kick, causing Stan to swallow the apple. Cut to closeup of Stan and show the impression of the apple going down his neck.

The guard realizes that the apple is gone and exits, followed by the two boys. He enters setup at the prison wall and throws Babe's apple over. Immediately from the other side of the wall are thrown implements of escape such as a rope ladder, hammers, saws, etc. The guard sees this and realizes the plot, gives Stan and Babe a dirty look, getting over he is wise to the trick and starts up the rope ladder which is hanging to the top of the wall.

Cut to shot from the other side and show the guard's head appear over the wall. Cut to the lower part and show two men holding the other end of the ladder. They look up and see the guard, take it big, let go of the rope and rush out of the scene.

Cut back to Stan and Babe's side. The rope ladder with the guard crashes to the ground, hitting Stan and Babe, and they all do a brodie. The guard jumps to his feet, grabs his gun and rushes to the iron gate, followed by Stan and Babe, and runs outside.

Cut to exterior of the wall. The guard enters just as the two thugs disappear around the far end of the wall. Stan and Babe walk out in back of the guard, who does not see them. The guard, realizing that the thugs got away, exits back through the gate and locks it, not knowing that he has left Stan and Babe outside.

Babe realizes that they are free, but Stan in a dumb manner walks to the gate and starts to knock. Babe quickly stops him, tells him they are free and both start to make a quick get-away, running out of the scene.

Cut around shooting away from the jail into open country. Stan and Babe rush into the scene and start away from the camera. Cut back to the iron gate; the same guard comes rushing out all excited, looks around for Stan and Babe and sees them running across the field. He fires twice in their direction. Stay with this setup for some time, with the guard watching off. Stan and Babe walk in very sheepishly and as they pass the camera we see that the seat of their pants have been shot out and are still smoldering. They enter the jail yard and the guard follows them and locks the iron gate. FADE OUT.

FADE IN on road camp, the convicts all lined up receiving implements like picks and shovels. As they file by the guards who are handing out the tools, we see Stan and Babe about fourth or fifth back in the line, Stan ahead of Babe. They ender and the guard hands Stan a large pick. Stan looks down and sees a smaller pick on the ground, picks it up, weighs both of them and hands the large one to Babe. Babe sees the small pick, snatches it away from Stan and gives Stan the large one. The guard sees Babe holding the small pick, snatches it away from him and hands him a pick twice the size of an ordinary one and tosses the small pick out of the scene. As they are about to exit, the guard stops Babe and also hands him a shovel.

Stan and Babe exit to where the other convicts are about to dig the road. Just as they start to work, a whistle blows and all the convicts drop their tools and exit. Stan and Babe realize it is lunch time and run out of the scene in the direction of the others.

Cut to an out-doors mess camp, two tents in the background with long tables. In the foreground is a single table neatly spread, which is for the warden. The convicts all rush in, take their seats and start banging on the table with knives and forks (See Coffee Dan). Stan and Babe are late and find that all the seats have been taken.

Cut to the far end of the table. A trusty enters and starts dishing out the soup and the convicts start passing it along, dumping one plate into the next. Babe and Stan are standing at the far end of the table. Babe has removed his derby and placed it on the table. A convict dumps a plateful of soup into Babe's hat. Babe puts the derby on and the soup runs all over his face. He takes a napkin or handkerchief and tries to clean himself up the best he can.

Cut to the small table where the warden is seated. A trusty enters and tells him he is wanted on the phone. The warden exits. Follow him to a telegraph pole where there is a telephone in a box nailed to the pole. He starts to talk, and from the conversation we are told that the governor is coming to inspect the road camp and that the warden should have everything in the best of condition on his arrival.

Cut back to Stan and Babe. Stan spots the neatly spread table with two chairs, taps Babe on the shoulder and calls his attention to it. They both sit in chairs at the warden's table. On the table there is a freshly cut white cocoanut cake. Babe takes a large piece and is about to eat it as the warden returns and stands behind him. Stan tries to pantomime to Babe that the warden is behind him. Finally Babe looks up, sees the warden and shoves the piece of cake into his pocket. The warden orders the boys away from the table, telling them to get back where they belong. They exit from the scene and the warden sits down.

Follow Stan and Babe into a setup where there is a couple of large rocks against some trees. They enter and sit down. Babe reaches into his pocket and gets the piece of cake. Stan watches him, getting over that he is hungry. As Babe is in the act of taking a bite of the cake, a fly lights on it and Babe has some difficulty trying to keep the fly off the cake. Stan watches this and finally gets an idea. He suggests to Babe that if he gave the fly a little piece of the cake he wouldn't bother him. He takes the cake from Babe, breaks it in two, puts one piece on the ground and gives the other back to Babe. The fly follows the piece of cake they have laid on the ground.

Babe turns to Stan and says with a smile, "That's the first spark of intelligence you have ever shown." As he is speaking, cut to insert of the piece of cake Babe is holding and show a large bee light on it. We also hear the buzz of the bee.

Cut to closeup of Babe. Not noticing the bee, he quickly takes a large bite of the cake. Stan has seen the bee light on the cake, and not wanting to tell Babe, he sits dumbfounded watching this action. Babe munches on the cake and finally swallows it. As he is about to take another bite we hear a faint buzz. Babe gets over he has swallowed something and starts feeling his stomach, realizing that the bee is inside. Stan jumps to his feet and by this time Babe is going through all kinds of contortions, the bee presumably flying around inside him. Stan gets a shovel and starts hitting Babe, trying to kill the bee.

As Stan swings back with the shovel, the warden enters and gets it in the face, knocking him to the ground. Stan realizes what he has done and Babe forgets about the bee for the moment. The warden jumps to his feet and is about to beat up Stan and Babe when we hear sirens.

Show the governor and his procession approaching. The warden turns to Stan and Babe quickly and says, "Here comes the Governor – I'll take care of you later."

Cut to the procession. A motorcycle cop who is leading and looking back rides into a ditch and upsets, and the procession passes by without noticing him.

The guard tells Stan and Babe to be as nice as possible to make an impression on the Governor. He spruces himself up before the Governor enters.

The cars enter and the warden opens the door of the Governor's car, respectfully tipping his hat to the Governor and guests. The Governor (Jimmy Finlayson) reaches out his arm to be assisted from the car by the warden, meanwhile looking around. The warden reaches for his hand to help him out, and as Finlayson steps from the car he disappears out of the picture.

Move back to long shot and show Finlayson has fallen into a ditch as deep as his height, and we just see his head sticking up. The warden quickly helps Finlayson out of the hole in an apologetic manner.

Cut to long shot and show the other guests in two cars approaching the camera. The Governor quickly brushes himself off, gives the warden a dirty look and forgets the situation for the moment.

Cut to the front of the Governor's car. Stan and Babe have been watching the Governor. Babe insists that Stan give him the smaller pick. Stan insists that he keep it and they go into a tug-of-war. In the tussle Babe gets the handle of the pick and snatches it away from Stan, and the sharp end is swung out of the scene. Show the end of the pick smash into the radiator of the Governor's car, piercing it and causing a stream of water to squirt out.

Babe and Stan realize what they have done and rush around excitedly trying to figure some way to repair the radiator. Go into short routine of Stan and Babe trying to stop the leak. A tough looking convict enters the scene, sees what has happened and tells Babe to get some rice and put it in the radiator. Babe thinks this is a good suggestion, and while still holding his finger in the radiator hole he tells Stan to get some rice. Stan excitedly rushes out of the scene toward the mess tent. He hurries into the tent and quickly returns with a five-pound box of rice.

Babe removes the radiator cap and starts pouring the rice into the radiator. As he is pouring and the box is nearly empty, the stream of water gradually stops. Babe gets over that they have accomplished their purpose. Babe quickly ditches the empty box as the warden enters.

The warden gives Stan and Babe a dirty look and asks them if they have been tampering with the Governor's car. They both look innocent, but the warden gets into the car to try the motor. He steps on the starter and races the motor a few times, listening to it. The radiator cap pops off and from the radiator a spray of rice pudding squirts into the air. Stan and Babe take this and realize what they have done.

Go into the mush routine, winding up with the Governor, guests, wardens and convicts getting into the mess. In the midst of the battle the Governor and his guests, who are very much humiliated, get into the other two cars and make a hurried exit to protect themselves from the barrage of flying pudding.

Cut to different shots of convicts who have been in the battle. They slowly realize it is a good time to make a getaway and exit. The wardens also completely disappear from the scene, leaving Stan and Babe alone madly throwing much in all directions. They suddenly stop, realizing that everybody has disappeared. Babe gets the idea it is a good chance to make an escape and both dash quickly out of the scene.

Cut to setup at a forked road. The boys run madly in and Stan starts one way and Babe the other. They come back to the point of the road and get into an argument about which way they should go. Babe finally wins out and they go in the direction that he first started. As they get fifteen or twenty feet away from the camera, we see ten or twelve convicts with their hands in the air, followed by guards with guns, walking directly toward Stan and Babe. The boys realize they are caught, turn and fall into line with the other convicts. As they walk toward the camera we fade out.

OUR WIFE

Production history: Production L-40. Script written late February through early March 1931. Dialogue script completed by H.M. Walker March 3, 1931. Filmed Monday, March 9 through Saturday, March 14. Filming resumed on Tuesday the 17th and finished Wednesday, March 18. Copyrighted by MGM April 27, 1931 (LP 2171). Released May 16, 1931. Two reels.

Produced by Hal Roach. Directed by James W. Horne. Photographed by Jack Stevens. Edited by Richard Currier. Sound by Elmer Raguse. Dialogue by H.M. Walker.

With Stan Laurel (Himself), Oliver Hardy (Himself), Babe London (Dulcie, the bride), James Finlayson (Dulcie's father), Ben Turpin (William Gladding, Justice of the Peace), Blanche Payson (Mrs. Gladding), Charlie Rogers (Meadows, the butler).

Ollie is about to marry his lovely girl friend, Dulcie, who is just as hefty as he. The home which Stan and Ollie share is gaily festooned with decorations, and a lovely wedding cake is on the dining room table. Thanks to various missteps, all of these are soon ruined, as are Mr. Hardy's original plans for the wedding: when Dulcie shows her father a picture of her intended husband, he goes berserk and adamantly forbids the marriage. The two lovebirds decide to elope. Later that night, Ollie and Stan help Dulcie escape from her father's house. Stan has helpfully rented the getaway car – a tiny Austin which can barely accommodate the three passengers and their luggage. Eventually, they arrive at the home of a Justice of the Peace, who, because of his cross-eyed condition, marries Ollie not to Dulcie, but to Stan.

The script for *Our Wife* differs from the film in only a few details. It's one of the very few scripts that includes the film's title as well as its production number.

Ollie's bride-to-be is named Dulcie in the film but is only referred to as "the girl" in the script. She is played by Jean "Babe" London (1901-1980); her real name was Ruth Glover, and from 1918 through 1960 she appeared in dozens of films, mostly comedies. She had appeared in two of the solo Stan Laurel shorts produced by Broncho Billy Anderson, and worked with Chaplin, Keaton, Langdon, W.C. Fields, Bob Hope and the Three Stooges in addition to making comedies for Al Christie, Vitagraph and Educational.

In the script for *Our Wife*, her squinting Scottish father declares that "no fortune hunter will ever marry the Finlayson millions," so presumably her character's full name would be Dulcie Finlayson. However, no fortune is mentioned in the film, so we can safely assume that Ollie is marrying her for love, not money.

During the scenes in which Stan and Babe are in their apartment preparing for the wedding, there's no phonograph playing the "Wedding March," but Leroy Shield's musical score provides a jazzy arrangement of it. Babe indeed tells Stan that he's the best man, but leaves the "pro tem" remark out of it; this sounds like a line from Beanie Walker, whose dialogue for L&H was occasionally a bit too grandiloquent for their characters.

Stan has made festive preparations for Ollie's wedding, but that cake and those dishes are not long for this world.

Mr. Hardy's slip on a stray ice cube has drastic consequences.

Stan helpfully explains to Mr. Finlayson's butler that Ollie is going to elope with his daughter. (This is Charlie Rogers, gag man, director and occasional actor.)

In the film, Ollie sustains many indignities, but Stan sitting on him is not one of them.

We never see Dulcie's full reaction to the Justice's error, but fainting was a predictable response.

For the final gag described in paragraph 27, we don't merely hear a big crash and then cut to Ollie with his face in the cake, we actually see him take a nosedive into the dining room table, which not only collapses to the floor but also pulls all of the festive decor from the walls. This spectacular shot is a tribute to Don Sandstrom, Charlie Oelze, Bob Sanders and the other members of the Hal Roach Studios prop department.

The car which Stan has hired for the eloping lovebirds is a 1931 American Austin Coupe. The script's suggestion of "ad lib business trying to get Babe and the girl into the car" develops into a lengthy sequence. One wonders how the two Babes, Stan, and the luggage all managed to actually fit in this tiny vehicle, but Miss London recalled, "It wasn't as uncomfortable as it looked. We all played it up, made it appear that the car was smaller than it was."

In the script, the scene where Stan has difficulty telling the Justice's wife that his friend wants to get married is a rare instance of a dialogue routine being fully written out. The only difference is that Dulcie's "nail on the head" remark was omitted in the film.

The ominous black cats crossing Ollie's path do not appear in the movie, nor does the outlandish gag involving Mr. Finlayson. Hal Roach was not fond of cartoonish gags such as the one that ends *The Live Ghost*, and one wonders if this strange bit of business was ever filmed.

Although the script makes no mention of him, nobody else could have played the cross-eyed Justice better than Ben Turpin, whose wonderful cameo was happily noted by reviewers in 1931. His error in determining the bride and groom was ultimately deemed to be enough of a "wow" finish without resorting to the Finlayson gag.

L-40 – "OUR WIFE"

1. FADE IN on bedroom of the girl's home. She is on preparing her trousseau, seeming very happy. Her father, Finlayson, enters and sees her. She turns and sees him, quickly tries to hide her things but realizes it is too late.

2. Finlayson suspects something is going on that he doesn't know about. He questions the girl and she finally breaks down and confesses that she is going to marry the dearest boy in the world. She gets over how wonderful Babe is. Finlayson is all delighted and showers her with his blessings, and asks her who the lucky boy is. The girl, all thrilled, runs to a drawer and takes out a big framed picture. She shows it to Finlayson and we insert picture of Babe. Finlayson does an extra big takem and gets over his utter dislike for Hardy, and swears that no fortune hunter will ever marry the Finlayson millions. The girl begs him to listen to reason. Finlayson is hot headed and refuses to listen to her any further, and forbids her to see Hardy any more.

3. The girl becomes defiant and says she will never give Hardy up. Finlayson gets sore and tells her she will remain in this room under lock and key till she comes to her senses.

4. Finlayson exits and locks the door, putting the key in his pocket. He starts down the stairs, accidentally steps on a carpet sweeper, goes out of sight down the stairs and we hear a crash as he reaches the bottom.

5. Cut to Stan and Babe's apartment. The phonograph is playing the wedding march. Babe is singing and laying out his clothes for the wedding. He gets over that his throat bothers him, goes to the dressing table and uses the throat atomizer, then sings again.

6. Cut to Stan in the little dining room with a big wedding cake on the table. He is arranging the table, and gets over that the flies are bothering the cake. He can't keep them off. He goes into the bedroom and gets the atomizer.

7. As Stan starts to exit, he steps on Babe's suspenders. Babe starts toward the bath room and his suspenders draw tight and pull

the seat of his pants out. Stan continues on his way and exits. Babe turns and discovers the pants all torn, and is bewildered; he can't figure out how he did it.

8. Cut to the kitchen; Stan is filling the atomizer with fly-killer liquid.

9. Cut to Babe, still wondering who tore his pants. he looks behind doors, under the bed, etc., then gets an idea that it might have been Stan.

10. Cut to Stan in the dining room spraying the cake. Babe enters, takes it big, grabs the atomizer from Stan and says, "What are you doing?" Stan says, "Killing the flies." Babe takes it again and says, "O-O-o-o—now you've ruined the cake!" The telephone bell rings and Babe exits, followed by Stan.

11. Cut to bedroom. Babe enters, with Stan trailing after him. Babe picks up the phone.

12. Cut to the girl at the other end. She says, "Oliver, something terrible has happened!"

13. Back to Babe. He takes it, and realizing that Stan is listening, he says, "Excuse me, darling." He lays down the phone and ushers Stan out of the room and closes the door. He starts back for the phone and is about to pick it up, but thinks a minute and tiptoes back to the door.

14. Cut to the living room, where Stan is on his hands and knees at the foot of the door listening. The door opens, Babe looks in but cannot see Stan. Satisfied that Stan isn't there, he exits back to the bedroom, picks up the phone and asks the girl what the trouble is.

15. Cut to the girl. She explains that her father has found out and forbids the marriage, and says "Whatever will we do?"

16. Back to Babe and he says, "There's only one thing to do – let's elope."

17. Back to the girl and she says, "How romantic! But father will

never forgive me."

18. Back to Babe and he says, "After we are married, nothing else matters." He tells her to be ready at midnight and that everything will be all right, and for further precaution Stan will help them. Babe then throws her a kiss and says, "Good bye, darling."

19. Cut to the girl; she throws a kiss and says, "Good bye, lover."

20. Cut to Stan at the extension phone and he says, "Good bye."

21. Cut to Babe; he gives a big takem, hangs up the phone and rushes into the other room just in time to see Stan hanging up the phone. He says to Stan, "Can't I have a little privacy? Well, now that you know my predicament, you've got to help me." Stan says, "What have I got to do with it?" Babe says, "What have you got to do with it? Why, you're the best man."

22. Stan takes it and says, "Does that mean that I'm better than you are?" Babe takes this and says, "Well – yes, pro tem. Now here's what you've got to do. Get a closed car and meet me at the girl's house." Stan nods, and Babe continues, "And I'll complete all other arrangements."

23. Stan picks up the telephone and Babe says, "What are you going to do?" Stan says, "Call a taxi." Babe says, "No, no, no! Don't you understand we're going to elope? Nobody must know about it. Hire a car that we can drive ourselves."

24. Stan nods and exits for his hat. Babe, all happy, starts singing again. He goes to the dressing table, picks up the atomizer, sprays his throat good, takes it big and starts yelling.

25. Stan enters and doesn't know what's the matter. Babe says, "Do something to help me! I'm on fire!" He starts running around the room like a mad man. Stan aimlessly runs around after him. Babe runs through the dining room into the kitchen, still hollering and asking Stan to help him.

26. Stan opens the ice box, gets the ice pick and chops off some ice. A big hunk of it slips onto the floor near the doorway. Stan gives

Babe a piece of ice. Babe puts it in his mouth and gets instant relief. He gives Stan a dirty look and says, "Come on!"

27. Babe starts into the dining room. Insert his foot slipping on the ice and stay with it while we hear a big crash, then cut to the dining room, table collapsed and Babe's face in the cake. FADE OUT.

28. FADE IN, front of the girl's home, night. Babe is on trying to attract the girl's attention. She comes to the window and Babe tells her everything is all arranged and that Stan is coming with the limousine. We hear an automobile Klaxon and Babe and the girl take it.

29. Cut to Finlayson in bed, and he wakes up.

30. Back to Babe. Stan enters and Babe "shushes him and says to the girl, "Where do you keep your ladders?" She says, "In the garage." Stan and Babe exit.

31. Cut to Finlayson coming along the hall listening at the girl's bedroom door.

32. Back to front of house. Stan and Babe enter with the ladder and place it against the window. Babe tells the girl to throw out her suitcase. Stan holds his arms out to catch it. The girl throws it and it hits Babe and breaks open. An alarm clock starts ringing and they try to stop it.

33. Back to the room. The girl hears Finlayson putting the key in the door, and she steps back as Finlayson opens the door. He looks around the room, sees the open window and says, "Ah-ha! So the bird has flown!" He rushes to the window and looks out, sees the ladder etc. He starts to crawl out of the window backwards and turns to go down the ladder. The girl exits from the room.

34. Cut outside. Stan and Babe have finally got the tings back into the suitcase. They start back for the ladder and Babe says to Stan, "You go up and help her." Stan starts up the ladder and takes it big when he sees Finlayson crawling out of the window.

35. The girl comes out the front door. Babe takes it when he sees

her and quickly pulls Stan down off the ladder, then moves the ladder aside, leaving Finlayson hanging on the window ledge. Babe and the girl embrace and Stan throws a handful of rice over them. Babe says, "Not yet." They exit to the sidewalk.

36. Babe looks around and says to Stan, "where's the car?" Stan parts the bushes and shows the Austin. Babe gives a helpless look and says, "What did you hire a thing like that for?" Stan says, "I didn't hire it. I bought it. It's your wedding present." Babe helplessly says, "Thanks."

37. Go for ad lib business trying to get Babe and the girl into the car, intercut with Finlayson still hanging and his cries for help getting weaker. Also a scene in the bedroom where the butler comes in, sees nobody there, shuts the window and locks it, turns the lights out and exits.

38. Babe and the girl are finally in the car. Stan tries to get in, but Babe pushes him out. Babe tries to get the car started, but can't. He finally tells Stan to give it a push. Stan goes to the rear of the car, puts one foot on the bumper and starts pushing the car down the street scooter-fashion. FADE OUT

39. FADE IN on sign "Justice of the Peace," and we hear door bell ringing. Pull back and show Stan on the porch ringing the bell. The door opens and a woman comes out. She looks at Stan and says, "What do you want?" Stan thinks a minute and then calls out to Babe, "What do we want?"

40. Cut to Babe with his head sticking out of the car. He takes it and says, "We want to get married."

41. Back to stan; he turns to the woman and says, "Yes, we want to get married."

42. Cut to Babe and he says, "Not we – US!"

43. Back to Stan; he again turns to the woman and says, "Not we – us." The woman takes it and says, "Well, how about it?" Stan looks over to Babe and says, "How about it?"

44. Cut to Babe and he says, "How about what?"

45. Stan turns to the woman and says, "How about what?" The woman becomes impatient and says, "What are you talking about?" Stan tries to think, then calls out to Babe, "Yes, what are we talking about?"

46. Cut to Babe. He says, "Tell her we want to get married!"

47. Back to Stan and the woman. He says, "We want to get married." We hear the voice of the Justice inside the house: "Well, how about it?" The woman turns and speaks into the doorway, "There's a couple here who want to get married." The voice replies, "O.K. I'll be right up." The woman turns to Stan and says, "He'll be right up." Stan asks, "Who?" The woman gives him a disgusted look and pokes him on the nose, then exits. Stan exits, holding his nose.

48. Stan enters to the car and Babe says, "Well, how about it?" Stan does a takem and says, "How about what?"
Babe: "Well, what did she say?"
Stan: "Who?"
Girl: "You sure hit the nail on the head. He's a great little man for detail."
Babe: "Well, as usual, I'll have to do everything myself!"

49. Go into routine getting Babe and the girl out of the car. They finally get the girl out and she stands waiting on the sidewalk while Babe is still struggling. He finally looks up and tells her to go on in, that he won't be a minute. Stay with Stan and Babe for the balance of the routine, intercutting with Finlayson still hanging at the window. Babe finally gets out and the car is a wreck. Stan throws another handful of rice on him and Babe says, "Not yet."

50. As they start to enter the house, a lot of black cats run out and Babe takes it. They finally get inside and line up in front of the table.

51. Out comes the Justice of the Peace with his eyes closed and yawning. He picks up the bible, then opens his eyes and we see he is cross-eyed.

52. Cut to Stan and Babe as they take this big. Stan crosses his fingers and nudges Babe.

53. Cut back to the Justice. He reads a short ceremony, mumbling the words unintelligibly, then cays "Do you take this woman to be your lawful wedded wife?"

54. Back to Stan and Babe and the girl. Babe says "I do."

Justice: "Do you take this man to be your lawful wedded
        husband?"
Girl: "I do."
Justice: "I now pronounce you man and wife."

55. The Justice comes around the table, shakes hand with Stan and says, "Congratulations!" He puts his arms around Stan and the girl, then says, "Do you mind if I kiss the bride?" Stan says, "Not at all." The Justice crosses to kiss the bride and kisses Babe.

56. Just then the door busts open and they all turn and see Finlayson standing in the doorway with his arms stretched about three feet. FADE OUT

ONE GOOD TURN

Production history: Production L-2. Script written late May 1931. Dialogue script completed by H.M. Walker June 3, 1931. Filmed Monday June 15 through Friday June 26. Previewed circa July 11. Copyrighted Oct. 5, 1931, by MGM. Released Oct. 31. Two reels.

Produced by Hal Roach. Directed by James W. Horne. Photographed by Art Lloyd. Edited by Richard Currier. Sound by Elmer Raguse. Dialogue by H.M. Walker. Uncredited: Assistant Cameraman, E.L. White. Props, Chet Brandenburg, Bob Sanders.

With Stan Laurel (Himself), Oliver Hardy (Himself), Mary Carr (Kindly elderly lady), James Finlayson (James Finlayson, director of the Community Players), Billy Gilbert (Generous drunk), Dorothy Granger, Snub Pollard, Gordon Douglas, Lyle Tayo (Community Players), Charley Young (Hard-of-hearing gentleman), Baldwin Cooke, William Gillespie, Hamilton Kinsey, Retta Palmer (Onlookers during auction).

Victims of the Depression, Stan and Ollie come to the door of a kindly old lady and ask if she might provide them with some food. In exchange, they attempt to chop some wood for her. While having their meal, they overhear a dastardly villain threatening to throw the woman out of her home; someone has stolen the $100 she needs to pay on her mortgage. They secretly decide to help her by going to the town square and auctioning off their faithful Model T. A drunk bids $100 and mistakenly puts his wallet in Stan's pocket. When Ollie finds this money on Stan's person, he assumes the worst and hauls his "one-time friend" before the woman as a thief, the "viper in my bosom" who has stolen her money. The elderly woman laughs and explains that nothing has been stolen; she and the "villain" were merely rehearsing a scene from the forthcoming production of the Community Players. Ollie's mild apology ("I must have made a faux-pas") is met with angry retribution from Stan.

Two scripts survive for *One Good Turn,* an "action" script presumably written by Stan and the gag men, and another consisting solely of dialogue and credited to H.M. Walker. The action script contains most of the important dialogue already, and since Beanie's verbiage for Laurel and Hardy tended to be a little stilted, it's not a surprise that ruthless cost-cutting executive Henry Ginsberg dismissed him from the studio in 1932.

In the film, Stan is tasting their precious kettle of soup rather than smelling it. The scripted gag with the fish and the handkerchief is not in the film, although a similar gag with a shark turns up in 1939's *The Flying Deuces.* When the boys' tent catches fire, instead of Ollie merely falling over the soup kettle, Stan deliberately throws it on the flames, without realizing that he's just wasted their last meal.

Instead of taking place at a School of Dramatic Arts as suggested in the script, the rehearsal more logically ensues at the private home of the kindly elderly lady. She's

Filming the opening scene. At the camera, assistant Edward L. White helps Art Lloyd (wearing the cap); director James W. Horne happily holds the umbrella, and Roach studios all-purpose utility player Chet Brandenberg is at extreme right.

played by Mary Carr (1874-1973), who was only 57 when she appeared in *One Good Turn*, but had been playing grandmotherly types in films for more than ten years. She had a starring role in *Over the Hill to the Poorhouse* (1920), which also featured four of her children. She worked steadily in films through 1940 and sporadically after that, her last appearance being a Quaker woman in *Friendly Persuasion* (1956). Fittingly, she lived to be as old as the ladies whom she portrayed, and died at age 99.

The action script refers to the "heavy" who threatens to throw the old lady out of her house as Silas Hemingway. Beanie Walker's dialogue script calls him Hector Hammerhead. The film gives him the most terrifying name of all, James Finlayson. (Using separate action and dialogue scripts could cause continuity problems. The action script for *Another Fine Mess* called one character "Leopold" while the dialogue script called him "Ambrose." Thelma Todd had used both names before someone caught the mistake and had her cover for it by calling out for "Leopold Ambrose....")

Stan's suggestion to help the lady move does not appear in the film, nor does the thunderous backfire of the boys' car.

One wonders why Ollie jumps to the conclusion of Stan stealing the old woman's money, as the boys have been together for the entire film; Stan would have had no opportunity to commit this thievery. (This makes the accusation even more unjust, helping to set up the film's final scene.) In the film, only the elderly lady hears Ollie's statement that his friend has a confession to make, the other players apparently having gone home from the rehearsal.

The original wrap-up brings back the drunk character from the auction scene. In the film, he's played by Billy Gilbert (1894-1971) a veteran of vaudeville and burlesque shows, who had been invited by Stan to become a gag writer at the Roach lot. Gilbert worked in this capacity before making his first appearance in a Roach

Filming the "victims of the Depression" sequence on the Roach backlot, in front of the façade for Mary Carr's house. *Courtesy of Richard W. Bann, Tracy Tolzmann and the late Bill Diehl.*

Ollie's comeuppance is not in the script. Stan's daughter provided the inspiration.

comedy, *The Panic Is On* (1931), starring Charley Chase. He would appear in ten Laurel and Hardy films and would star in Roach's Taxi Boys series and several musical shorts. His famous sneezing routine won him the part of Sneezy in Walt Disney's *Snow White and the Seven Dwarfs* (1937), and he was a very busy supporting player in major studio releases such as *His Girl Friday* (1940), working in films through the early 1960s.

The drunk's reappearance may not have been filmed; in any event, the film contains an entirely different ending. Stan's three-and-a-half year old daughter Lois had become frightened of her "Uncle Babe" after seeing him abuse her daddy too many times on the screen. (A Laurel family home movie shows Babe trying to give little Lois a hug, and she all but runs back to Stan's protective arms.) In order to show young Lois that his movie character could take care of himself, Stan created a sequence where he gets his revenge by chopping down a shed in which his accuser is hiding, and bringing its roof down on Ollie's cranium. Stan gets his own comeuppance when a stray log hits him on the head, and of course there's no doubt that the boys' friendship will prevail.

L-2
LAUREL & HARDY.

1. Fade in on a typical hobo camp – home-made tent made of sacks, etc., and a fire out in front with a big can of mulligan stewing. Stan enters, throws down a pile of wood near the fire, then stirs the soup and tastes it, making a big noise.

2. Cut to Babe down by the stream washing out some clothes. The noise of Stan tasting the soup comes over his scene. He takes it and calls for Stan. Stan enters from around the tall bushes.

BABE: What are you doing?

STAN: I was smelling the soup.

BABE Well, don't ever do that again. If there's anything I detest, it's a soup-sniffer. Come here and help me wash these clothes.

3. Stan takes one of Babe's shirts, dips it in the water and scrubs it up and down on a rock, native fashion.

4. Cut to Babe wringing out a suit of long underwear.

5. Cut back to Stan; he has finished scrubbing. He dips the shirt back in the water, wrings it and as he opens it out it is full of holes and torn badly. Babe sees it and takes it and smacks Stan, then hands him the long underwear and tells him to go and hang it on the line. Babe lays a handkerchief in the water and turns to get something else to wash. A fish comes up and takes the handkerchief away. Babe sees it and does a pitiful takem.

6. Stan enters from behind the bushes with a tin cup, walks through the stream to a pump on the other side, draws a cup of water and goes back through the stream and exits. He does this two or three times, then stops and says to Babe:

STAN: You haven't got another cup, have you?

BABE: What for?

STAN: The tent's on fire.

Stan exits, followed quickly by Babe.

7. Cut to the tent set. Babe enters in time to see Stan throwing the cup of water on the blazing tent. Babe goes to make a pass at Stan but falls over and upsets the pot of mulligan. Babe says, "What next?" Stan points to the clothes line and as Babe looks we cut and show the underwear all shrunk up to kid's size. FADE OUT.

8. Fade in on sign reading, "School of Dramatic Arts." Lap

dissolve to living room, with about half a dozen characters on, getting ready to rehearse a play, all with parts in their hands. The director has a script and is arranging some furniture. He says to the leading woman, "As the scene opens, you are seated here knitting. You are supposed to be a poor widow. I am going to play the crooked landlord who is going to foreclose the mortgage." He turns to some of the other characters and tells them to please study their parts well as he wants this annual show to be a howling success.

9. Cut to the back yard of the house. Stan and Babe enter and Babe says, "Let's try our luck here." They knock on the door and the old lady opens it.

BABE: Pardon the intrusion, Lady, but my friend and I are victims of the depression. We haven't eaten food for three days.

LADY: You poor things! Fancy not eating for three days.

STAN: Yes, ma'm. Yesterday, today and tomorrow.

BABE: We were wondering if you would be kind enough to provide us with a slice of buttered toast.

LADY: If you will wait a few minutes I'll fix you something to eat.

BABE: Thank you, ma'm. Is there anything we can do for you while we're waiting?

LADY: No, I don't think so.

STAN: (To Babe) How about you chopping some wood?

LADY: That would be splendid.

BABE: Yes, ma'm.

Babe gives Stan a dirty look and they exit.

10. Cut to the wood shed. Stan and Babe enter.

BABE: Well, you suggested it, you cut it.

Babe sits down and makes himself comfortable.

STAN: I don't know anything about cutting wood.

BABE: You should. You told me once your father was in the lumber business.

STAN: I know, but he was only in it in a small way.

BABE: What do you mean, a small way?

STAN: He used to sell toothpicks.

BABE: Well, go ahead and make some toothpicks.

Stan places a log on another one, picks up a big axe and hits it. One end flies up in the air and lands on the roof of the shed and starts to roll down.

BABE: Why don't you be careful? That might have hit me.

The log end drops into the scene and clunks Babe. At this point the old lady looks out of the back door and calls them. They exit into the kitchen.

11. Cut to the kitchen. Stan and Babe enter. The table is set for two, with sandwiches, etc. The lady puts coffee on the table and tells them to help themselves, then exits to the living room, closing the door. Stan and Babe sit at the table, getting over how nice the old lady is, and do the coffee pouring gag.

12. Cut to the living room. The old lady sits in a chair and starts to do her knitting. The director goes out and closes the front door. We hear the door bell ring and the old lady gets up and opens the door. She takes it big and reads from her part: "Silas Hemingway! You here again?" This is played in the old melodramatic spirit. He tells her he has come to foreclose the mortgage. The poor old lady says, "So, Silas Hemingway, you thought you were going to catch me with my pants down! But this time you are foiled! I have prepared for this emergency. I am going to pay you – then you can get out and never darken my doors again!"

13. She exits into the kitchen, paying no attention to Stan and Babe, reaches to a cupboard and gets an old coffee can, then exits back to the living room, closing the door.

14. In the living room she opens the coffee can to get the money, discovers it is gone, lets out a scream, drops the can and says, "I've been robbed!"

15. Cut to Stan and Babe; they take this.

16. Back to the living room; the Heavy continues: "Ha, ha, ha! The same old story. Well, me proud and haughty beauty, at last I have you in my clutches." The old lady pleads, "Spare me, spare me. It's only a hundred dollars. Give me a little more time." The Heavy says, "Not another minute! If you are not out of this house by three o'clock I will throw you out, bag and baggage."

17. Cut back to Stan and Babe and they take it again.

18. Back to the Heavy. He gives a dirty laugh and a sneer, snaps his fingers and exits, slamming the door. The old lady sits back in the rocking chair sobbing loudly, "What will I do? What will I do?"

19. Back to Stan and Babe; they take it again. Babe looks through the key hole, and we see a shot of the old lady still acting and crying her heart out. Babe gets very dramatic and says, "We've got to do something. We've got to help her."

STAN: What for?

BABE: What for? One good turn deserves another. Quick, think of something we could do to help her.

STAN: Maybe we could help her move.

BABE: She's not going to move! I'll save this home if it's the last
thing I do. We've got to get our brains – my brains
together and see what can be done.

Babe paces up and down the kitchen, suddenly looks through the
door to the yard and sees the old car. He turns to Stan and says, "I
have it! We'll sell the car to raise the money." Stan says, "Let's go and
tell her." Babe holds him back and says, "No, no. Don't do that. We'll
surprise her. We've got to hurry and get back here before three
o'clock." They start to tiptoe out of the kitchen. Stan exits, then comes
back for another sandwich and exits again.

20. Cut to the yard. They tiptoe quietly up to the car. Babe says,
"Don't make a noise – let's sneak away quietly."

21. Back to the living room. The director is telling the
characters, "Now you come in the door just like you're terribly cold,
and your line is, 'What a terrible night!'"

22. Back to the yard; Stan and Babe get into the car and prepare
to start it up.

23. Back to the living room. The door opens and the guy comes in
and says, "What a terrible night!" They hear a terrific noise like
thunder and all take it big.

24. Cut to Stan and Babe in the noisy car. They look back at the
house and pull out quickly. FADE OUT.

25. Fade in on corner of street, the car parked by the sidewalk.
Babe is standing up in the car with a crowd gathering around him. He
starts to give them a sales talk, giving them a sympathy angle that
the car belongs to an old lady who is about to lose her home and he is
trying to raise money for her by selling this car to the highest bidder.
Babe says, "In the name of charity, what am I offered?" Nobody
answers, and Babe says, "Won't somebody start it?" Still nobody
answers. Babe pleads with them and again says, "Please, won't
somebody start it?" Stan starts the motor and the noise is so terrific
the crowd take it big and run, thinking it is going to explode.

26. Babe frantically tries to stop the motor from running, but
can't do it. Stan finally picks up a hammer out of the back seat, lifts up
the hood and smacks the engine with the hammer, and the noise
stops. Babe says, "What did you go and do that for?" Stan says, "I
thought you wanted somebody to start it." Babe gives him a dirty look
and starts trying to entice the crowd, finally getting them back again.

27. Babe says, "Now, folks, what am I offered?" A crying drunk
speaks up and says, "A hundred dollars. Poor old lady – if she's worth

anything at all she's worth a hundred dollars." He takes out a wallet, removes some money and puts the wallet back in Stan's pocket by mistake. Babe continues trying to raise the bid.

28. Cut to a character alongside of Stan. He asks Stan what time it is. Stan looks out of scene and we show a big clock with hands pointed to 1:25. He turns to the character and says, "One twenty five." The character being deaf puts his hand to his ear and says, "Hey?" Over this scene we hear Babe calling, "Going at one hundred dollars." Stan yells at the top of his voice, "One twenty five!" The old guy thanks him. Babe says, "Sold to the gentleman for one hundred and twenty five."

29. The crowd disperses, just leaving Stan. Babe says, "Who said one twenty five?" Stan replies, "I did. He was asking me the time."

30. Babe sits on the running board of the car with utter disgust, then discovers the wallet sticking out of Stan's pocket and says, "What's that?" Stan takes it, pulls the wallet out, opens it and sees a lot of money. Babe says, "Where did you get it?" Stan looks blank and can't explain.

BABE: I see it all now. After all these years you've shown up in your true colors.

STAN: What do you mean?

BABE: What do I mean? I mean you're going to give this money back to the old lady and make a full confession!

STAN: Of what?

BABE: Don't try to alibi. You know you stole that money from the old lady! Guilt is written all over you!

Stan quickly looks himself over, then looks blank again.

BABE: To think that all these years I've been fostering a common thief!

STAN: What are you talking about?

BABE: Don't bluff me, you snake in the grass. You sheep in wolf's clothing! You double-crosser! You Judas! You despicable viper! You – You ---

STAN: Don't you call me a You-You!

Stan starts out but Babe pulls him back and says, "No you don't. You're going back to that house and tell the whole truth! Get in that car!"

STAN: I won't get in that car. I haven't done anything.

BABE: You get in that car!

STAN: I won't!

31. Babe grabs Stan and starts to wrestle with him to get him

into the car. He finally gets him in the back seat, and after an ad-lib struggle we move back to longer shot and show the car collapse.

32. They pick themselves up out of the wreck. Babe tells Stan to go on, like he was herding him. Stan refuses to go. He runs away and stops as Babe stops. Babe picks up a rock and throws it at Stan. Stan picks up one to throw back at him, but Babe makes a run at him and Stan puts the rock down and runs. They both stop again and Babe throws another rock. It hits Stan and he does a Brodie. He gets up sore, picks up another rock and throws it back at Babe. Reverse angle, Babe in small figure; the rock knocks his hat off. Babe goes crazy, picks up his hat and makes a wild rush after Stan. They exit around the corner.

33. Cut to the living room of the house. The characters are on still rehearsing. The Heavy has the old lady by the throat and she is on her knees screaming for help. The door bursts open and Stan and Babe enter. Babe very dramatically says "Stop!" He throws the Heavy over a settee, helps the old lady to her feet. The characters all take it, wondering what it is all about. The old lady says, "What on earth is the matter?"

    BABE: Madam, my friend Mr. Laurel here has a confession to
          make.
    LADY: Confession?
    BABE: Yes, he's the one who stole your money and put you into
          that villain's clutches.
    LADY: There must be some mistake.
    BABE: There is no mistake. I caught him red-handed.
    HEAVY: You must be off your nut. We're only rehearsing a play.

34. Babe takes it big, and at this point the drunk staggers in and says, "Sorry I'm late for rehearsal, folks. I was trying to save an old lady from losing her home." The drunk looks over and sees Babe with the wallet and sys, "What are you doing with my money?" He grabs it from Babe and hollers, "Help! I've been robbed! Police!" Stan and Babe take it big and run out of the house. FADE OUT

Walker
DIALOGUE
Wednesday
June 3
1931.

L2.

Stan   Oliver

and

Laurel   Hardy

In

“ONE GOOD TURN”

HARDY   What are you doing now?

LAUREL I was just smelling the soup.

HARDY   Well, don't ever do that again! If there's anything I
can't stand, it's a soup-sniffer!

LAUREL It wasn't really a sniff ---

HARDY   Come here and help me wash these clothes!

Here, hang this Haberdashery on the line!

LAUREL Haber --- ?

HARDY   Hang IT on the line!

LAUREL You haven't got another cup, have you?

HARDY   Another cup, what for?

LAUREL The tent's on fire!

HARDY   What next?

               . . .
               . . .

DIRECTOR As the scene opens, you are seated here, knitting.
          You are supposed to be a poor widow.

LADY   A poor lorn widow.

DIRECTOR That's it. I am going to play the crooked landlord
          who is going to foreclose the mortgage on your home.

          Now, listen all, please. Study your parts, be dead
          letter perfect. I want this annual show to be a
          howling success; the biggest hit in years!

               . . .
               . . .

HARDY   Let's try our luck here.

          Pardon the unseeming intrusion, lady, but my friend
          and I are victims of the depression. We haven't tasted
          food for three days.

LAUREL --- And three nights.

LADY   You poor things. Fancy not eating for three days.

LAUREL Yes, Ma'm. Yesterday, today and tomorrow.

HARDY   We were wondering – pondering, as it were – if you
          would be kind enough to provide us with a slice of
          buttered toast?

LADY   Why, certainly, if you will wait a few minutes I'll fix
          you something to eat.

HARDY   A thousand thanks, Ma'm. Is there anything we can
          do, some slight chore, while we're waiting?

LADY   No, I don't think so.

LAUREL   How about you chopping some wood?

LADY   That would be splendid!

HARDY   Yes Ma'm, splendid it shall be.

               . . .
               . . .

HARDY   Well, you suggested it, you cut it!

LAUREL   I'm no mechanic. I don't know anything about cutting
          wood.

HARDY   You should. You told me once your father was in the
          lumber business.

LAUREL   I know, but he was only in the lumber business in a
          small way.

HARDY   What do you mean, in a small way?

LAUREL   He used to sell toothpicks.

HARDY   Well, go ahead and sliver – Make some toothpicks.

          Why don't you be careful? That might have hit me.

LADY   All ready. Come right along.

               . . .
               . . .

LADY   Now just help yourselves, won't you?

LADY   (Reading her part)

          What, Hector Hammerhead, you here again!

DIRECTOR Let us not bandy words! I have come to foreclose the mortgage. Out you go.

LADY   So, Hector Hammerhead, you thought to catch me unprepared and at your mercy!

          But this time you are foiled! I have been ready for this dire emergency. I am going to pay you! Pay you, dollar for dollar! And then you can go! Go, and never darken my door again!

          I have been robbed!

DIRECTOR Ha! Ha! Ha! You have been robbed! The same old story! Well, Christine De Mannville, at last I have you in my clutches!

LADY   Spare me, Hector Hammerhead, spare me! It is only a hundred dollars! Give me more time! Just a little more time!

DIRECTOR Not one more minute! If you are not out of this house by three o'clock, I'll have my minions throw you out, bag and baggage!

LADY   My hour has come! What will I do? What will I do?

HARDY   We have got to do something!

          Are we men or are we fish?

          We've got to help her!

LAUREL   Why, what for?

HARDY   What for? You ask me, what for?

          Because one good turn deserves another!

          Quick, think of something we can do to help her!

LAUREL   Mebbe we could help her to move.

HARDY   She's NOT going to move!

I'll save her home if it's the last thing I ever do!

We've got to get our- our- our – MY brains together and see what's to be done!

Eureka! I have it!

LAUREL   Eureka! What is it?

HARDY   We'll sell the car to raise the money, the hundred dollars!

LAUREL   Let's go and tell her.

HARDY   No! No! Don't do that! We'll surprise her!

We've got to hurry, and get back here before three o'clock!

. . .
. . .

HARDY   S-s-h! Don't make a noise! Let's sneak away, quietly!

. . .
. . .

DIRECTOR   Now then, you enter through the door. It is storming, and you are cold, frozen. Your line is: "What a terrible night!"

MAN   What a terrible night!

. . .
. . .

HARDY   The bargain of a century, good people. This car, just as it stands, one hundred dollars.

             Pause! Consider! This car belongs to a dear old lady, she might be your mother, who is about to lose her home. It is to save and preserve this home that I am trying to sell this car.

             In the name of charity – sweet charity – what am I offered?

             Won't somebody please start it?

             Please, please, somebody start it! That's all, just start it!

             Now, just what did you do that for?

LAUREL   I thought you wanted somebody to start it.

HARDY   Now, folks, what am I offered?

DRUNK   One hundred dollars! Poor ol' lady, if she's worth anything at all, she's worth a hundred dollars.

HARDY   One hundred dollars is bid! Do I hear one hundred and five?

MAN   What time is it, Buddy?

LAUREL   One twenty five.

MAN   Hey?

HARDY   Going! Going at one hundred dollars!

LAUREL   ONE TWENTY FIVE!

HARDY   Sold to the gentleman for one hundred and twenty five!

Who said one twenty five?

LAUREL   I did. He was asking me what time it was.

HARDY   What's that?

Where did you get it?

I see it all! I wouldn't have believed it! After all these years you have shown up in your true colors!

LAUREL   What do you mean?

HARDY   The leopard cannot change his spots!

LAUREL   What spots? What do you mean?

HARDY   You know what I mean! You're going to give this money back to that dear old lady! And you're going to make a full confession!

LAUREL   Confession of what?

HARDY   Don't try to alibi! You know you stole the money from the old lady! Guilt is written all over you!

To think that all these years I've been fostering a common thief! A viper in my bosom!

LAUREL   Whose bosom? What are you talking about?

HARDY   Don't try to bluff me, you snake in the grass! You sheep in wolf's clothing! You double-crosser! You Judas! You traitor! You, you !!!

LAUREL   Don't you call me a You-You!

HARDY   Oh, no you don't! You're going back to that house, and tell the whole truth! Get in that car!

LAUREL   I won't get in no car! I haven't done anything!

HARDY   You get in that car!

LAUREL   I won't!

HARDY   Go on, and keep going!

                   . . .
                   . . .

HARDY   Stop!

LADY   What on earth is the matter?

HARDY   Madame, my one time friend here, Mr. Laurel, has a
           confession to make!

           Yes, he's the one who stole your money, and placed
           you at the mercy of that villain!

LADY   Why, there must be some mistake.

HARDY   There's no mistake! It's all too true! I caught him
           red handed!

DIRECTOR   You must be off your nut; crazy as a loon! There's
           been no money stolen! We're only rehearsing a play!

DRUNK   Sorry I'm late for rehearsal, folks. I was trying to
           save some old lady from losing her home.

           What are you doing with my wallet, my money?

           Help! Robbers! Police!

"SCRAM!"

Production history: Production L-9. Script and H.M. Walker dialogue script written early June 1932. Filmed Tuesday June 14; Thursday June 16 – Thursday June 23. Retakes shot Monday July 4 through Saturday July 9. Released Sept. 10. Copyrighted Sept. 12, 1932, by MGM (LP 3237). Two reels.

Produced by Hal Roach. Directed by Raymond McCarey. Assistant Director (uncredited), Lloyd French. Photographed by Art Lloyd. Edited by Richard Currier. Sound by James Greene. Dialogue by H.M. Walker.

With Stan Laurel (Himself), Oliver Hardy (Himself), Richard Cramer (Judge Beaumont), Arthur Housman (Genial drunk), Vivien Oakland (Mrs. Beaumont), Wilson Benge (Hawkins, the Beaumonts' butler), Charles McMurphy (Policeman who hears razzberry), Sam Lufkin (Bailiff), Baldwin Cooke (Court clerk), Charles Dorety (Defendant).

On a rainy evening, vagrants Stan and Ollie are in night court, being ordered to "Scram!" in one hour by an angry judge who detests drunks and homeless people. While walking out of town, the boys encounter a friendly, well-to-do drunk who has lost his car key down a street grating. In thanks for their finding it, he drives them to his lavish home and invites them to spend the night in a warm, comfortable upstairs guest room. As the boys prepare for bed, the drunk encounters a butler downstairs, who informs him that he is in the wrong house. The drunk departs, unbeknownst to Stan and Ollie; they begin to look for him and find the lady of the household, who screams and faints when she sees two strangers in her home. They revive her with what they think is water – actually gin from a jug left behind by the drunk. A couple of glasses of this make the lady very convivial indeed. Inviting the boys into her bedroom, she dances energetically and begins laughing uncontrollably. Before long, Stan and Ollie are also screaming with laughter, a sound which alerts the true master of the house, who has just returned home. It's the angry judge, and when he sees his drunken wife in their bedroom, laughing uproariously with the two vagrants, he is not amused.

"*Scram!*" benefits enormously from three great supporting performers. Vivien Oakland (1895-1958) had portrayed Mrs. Laurel in *Love 'em and Weep* and Mrs. Hardy in *We Faw Down* and *That's My Wife*; she would later have a memorable scene sharing a stagecoach with Stan and Ollie in *Way Out West*. But her great moment with the team is here, as the very proper Mrs. Beaumont whose inhibitions are curiously unleashed after the boys innocently revive her with a glass of water.

Richard Cramer (1889-1960) was a stage actor for twenty years before embarking on a film career in 1927; he appeared in more than 250 films, the vast majority of them Westerns, before retiring in 1952. Occasionally, he was allowed to display a gift for comedy, as in his portrayal of "Officer Postlewhistle" in the surreal W.C. Fields short *The Fatal Glass of Beer* (1933).

Making his first of five appearances with Stan and Ollie is Arthur Housman (1889-1942), who worked in vaudeville before beginning his work in movies with the Edison company in 1912. He was teamed with William Wadsworth for a series of "Waddy and Artie" comedy shorts in 1915; in the early '20s he was working in features,

In the 1920s, Arthur Housman was often cast as a debonair villain. *Photo courtesy of Jack Taylor.*

After 1930, Mr. Housman was almost exclusively seen as a genial tippler.

Richard Cramer is not pleased at the sight of his houseguests.

Vivien Oakland in a dignified pose...

sometimes as a suave villain. He had memorable scenes in *The Bat* and *Sunrise*, and transferred well to sound films. His appearance as a drunk in Harold Lloyd's 1930 feature *Feet First* brought him acclaim – and so many similar roles that he became typecast as a perennial souse. For most of his remaining films (of about 320), he played "Drunk on Subway," "Drunken Voter," "Drunk on Train" and so on. He added his comic expertise to Laurel and Hardy's *The Live Ghost, The Fixer Uppers* and *Our Relations*, and had a very brief moment as "Drunken Legionnaire" in *The Flying Deuces*. In *"Scram!"* he demonstrates that while his liver may be in jeopardy, he has a good heart. He means well for Stan and Ollie, and it's only though his tipsy confusion that he accidentally places them in harm's way.

The script, which consists of seven legal-sized pages, proposes that the boys should be asleep on a bench in the night court when the bailiff calls them; in the film, they're too nervous about their fate to be drowsy.

When we first encounter the drunk in the film, we can tell from his elegant suit and top hat, and his fancy touring car, that in his sober moments he's quite prosperous. We never do find out where he's been for the past few hours, but the script makes it clear that he makes his acquaintance with Stan and Ollie at the "exterior of a speakeasy." Prohibition was still in effect when *"Scram!"* was made, and wouldn't be repealed for another year and a half. As Mr. Housman's condition indicates, a gallon jug of gin was still readily obtainable.

Someone thought better of "closing the cop in" under the grating after his pursuit

...and in one less dignified, trying to make Ollie her dancing partner.

The original one-sheet poster from 1932.

of Ollie comes to an end; we see him emerging from the hole in the sidewalk just as the drunk's car speeds away. We wouldn't want to see one of our brave men in blue trapped underground.

In the script, the butler of the house seems more accommodating to the drunk and a little more harsh to Mrs. Beaumont than he is in the film. He's played by Englishman Wilson Benge (1875-1955), who was typecast as waiters and butlers just as indelibly as Housman was tagged as a drunk. His best role in movies may be in the 1930 Ronald Colman film *Raffles*. *"Scram!"* was his last of four appearances with Laurel and Hardy, the others being *Do Detectives Think?* (as a butler), *The Battle of the Century* (as the top-hatted mayor who tries to stop the pie fight), and *You're Darn Tootin'* (as a fellow member of the orchestra). While most of his work was in feature films, he occasionally returned to short comedies, as in *A-Plumbing We Will Go* (1940), where he was, of course, a butler – bedeviled this time by The Three Stooges.

Other bits of business suggested by the script but not in the film include the wife getting an attack of the hiccoughs, or hiccups if you prefer; the butler's accident and subsequent "revival"; and the ending scene with Stan and Ollie making little ones out of big ones in a prison rock quarry.

The ending of the movie, evidently the product of on-the-set inspiration, instead provides a great moment where the revelry of Stan, Ollie and the wife is contrasted with a repeating close-up of the baleful glare of the judge, who of course thinks that the boys have gotten his wife drunk in retaliation for ordering them out of town. This is a great example of getting laughs purely through editing, and is a testament to Laurel and Hardy's talent as film comedians in addition to their skills as performers.

L-9 – Laurel & Hardy

Fade in on long shot of a small night court. The judge has just sentenced a character who is being taken to the tank.

Closeup the Judge says "Next."

The Bailiff calls out, "Laurel and Hardy."

Cut to benches with a bunch of prisoners looking around for Laurel and Hardy. The bailiff again calls and there is no answer. The Judge getting impatient hits his gavel on the desk and says, "Laurel and Hardy!"

The cop looks among the benches and discovers Stan and Babe asleep on the rear bench. He awakes them, shoves them up to the Judge who gives them a dirty look. Babe is all fussed; Stan looks kind of groggy and half asleep. He takes a drink of water from the Judge's glass.

The Judge says, "You are charged with vagrancy. Guilty or not guilty?" Babe says, "Not guilty." The Judge says, "On what grounds?" Stan says, "We were only sleeping on a park bench." Babe agrees with Stan, then gives him a double takem. The Judge by now is burning up. He looks menacingly at them and says, "If the jail wasn't full I'd give you 180 days -- " Stan says, "Is that as much as a month?" The Judge continues, "But being that it is full I'm going to give you just one hour - - " Babe very elated says, "That you, sir." The Judge continues, "—to get out of town!" Stan and Babe take it. The Judge continues and gives them a severe lecture, ending up with, "Now never let me set eyes on you again. Case dismissed!" Babe says "Thank you, sir," and Stan says, "Does that mean we can go back and sleep on the park bench?" The Judge blows up and says, "Get out of here or I'll build a jail for you!"

Cut to exterior of a speakeasy. There is a slight drizzle of rain as the last few guests are seen departing, the last of which is a drunk who staggers out onto the sidewalk. He starts toward an expensive touring car parked at the curb. He has a gallon jug of gin in his hand. He places this in the car and starts feeling for his key. He is standing directly over an iron grating in the sidewalk. He finds the key and takes it out of his pocket. He starts to get into his car but slips on the running board, doing a brodie and losing the key.

Insert the key falling down into the grating.

The drunk starts looking around the sidewalk trying to find it.

Stan and Babe enter and ask the drunk what he is looking for. He tells them he has lot the key to his car. They help him in the search and discover it at the bottom of the grating. Babe says, "Here it is." The drunk bends over to see and nearly falls. Babe grabs him just in time and says to Stan, "You hold him while I try and get it."

Stan holds the drunk while Babe tries to get his hand through the grating to get the key but fails to get it. Stan says, "Wait a minute – I've got an idea." Babe asks him what, and Stan says, "You hold him." Babe gets up and holds the drunk.

Stan pulls back the lapel of his coat and we insert a piece of chewing gum there. Stan puts it in his mouth and starts chewing it to moisten it. He then takes the umbrella from the drunk, puts the gum on the end of it and pokes it down the grating.

Insert the gum sticking to the key.

Stan starts to pull it up out of the grating but the umbrella opens. Babe looks at this very disgusted and says, "You hold him – I'll fix it." Stan then gets up and holds the drunk while Babe gets hold of the grating with both ands and lifts it out bodily. The grating is pretty heavy. Babe says to Stan, "Now get the key." Stan lets go of the drunk, walks around in back of Babe to the other side of the hole to get the key. The drunk staggers backwards and falls into the hole. Stan helps him out. Babe can't hold the grating any longer and he has to put it back. They start to put the drunk into his car.

The drunk thanks them and tells them if they will jump in he will drive them home. Babe tells him that they have no home. The drunk immediately becomes very sorry for them and right away invites them to stay at his place for the night, saying, "Fancy having no home. I wouldn't let a dog stay out on a night like this. You're going to come with me." Babe thanks him and they start into the car.

The drunk says, "Give me the key." Babe looks to Stan for it and Stan says, "I didn't get the key." Babe says, "Will you please hold him while I get it?" The drunk starts to stagger. Stan grabs him as Babe lifts the grating as before. The drunk gets a little more staggery, becomes too heavy for Stan and both stagger back and fall into the hole.

Babe takes it with a disgusted look. He looks off and sees a cop coming, quickly puts the grating back over the hole and tells Stan, "Keep quiet – here's a cop." Babe stands up quickly and looks very nonchalant. The cop enters, looks suspiciously at Babe and starts on his way.

Cut inside the hole; Stan motions to the drunk with a "Sh-h-h—" The drunk looks at him and gives him a razzberry.

Cut to Babe; the cop turns around quickly thinking Babe has made the noise at him. Babe gets all bashful. The cop walks back to him, gives him a dirty look and hits him on the head with his night stick. Babe takes it with an "Ouch" and the cop starts on his way again.

Cut back again to Stan and he "shushes" the drunk, who gives him another big razzberry.

Cut back to Babe and the cop; the cop just turns quickly and looks at Babe. Babe starts backing away. The cop starts after him and they chase out of the scene.

Stan lifts up the grating, helps the drunk out and puts him into the car, leaving the top of the grating still on the sidewalk. We hear Babe's "Oh-h-h—" coming out of scene and Babe enters on the run, followed by the cop. Babe passes the hole in the sidewalk and the cop does a high gruesome into it.

The drunk has the car started by this time. Stan gets out of the car, goes over to the hole, and starts to help the cop out. Babe grabs him, rushes him into the car, then gets a second thought, goes back and puts the grating back over the hole, closing the cop in.

Babe goes to do a running leap into the car as it pulls out, and he does a high gruesome onto the street. He jumps up and starts after it as we fade out.

Fade in on front of the house. The car drives in. Stan and Babe and the drunk get out and go up to the front door.

The drunk starts feeling in his pockets for the key to the house. Babe says, "Did you lose something?" The drunk says, "Yes, I can't find my key." Babe says, "Do you mind if I help you?" and the drunk tells him to go ahead. Babe starts feeling in the drunk's pockets. Stan helps him and ends up feeling through Babe's pockets. Babe smacks him away and says to the drunk, "Is there anybody home?"

Drunk: "Sure – my wife."

Babe: "Why don't you ring the bell?"

Drunk: "We can't do that – might wake her up."

He then gets an idea and says to Babe, "How about you climbing through one of the windows and opening the door from the inside?" Babe says that's a good idea. He turns to Stan and says, "You take care of him till I open the door." Babe exits down the stairs.

Bring Babe in to a window alongside the porch, which is partly open. He tries to climb up to it but it is a little bit out of his reach. He then calls to Stan in a whisper and tells him to lean the drunk against the door and come help him. Stan does so and comes in to Babe. They go into a routine of climbing up to the window.

During this action we cut back to the drunk. The door suddenly flies open and he falls inside. He picks himself up, quietly closes the door and lies down on the settee or whatever happens to be handy.

Back to Stan and Babe. They finally make the window. Stan gets inside and helps Babe in.

Cut inside; Stan and Babe tiptoe to the door, open it and exit.

Cut to exterior. Stan and Babe enter and the door closes in back of them. Babe pushes Stan for being so careless and they start looking for the drunk. Babe exits, followed by Stan.

They come in to the window set. Babe gets on his hands and knees again for Stan to climb up on his back and says, "See if he's inside." Stan starts to climb on Babe's back.

Cut to the door. It opens and the drunk comes out and looks around.

Cut to Stan and Babe. Stan looks inside the room and whispers back to Babe, "He's not in there." He starts down off Babe's back.

Back to the drunk; not seeing Stan and Babe he goes back into the house and closes the door.

Stan and Babe come back up on the porch, still a little worried as to where the drunk is. They hear a couple of hiccoughs inside and both take it. Stan rings the door bell. A loud bell is heard and the drunk opens the door quickly and says "Sh-h-h—"

Cut to the butler in bed just being awakened. He gets up and starts putting on his pants.

Back to Stan and Babe, and the drunk invites them in. He then tells them, pointing in the direction, that his room is upstairs at the end of the hall; for them to go on up and make themselves comfortable. Babe thanks him and the drunk says, "Don't mention it. I want you to feel that this house is a much yours as it is mine." Stan and Babe are both pleased at this. The drunk continues and says, "I'll go put the car away and fix up a nice little drink, and I'll be right up." Stan and Babe exit up the stairs.

The drunk starts for the door. On a little table he sees a pitcher of water and a couple of glasses. He stops and looks and it gives him an idea. He still has the jug of gin through all this previous business. He empties the pitcher of water out into a flower bowl or something and pours the gin into the pitcher, picks up the tray and starts upstairs.

The butler enters through the living room and takes it when he sees the drunk going upstairs with the tray, and quietly follows him up.

Cut to the upper hall. The drunk enters, the butler behind him.

The butler finally stops him and asks him where he is going. The drunk turns and sees the butler, starts away, gives a double takem, then places the tray down and starts to look around the house a little bewildered, and says to the butler, "Excuse me – I must be in the wrong house." The butler says, "I'm afraid you are, sir."

The drunk gives a silly laugh and says, "Every time I get drunk I do that." The butler says, "Do what?" and the drunk says, "Get in the wrong house. Excuse me." He misses the top step and goes out of the picture. We hear him falling down the stairs and a crash.

Cut to the woman's bedroom. She wakes up, hearing the noise, and quickly exits to the hall.

She says to the butler, "What on earth was that?" and the butler replies, "Don't get frightened, madam. It was just a stranger under the influence of liquor – made a slight mistake – thought this was his house." The wife says, "It's a good thing my husband wasn't home. He'd have killed him. He detests drunken people. Good night, Jenkins." He says good night and they both exit, he downstairs and she to her room. Fade out.

Fade in on another bedroom; Stan and Babe are on dressed in pajamas etc., Babe using a perfume spray on himself. He says, "This is the first time we ever had a break."

Stan: "I wonder where our friend is."

Babe: "Maybe he lost his way again – let's go see."

They exit.

Cut to hall. Stan and Babe enter from bedroom. As they are passing the wife's room she enters to the hall, sees them, screams and faints. Stan and Babe run to her assistance. Babe says, "Quick – get me a glass of water." Stan turns and sees the pitcher of gin on the table. He pours out a glass. Babe takes it and gives it to the wife. She comes to and Babe says, "Don't be alarmed, lady. Everything's all right. We are friends of your husband."

Wife: Where is he?

Babe: He went to put his car away. He'll be right in.

Wife: What are you doing here?

Babe: We helped him out of a little difficulty and he was kind
 enough to invite us to stay all night.

Wife: You've got his pajamas on.

Babe: Yes, you see it was raining and we got all wet. So he told us
 to take off our clothes and make ourselves comfortable.

Wife: Is my husband wet too?

Stan: Wet? He's soaked!

Babe helps her to her feet and she says, "The poor dear. Won't you come in and wait?"

Stan and Babe follow her into the bedroom.

In the bedroom the wife is weaving a little bit. She says, "Won't you sit down? He won't be long." They get seated and the wife hiccoughs. Stan and Babe take it.

Wife: Excuse me. I always do that when I get nervous.

Babe: That's perfectly all right.

The wife hiccoughs again and says, "Pardon me, it's most embarrassing." Stan says "It sure is." Babe kicks him. The wife hiccoughs again and Babe says, "If I am not being too bold, I think I could stop that for you." She hiccoughs again and says, "That's most encouraging. I'd try anything once." Babe tells Stan to get another glass of water.

Stan exits to the hall and brings in the tray with pitcher and two glasses. Babe comes over to the wife and Stan hands him a glass of gin. Babe pantomimes to her and says, "Now hold your nose and count three." She says, "How many sips?" and Babe says, "No sips – drink it all." She does so, emptying the glass. Babe takes the glass from her and hands it to Stan, who places it back on the tray. Babe looks at the wife and says, "If that doesn't stop it nothing will." Stan and Babe sit down.

The wife starts into a silly little laugh, which grows into hysterical laughter. Stan and Babe keep looking at each other wondering what on earth is the matter. The woman's laugh becomes infectious and Babe starts to laugh, followed by Stan.

The wife starts kicking her shoes off and gets very wild. Stan tries to put them back on. They are all laughing hysterically. She keeps pushing Stan on his fanny. Babe gets a big laugh out of this. Stan says, "I wonder what's the matter with her?" Babe says, "I think we better put her t bed and go downstairs and wait for her husband. If he saw us in here he might not like it." He crosses to the wife, takes her by the arm and says, "I think you better go to bed." She says, "I don't want to go to bed. Let's play."

She staggers to the electric piano and turns on the music. Insert the roll and the title is "I love my baby." The music starts. Babe tries to insist that she go to bed, but she tries to dance with him. Stan and Babe try to assist her to bed, all still laughing. She pokes Stan in the neck and it causes his tongue to pop out. Babe and the wife both laugh hilariously at this, but Stan doesn't think it is so funny. She repeats the same business. Stan gets mad and does it to her, which makes her mad for a minute. Babe laughs. The wife kicks Stan in the fanny and starts laughing again. Stan gets mad and kicks her. She takes it and stops laughing.

Babe sits down, screaming hysterically. Both the wife and Stan turn and poke him in the neck and his tongue pops out. He stands up indignantly and says, "Don't you do that!" The wife kicks Babe in the fanny and goes into hysterical laughter again, then starts dancing around the room with him.

Cut down to the butler in bed. Some plaster drops on his face, which wakes him up and he hears the terrific revelry going on. He gets up and starts to put on his pants.

Back to the room, the dance still going on. There is a knock on the door and everything stops. The wife says, "Come in." The butler enters and is standing with his back to the piano.

Butler: "What's the meaning of all this noise? What are you doing in this house?"

Wife: "Jenkins, these are friends of my husband."

Butler: "This revelry stops or I leave in the morning."

Wife: "Oh, don't go, Jenkins."

Butler: "I will have to go if this noise keeps up. How do you expect a man to sleep?"

In saying this, he spreads his arms out with a broad gesture to emphasize his statement, and accidentally knocks away the stick holding up the piano lid, which drops down, hits him on the head and knocks him out. Stan and Babe take it and run over and pick him up. Babe tells Stan to get him another glass of water.

Stan quickly pours another glass of the gin and they give it to the butler. He comes to a bit dazed, pushes Stan and Babe aside and says, "Leave me alone – I'm all right." He tries to make the door, misses it and bumps against the wall. He turns with a silly grin, then motions a high-sign with his hand and says, "On with the dance, baby." He exits.

Babe turns to the wife and says, "Listen, this has gone far enough. You've got to go to bed." The wife says, "All right. You close your eyes and I'll go to bed." Stan and Babe stand with their eyes closed. She pokes them both in the neck and their tongues come out. They get mad at this. They take the wife by the arms and start to lead her to the bed. She continues singing and dancing and they have an awful time trying to persuade her to go to bed.

Cut downstairs. The front door opens and the Judge that we saw in the night court enters. As he is hanging up his coat the butler enters down the stairs dancing in time to the music. The Judge takes it when he sees him. The butler gives the high sign and says, "Hi, Judge." The Judge says, "Jenkins, what's the meaning of this? Where's my wife?" The butler says, "Alice is upstairs entertaining a couple of your pals." The Judge starts upstairs.

Cut to the bedroom. Stan and Babe are still having a hard time trying to get the wife into bed. By this time they are all laughing again. The wife does another big hiccough. Babe says "Get me another glass of water." He continues to struggle with her as Stan goes back to the table and doesn't see the Judge standing in the doorway. He pours out another glass of gin and runs back to Babe and the wife. Babe holds the wife's nose as she is kicking, and pours the glass of gin down her throat. The Judge is watching this. He looks at the pitcher, picks it up and smells it and looks wild-eyed.

Babe says to the wife, "Now you've got to go to bed!" She says she doesn't want to and starts a chase. She runs out around the piano, followed by Stan and Babe. The Judge is standing on watching them. As Stan and Babe pass the Judge, Stan does a big double takem and Babe continues on, not seeing him. Stan is trying to motion to Babe, who is struggling with the wife to put her to bed. Babe finally says, "Come on, do something to help me." He turns and sees the Judge. The Judge starts taking off his coat as Stan and Babe run frantically around the room. Fade out.

Fade in on two little figures in a prison quarry, their backs to the camera. A warden is walking up and down. The two figures are breaking rocks.

Cut to front shot and show Stan and Babe with black eyes and court plaster all over their faces, and Babe's arm in a sling. Fade out.

TWICE TWO

Production history: Production L-12. Script written early Dec. 1932. Filmed Friday Dec. 9 through Thursday Dec. 15. Previewed late Dec. Copyrighted Feb. 20, 1933, by MGM (LP 3668). Released Feb. 25. Two reels.

Produced by Hal Roach. Directed by James Parrott. Photographed by Art Lloyd. Edited by Bert Jordan. Sound by James Greene.

With Stan Laurel (Himself/Mrs. Hardy), Oliver Hardy (Himself/Mrs. Fannie Laurel), Baldwin Cooke (Diner counterman), Charlie Hall (Cake delivery boy), May Wallace (Voice of Mrs. Laurel), Carol Tevis (Voice of Mrs. Hardy), Ham Kinsey (Passerby).

Mr. Hardy makes his living as a brain surgeon. (One shudders to think of his patients.) Mr. Laurel is his switchboard operator and secretary. Each has married the other's sister, and tonight is their shared wedding anniversary. An attempt to have a celebratory dinner party (at what seems to be their shared residence) is marred by Mrs. Hardy dropping a cake on the head of Mrs. Laurel; on Mr. Laurel's unsuccessful attempts to buy fifteen cents' worth of ice cream; and by Stan having accidentally revealed to Ollie that his sister has a surprise for him. We never do find out what the surprise is, because the bickering of the two couples ends with the Hardys going "to the Ambassador, where we can get something good to eat." Another cake aimed at Mrs. Laurel is the parting shot.

Laurel and Hardy had played their own small sons in *Brats* (1930), and possibly because that worked so well, they tried playing their own sisters – and each other's wives – in this film. Stan, of course, had dressed in female attire for comic purposes many times; in vaudeville, he and his partner Mae had performed a sketch for years called *No Mother to Guide Them*, with Stan playing an old maid. Since teaming with Babe, he had donned a wig and a dress in *Duck Soup, Why Girls Love Sailors, Sugar Daddies, Their Purple Moment, That's My Wife,* and *Another Fine Mess*; there would be more of these female impersonations in future films. Babe had appeared in drag in some of the comedies he made for Vim in Jacksonville, Florida: *Busted Hearts, A Day at School, Maid to Order* and *A Warm Reception*. Cross-dressing was a tradition of long standing in English "pantomimes" and in screen comedy. The distinction in *Twice Two* is that Stan and Ollie are not pretending to be women, they're really supposed to be members of the fairer sex.

Twice Two is not quite as successful as *Brats*, possibly because an elaborate planned sequence turned out to be technically problematic. In any event, Stan told his official biographer, John McCabe, that he thought it was "the worst film we ever made." It's certainly not that bad, but it could have benefited from a quicker pace; Leroy Shield's background themes also would have benefited the movie's often barren soundtrack.

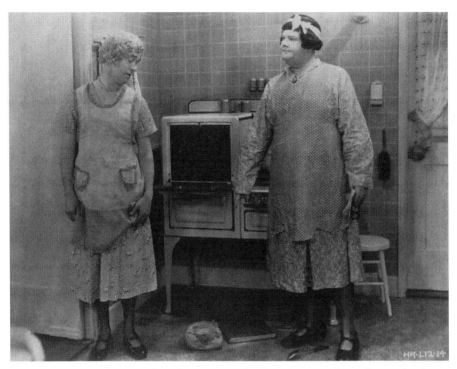

In a deleted gag, the ladies are floored by the task of making dinner, and so is the roast beef.

The babyish voice of Stan's sister – or Ollie's wife – was provided by Carol Tevis (1907-1965), who at one point provided the voice for Minnie Mouse, and also starred in a series of RKO comedy shorts, *Blondes and Redheads*. Ollie's sister – or Stan's wife – was voiced by May Wallace (1877-1938), a veteran of the Mack Sennett studio who became a mainstay at the Roach lot in the late '20s. She had appeared with Laurel and Hardy in *County Hospital* (1932) as a head nurse ("He'll sleep for a month!"), but made more appearances with Our Gang. She's especially memorable in *Love Business* (1931), where she's Wheezer and Jackie's mother – and the new landlady to their teacher, Miss Crabtree.

Another supporting player is Baldwin "Baldy" Cooke (1888-1953), who with his wife Alice had partnered with Stan Laurel in vaudeville as "The Keystone Trio." Baldy plays a counterman who frustrates Stan's attempts to buy some ice cream. He appeared in close to 90 films between 1928 and 1942, almost all of them produced by Hal Roach. He'd been the next-door neighbor in *Perfect Day* (1929), and was also prominent in Charley Chase's *The Pip from Pittsburg* (1931).

A scripted sequence in which the ladies attempt to prepare a roast for the anniversary dinner may have been filmed – a surviving photograph suggests this – but it's not in the finished movie.

After a mishap with a cake, Fannie is too immobilized in the film to go to the

Ollie is scolded by his lovely bride...

...and also by his own sister.

Delivery man Charlie Hall wants to make sure that Mrs. Laurel gets this cake. She will.

telephone herself, as suggested in the script; instead she just glowers at Stan's sister and sighs, "Phone the bakery and order another cake."

The entire last section of the script details an elaborate sequence in which the two couples attempt to watch home movies. This is nowhere to be seen in the film. It would have required an inordinate amount of expensive and time-consuming optical-effects and split-screen work; as the Roach studio's special effects wizard Roy Seawright observed, "The minute a script was written, the production office would mark the special-effects scenes with red lines in the margins, then they'd come to me and say, 'Roy, what do we do?' Then I would analyze it, and figure out the best and most economical way to do it. We had to have the ingenuity to solve each problem as economically as possible — if you needed a lot of money, they'd say, 'Forget it! We'll write something else!' We just didn't have the money — the production department would hammer you over the head with that until you were black and blue, that you had no money."

In the film, this was replaced with an ever-escalating argument between the two ladies, which climaxes with Ollie and his wife leaving. Just as they reach the door, Charlie Hall, a delivery man from the bakery, arrives with a replacement cake and asks Mrs. Hardy if she'll see that Mrs. Laurel gets it. Fannie gets the cake in a more direct way than she anticipated, and Stan tastes a little of the frosting that has splattered his wife as the film fades out.

L-12 Laurel & Hardy

Fade in on office door with sound of typewriter going over scene. The reading matter gets over "Oliver Hardy, M.D., Brain Specialist. Associate Advisor, Mr. Laurel."

Dissolve to inside of office. Babe is busy typing.

Cut to Stan in the outer office sitting at a small switchboard, plugging in the telephone calls. He suddenly thinks and exits to Babe's office.

STAN: Say, do you know what day this is?

Babe thinks a minute and says, "What?"

STAN: It's a year ago today that I married your sister, and you married mine.

BABE: That's right, it's our anniversary. That was a good idea of yours, marrying into each other's family. It made it so much easier, knowing each other's ways. Now, I get along swell with your sister and get along good with mine, don't you?

Stan gives a little doubtful nod.

BABE: I know what we'll do. Let's get the girls and we'll go out tonight and celebrate our anniversary. Get my domiciliary edifice.

Stan looks puzzled, and Babe says, "Call up my home!"

STAN: What's the number?

BABE: Why can't you remember? It's Waterloo—Two-Two.

STAN: Two-two?

BABE: Two-two.

Stan starts to look, turns and says, "Two two!" Babe gives him a dirty look as he exits.

Stan enters to the switchboard and puts in a plug.

Cut to Babe's home. The phone rings. Babe's wife, a blonde girl, enters with back to camera. She picks up the phone and in a baby voice says, "Hello."

Back to Stan, and he says, "Is that you sis?"

Back to the girl. She turns, facing the camera, does a silly giggle, and says, "Uh huh." We now see that it is Stan dressed as the girl.

Back to Stan, and he says, "Ollie wants to talk to you." He puts in another plug.

Cut to Babe. His phone rings and he answers it, saying, "Is that you, honey?"

Back to the home. The girl giggles again and says, "Uh huh."

Back to Babe, and he says, "Do you know what day it is?"

Back to the wife. She says, "How could I ever forget it?" and does a silly giggle.

Back to Babe. He gets all giggly too, and says, "How about you and sis and Stan and I going out tonight to celebrate our anniversary?"

Cut to Stan, and he says "That would be swell. Let's go to the Montmartre."

Back to Babe, very annoyed. He speaks over the phone and says, "Just a minute." He lays down the phone, exits to Stan, and says, "Don't you listen to my conversation when I'm talking privately. Just because it's your sister, you don't have to listen to everything we say."

STAN: Well, you listen to me when I talk to your sister.

BABE: No, I don't.

STAN: Yes, you do!

BABE: Well, what about it?

STAN: What about what?

Babe gives him a dirty look and exits and picks up his phone again. Stan pushes in a plug or does something at the switchboard to cause a whistling noise in Babe's ear. Babe takes it very annoyed, and puts the receiver to his phone.

Back to Stan. There is a terrific whistling noise, and all the plugs jump out. Stan gets made, pours some water into the mouthpiece of his phone, and blows into it.

Cut to Babe. Water comes squirting out of the mouthpiece and into his face. Babe, very annoyed, pours some ink from a bottle into the receiver of his phone and blows that. The ink comes out of the mouthpiece and hits him right in the face. He hangs up the phone, disgusted.

Cut to the home. Babe's wife is jiggling the hook and says, "Hello? Hello?"

Back to Stan. He says, "Is that you sis?"

Back to the wife, and she says, "Yes."

Back to Stan. He says, "Is Fannie there? Tell her I was to speak to her."

Babe's wife calls out of the scene, "Fa-a-nnie, your husband Stanley wants to talk to you."

Cut to the kitchen and show Babe, dressed in women's clothes, taking a big roast out of the oven and basting it. She turns in the direction of Babes wife and says, "Just a minute," and leaves the meat on the drainborad, closes the oven door, and exits wiping her hands on her apron.

She comes into the telephone, takes the receiver from Babe's wife and says, "What is it, honey?"

Stan does a big grin and says, "Ollie wants to take us all out tonight to celebrate our university."

Back to the wife. She says, "Tell Ollie we can't go. I'm cooking a dinner and we'll have a nice quiet evening at home. We've got a nice surprise for him, but don't tell him."

Stan says, "All right, I won't."

Back to the wife. She says, "Hurry home. Goodbye." She hangs up the phone and motions to Babe's wife, and they exit to the kitchen.

Back to Babe's office. Stan is on.

BABE: Who were you talking to?

STAN: I was talking to Fannie.

BABE: What did she say?

STAN: She said we had to come right hom. She's got a surprise for you.

BABE: What else did she say?

STAN: She told me not to tell you.

BABE: Well, don't tell me!

STAN: All right, I won't. I can keep a secret.

Babe gives him a big takem as we fade out.

Cut to the kitchen of the home. Stan's wife picks up the roast in the pan with both hands, can't open the oven door, and calls to Babe's wife to open it. Babe's wife opens the oven door which drops onto the end of the roasting pan, knocking it out of Fannie's hands to the door, and the roast slides under the sink. Fannie looks very disgusted. Babe's wife gets on her knees and crawls under to get the roast. As Fannie is picking up the pan, Babe's wife comes from under the sink, and her head accidentally gets up under Fannie's clothes. Fannie by this time has the pan with the hot gravy in her hands. She runs around, finally doing a Brodie and spilling gravy all over the place.

They pick themselves up, and Fannie gives Babe's wife a dirty look. Fannie picks the meat up, puts it in the oven, and says "Why don't you do something to help me? Now, let's get the table set, so we can have everything ready for the boys." She looks around and says, "Where's the tablecloth?" Babe's wife says, "It's up there," pointing to a cupboard up high over the gas range. Fannie gets up on the stove and starts to reach for the cupboard. Babe's wife puts a kettle of water on the stove, turns on the gas, gets a match, strikes it and lights the gas, which gives a little explosion, and the flame shoots high up in the air.

Cut to Fannie, just reaching in the cupboard for the tablecloth. There are also some platters in the cupboard. The big flame shoots up, catchers her in the rear, she takes it big and does a high gruesome to the floor. The concussion of the fall causes the oven door to drop open, and either the meat or the mashed potatoes falls out of the oven and into her lap.

Fannie picks herself up, puts the meat back into the oven, gives Babe's wife a dirty look, grabs the tablecloth and exits to the living room. Babe's wife picks up the birthday cake and follows.

Cut to the living room. Fannie is on, putting the tablecloth over the table. She discovers the table is a little small, tells Babe's wife to put the cake down, and help her with the table. Babe's wife says, "What do you want me to do?" Fannie tells her, "When I unhook it from underneath, you pull it out."

Fannie starts under the table. Babe's wife puts the cake on the center of the table. Fannie, from under the table, says, "Now—pull it open." Babe's wife grabs the table and pulls it apart from the center, and the cake topples over and goes out of sight. Babe's wife looks down at the opening and gets a little fussed. Fannie comes up from under the table with the cake around her neck. The cake looks like an Elizabethan collar, and the round center of the top of the cake, with several candles on it, is sitting on top of her head, which gives the appearance of a crown. Try to get a bust picture of a queen of that period that would resemble Fannie's makeup to hang in the living room. Babe's wife takes it when she sees Fannie, then turns to look at the picture of the queen. Fannie gives her another dirty look, goes to the phone, dials a number and says, "Is this the Acme bakery? This is Mrs. Laurel speaking. Would you kindly send another birthday cake as you sent this morning? No, we didn't eat it, we had a slight mishap." She gives Babe's wife another dirty look as we fade out.

Fade in on an exterior of the house. Stan and Babe enter to the front door. Babe has a bunch of roses. He takes out his key, tries to open the door, but it is the wrong key. He turns away to find another one amongst the bunch. Meantime, Stan opens the door, goes in, and closes it. Babe turns back with another key, and takes it big when he sees Stan isn't there.

Cut to the inside. Standing near the door is a hall tree. Stan is dusting off his hat. Babe enters and stands alongside him. Stan turns to put his hat on the hall tree and accidentally puts it on the bunch of

roses that Babe is holding. Babe throws the hat off and very
disgustedly leans against the door with his hand, which is holding the
roses. Stan, not thinking, closes the door which cuts off the roses,
leaving the stems. Babe opens the door and shows the stems. He gets
infuriated, pushes Stan outside and locks the door. Stan uses the
knocker but Babe pays no attention. The second time, Stan hits it
hard.

Cut to the inside and show two pictures fall off the wall, which
scares Babe.

Cut to Stan. He realizes he has done something wrong, and exits
toward the back of the house.

Cut to interior. Babe walks to the front door, and opens it as
though to bawl Stan out, and is surprised to see Stan is not there. He
starts looking around outside. Stan comes walking in from the back
porch, and in a double-exposure shot we see his sister fixing some
dishes. Stan says, "Hello, sis," and she says, "Hello, Stannie. Where's
Ollie?" Stan says, "He'll be in to see you in a minute." Stan starts for
the kitchen door.

Cut to living room, Babe coming across to the kitchen. The door
opens and hits Babe a terrific bump on the nose. Stan half enters, sees
what has happened, exits back into the kitchen. Babe gets up to make
a terrific lunge at the door.

Cut to interior of kitchen. Babe's wife enters on the kitchen side
of the door and turns around to back out with an armful of dishes.

Cut to Babe. He slams the door, catching his wife on the fanny
and knocking her out of the scene, and we hear a terrific glass crash.

Back to Babe. He gives a nod of satisfaction, and his wife comes
out and kicks him in the rear.

Cut to kitchen door. Stan is looking through, and seeing his sister
coming, he backs into the kitchen, closing the door (make hold shot of
this) and the sister goes into the kitchen and immediately Stan comes
into the living room. He looks through the door into the kitchen, and
nods to his sister as to say, "That's the way to handle Hardy."

Cut to the sister, and she nods back with the same attitude. Stan,
realizing that Babe is alongside him, does a double takem, then gets a
little brave and nods at Babe. He starts to walk up and down in a
cocky manner. Over the scene comes the voice of Stan's wife calling,
"Stanley--" Stan loses his cockiness and looks at Babe a little helpless,
and Babe gives him one of those dirty nods, as if to say, "She will take
care of you." Stan exits to the bedroom.

Stan enters his wife's bedroom. The wife very confidently tells him to close the door. He does so and comes down to her, and she says, "I've had an awful time with your sister today. She's getting dumber and dumber." Stan says, "I can't understand it. I don't know who she takes after." They do a bit of business, either powdering the back or the perfume spray, at which Stan's wife gets very annoyed. She gives him fifteen cents and tells him to go to the store and get some strawberry ice cream. He exits from the bedroom.

Lap dissolve to the store. Stan walks into the counter and says, "Give me fifteen cents' worth of strawberry ice cream." The clerk says, "We haven't any." Stan crosses to the phone.

Cut back to the house. The phone rings. Stan's wife comes to the phone and says "Hello," then turns and looks across the room.

Cut to Babe and his wife. Stan's wife says, "They haven't any strawberry." Babe's wife giggles and says, "Get tutti-frutti. I love tutti-frutti." Babe gives a disgusted look.

Back to Stan's wife, and she says, "get tutti-frutti."

Cut to Stan. He takes it, then goes to the clerk and says, "Give me some frutti-tutti." The clerk says, "We haven't any." Stan goes back to the phone.

Cut to the house. The phone rings again. This time Babe comes to the phone and sys, "Hello. Well, get chocolate. If you can't get chocolate get anything." He hangs up.

Back to Stan. He says to the clerk, "I'll have chocolate." The clerk says, "We haven't any." Stan says, "Well, what flavor have you got?" The clerk says, "We haven't got any. We don't sell ice cream."

Back to the house. Babe and the two wives are on, seated at the table. The door opens and Stan enters. Stan's wife says, "Where's the ice cream?" Stan says, "They didn't have any."

Cut to Babe, and he says, "Well, why didn't you go to some other place?"

Back to Stan, and he says, "I didn't have any money. I spent the fifteen cents calling you up." Babe and his sister exchange dirty looks. Stan's wife says, "Come on, sit down." Babe says, "I'll get it later."

We now go for a routine of Stan and his wife on one side of the table and Babe and his wife on the other side. Stan is helping his wife to various dishes and on the other side, Stan as Babe's wife is helping Babe to several dishes, so Hardy is getting the worst of it on both sides. Get a gag to fade out.

Fade in. The girls are clearing the table to wash the dishes, and Stan comes over and whispers in his wife's ear, "What about the surprise?" Babe hears this and says, "Oh, yes. What about that surprise?" Stan's wife gives Stan a dirty look and says to Babe, "Now that you know about it, you'll find the packages behind that chair." Babe, all excited, asks, "What is it?" and she says, "We bought you a moving picture machine. Now you get it set up while we girls wash the dishes, and afterwards we'll run pictures."

The girls go into the kitchen while Stan and Babe unpack the projection machine and try to put up the screen. Arrange business in the kitchen to intercut with the business of fixing the machine up. Stan and Babe get the machine unpacked. While Babe is examining it, Stan plugs in the switch. The machine starts going with a buzzing noise and scares Babe. Babe pulls out the plug and says, "Will you leave it alone? You put up the screen, I'll attend to this." Stan unpacks the screen and has difficulty getting it up, with a routine on the order of a deck chair. He finally breaks up the screen, and Babe sends him into the kitchen to get a tablecloth to use for a screen.

Stan's sister is on drying the dishes, which she has stacked on top of the folded tablecloth. Stan comes in and says, "Sis, give me a tablecloth." His sister pulls the cloth from under the plates, breaking them all.

Stan comes out and hands the cloth to Babe, who figures to hang it up over a curtain rod. Thorugh Stan's dumbness, the chair that Babe is standing on slides away from under him, and Babe goes through the front door, sheet and all. The two girls come running out of the kitchen to see what the excitement is. Babe's wife says, "Oliver, why don't you be careful?" Babe gets burned up and tells her to mind her own business. A near scuffle starts. Fade out.

Fade in. The screen is all set and the picture ready to go. Babe tells Stan and the two wives to take their seats in front of the screen. Babe puts out the lights and starts the machine. The picture comes on, but it is upside down. Stan suggests that Babe turn the machine over. Babe says, "Mind your own business. I'll fix it." He puts up the lights again and starts to fix it.

Lap dissolve back to the group, and Babe says, "Now we're all ready to go." The picture starts again, and this time it is reversed, the characters on the screen walking backwards. Babe says, "Will you mind your own business?" He starts to fix the machine, and we lap dissolve.

This time he gets it right, and the picture starts. Use stock shot of some wild animal—jungle picture. Get scene where lions come running out of bushes and start toward foreground. Stan gets scared and says, "Look out!" Stan and the two wives start to run, knocking Babe over, turning the machine around, and we see the picture on the wall wherever the machine is pointing. Show the film pouring out onto the floor. The lights are finally turned on. Babe kicks Stan on the fanny. Stan's sister comes to the rescue, kicking Babe and saying, "You can't do that to my brother." They go into a little free-for-all. Finally, Babe says, "Wait a minute! This has gone far enough. Stan, you take that sister of yours and get out of here!" He looks over to his sister and says, "It serves us right for marrying into the family." Stan's sister starts to cry, and Stan looks mad and says, "You can't talk like that to my sister." Babe says, "Well, what are you going to do about it?" At this point, the front doorbell rings. Stan opens the door, and a messenger boy says, "Mr. Hardy live here?" Stan says, "Yes," and the boy says, "Will you see that he gets this cake?" He gives Stan a big cake, and Stan says, "I certainly will."

Cut to Babe, and the cake hits him right in the face. Fade out.

ME AND MY PAL

Production history: Production L-13. Script written mid-March 1933. Shot circa March 15-25. Musical score assembled April 15. Released April 22. Copyrighted May 10, 1933, by MGM (LP 3867). Two reels.

Produced by Hal Roach. Directed by Charles Rogers. Assistant director, uncredited, Lloyd French. Photographed by Art Lloyd. Edited by Bert Jordan. Sound by James Greene.

With Stan Laurel (Himself), Oliver Hardy (Himself), James Finlayson (Mr. Peter Cucumber, father of the bride), Marion Bardell (The bride), Eddie Dunn (Cab driver), Bobby Dunn (Telegraph messenger), Frank Terry (Hives, Hardy's butler/Radio announcer), James C. Morton (Policeman), Charlie Hall (Florist's delivery boy), Mary Kornman, Carroll Borland (Bridesmaids), Charley Young (Usher), Eddie Baker, Charles McMurphy (Policemen at finale).

Ollie is a successful businessman, engaged to marry the daughter of his boss, a big oil magnate. Stan is to be the best man; not only does he secure the railroad tickets for the honeymoon and buy the wedding ring, he also brings to the Hardy abode a wedding present – a jigsaw puzzle. While waiting for a taxi to take them to the bride's home where the wedding is to be held, the boys become absorbed in assembling the puzzle; so do the cab driver, a telegraph boy, and a policeman. Ollie's future father-in-law wonders why the intended groom hasn't shown up, and beats a path to Hardy's house, where a fracas ensues. Soon, Stan's gift has caused Ollie's marriage, fortune and career to be torn asunder, along with the puzzle.

Hal Roach would frequently remark, "Fifty percent of what's in the script will not play," and that's just about the percentage of unused material in the script for *Me and My Pal*. The first half is very similar to what wound up in the movie, with a few slight differences, while the second half bears little relation to the film.

The opening scene has Ollie listening to the radio in his living room, beaming with pride when his imminent wedding is announced. The script has the radio announcer calling the groom "the Middiesville boy who made good in the city." This is a reference to Babe's hometown of Milledgeville, Georgia. The script also refers to him as Oliver Norval Hardy, but Babe's middle name, which was also his mother's maiden name, was spelled Norvell.

In the script, Ollie jumps up and turns off the radio at the first mention of Stan; in the film, the announcer goes on to note that Mr. Laurel believes the motion picture industry is still in its infancy – a comment made so often by movie moguls that it had become a joke in the film business. The announcer begins to detail Mr. Laurel's views on "technocracy" before Ollie switches off the radio in exasperation.

The script has Stan further annoying Ollie by getting train tickets for two upper berths. In the film, Ollie asks him, "Now, why did you get two tickets for Chicago

The boys while away the time while waiting for a taxi. Eventually, they while away Ollie's wedding and career.

Policeman James C. Morton, cab driver Eddie Dunn, and butler Frank Terry are soon just as preoccupied as Stan and Ollie.

when you knew I wanted to spend my honeymoon in Saskatchewan?" Stan replies, "Well, the man said there was no such place as Skatch...Sesquatch...," unwittingly revealing the reason for the change in destination.

The scripted telephone conversation between Ollie and his bride is not in the movie. Poor Marion Bardell; although she gets screen credit, she has only one line: "Oh, daddy, whatever could have happened to him?" It's too bad that the wedding gets called off, as Marion seems like she might have been one of the nicest of Ollie's screen wives.

Floral delivery man Charlie Hall arrives at the bride's home with a large wreath bearing the message "In Memory" much later in the film than in the script. By the time Charlie gets there, Mr. Cucumber is so angry at Hardy that he grabs the wreath and storms off, growling, "I may have some use for this!"

The original 1933 one-sheet poster.

The script takes up seven pages, and in the middle of the third one it begins a significant detour from the film. The tramp character is not in the movie, nor the suspicious neighbor or plainclothes detective. The specifics of the climactic battle are very different, and no pies are thrown.

At the very end, Ollie does indeed come down the chimney in the film as per the script, but since the puzzle has long since been scattered, the film provides a new ending. While the boys were preoccupied with the puzzle, a telegram had arrived, and only now does Ollie read it. He has the opportunity to sell his stock for a two million dollar profit if he calls his broker immediately. Just as Stan brings him the phone, a radio bulletin announces that the same stock has just taken "a tremendous dive and failed."

Me and My Pal was filmed during the week that newly installed President Franklin D. Roosevelt declared the "bank holiday" to stop the panicked withdrawal of funds which was causing the failure of financial institutions all over the country. It's likely that most people who saw this movie in 1933 could empathize more with Mr. Hardy as a ruined businessman than as a big oil magnate.

Just so you don't suffer the same fate as Ollie, here's the puzzle all put together: "White Feather," painted by R. Atkinson Fox in 1930 for promotional products distributor Brown & Bigelow.

L-13 – Laurel & Hardy.

Fade in on living room of Babe's home. Babe is all dressed up, seated at a coffee table on which there is a silver tray with silver coffee pot, creamer, cup and saucer, and a plate with some toast. He is apparently very happy.

The radio is playing music. It finally stops and an announcer starts to speak. He says, "Pardon me, ladies and gentlemen, I want to interrupt this program for a very important news flash. You will all be interested to know about the Middiesville boy who made good in the city. It is with pleasure that I announce that Oliver Norval Hardy today at high noon is to marry the only daughter of the well known oil magnate, Mr. Peter Cucumber. The wedding will be held at the bride's home and will be one of the high lights of the social season. You will remember that Mr. Hardy started with this firm as elevator boy and worked his way to the top, and after the wedding today he becomes general manager of this vast concern. It may also be interesting to know that Mr. Hardy's life long friend, advoser and severest critic, who guided him to the pinnacle of success, is to be his best man – Mr. Stan Laurel. Mr. Laurel says ---"

Babe jumps up and turns the radio off, looking very annoyed. He rings a little bell which is on the tray and the butler enters. Babe says to the butler, "Hives, take this away and as soon as Mr. Laurel arrives order me a taxi." The butler picks up the tray and starts to exit as the door bell rings.

Cut to interior of front door. The butler enters still with the breakfast tray in his hand. He opens the door and Stan enters with a package under his arm, and he is also dressed up. He hands his hat to the butler, and seeing a piece of toast left on the plate he takes it and starts to eat it as he exits. The butler looks very disgusted at this. He hangs Stan's hat on the hat rack and exits.

Stan enters the living room to Babe. Babe looks at him very disgusted and says, "Mr. Laurel says!" He continues, "Did you get everything?" Stan takes some tickets out of his pocket, hands them to Babe and says, "I got the railroad tickets." Babe starts to open them. Stan continues, "And I got the ring and ordered the flowers. They'll be there in time for the wedding." Babe looks at the tickets, becomes very disgusted and gives Stan a push. Stan says, "What's the matter?" and Babe says, "Why did you get two upper berths?" Stan says, "Well, that's all they had next to the engine." Babe gives a disgusted look, then seeing the package under Stan's arm he says, "What's that?"

Stan: "I bought you a wedding present."

Babe: "That's very thoughtful. What is it?"

Stan: "Guess."

Babe: "I haven't time to guess!"

Stan opens the package and shows it to Babe, and we see that it is a Jig-saw puzzle. Babe again looks disgusted and says, "No what did you want to buy a thing like that for?" Stan says, "Well, when you're married you won't be going out much at nights, and I thought it would be something for us to play with." Babe says, "My play days are over. From now on my mind is made up to become a big oil magnate." Stan looks at him with a puzzled expression. Babe realizes that Stan doesn't quite understand what he means and says, "You know what a magnate is, don't you?" Stan with a look of full realization says, "Sure – a thing that eats cheese."

Babe throws his hands up in the air, getting over, "What's the use trying to explain any further?" The butler enters and Babe says, "Did you order the taxi?" The butler replies, "Yes sir, he'll be here any minute."

At that moment the telephone bell rings and Babe, who is right near the phone, picks it up. He is still burned up over Stan's reply and shouts into the phone, "Hallo!" Suddenly a transition comes over his face, and twiddling his tie he says, "Oh, is that you, sweet?"

Cut to the other end of the line and we show the bride all dressed up for the wedding. Her father, a character like Jim Finlayson, is listening over her shoulder trying to get an earful. She says to Babe, "Are you all ready, honey?"

Back to Babe. He says, "Yes, darling; I'm all ready – I've ordered the flowers, I've got the ring and the railroad tickets – it's just a question of minutes till you and I will be one."

At that moment the florist arrives at the girl's house with a bunch of funeral wreaths. Finlayson seeing these gives it a big takem.

Back to Babe; he just finishes his conversation over the phone by saying, "I'll see you at high noon, darling," and he hangs up.

Babe looks at his watch, starts to get a little impatient, sits down and strums his fingers on the chair.

Cut to Stan, who is absorbed with the jig saw puzzle. He has two pieces in his hand is trying to fit them together. Babe sees him and says, "What are you trying to do?" Stan says, "I'm trying to put this foot into this face." Babe corrects him and shows him how to put the two pieces together, then goes back to the chair, looks at his watch and becomes more impatient. Unconsciously he is watching Stan. He becomes a little more interested in the puzzle, and gradually moves his chair closer, finally becoming absorbed in it.

There is a ring at the door bell and thebutler crosses and opens the door, and we see the taxi driver there. The butler comes over to Babe just as he is putting a piece of the puzzle in position, and says, "Your taxi is here, sir." Babe jumps up and says to Stan, "Come on – we can't fool any more of time away with that thing."

As Stan and Babe reach the door, Babe turns to the taxi driver and says, "Bring my bags." Stan and Babe exit.

The taxi driver picks up the bags and seeing the puzzle he puts down the bags for a minute and slowly becomes absorbed in it.

Cut to Stan and Babe in the taxi. Babe is getting burned up as we cut to insert of the meter, which registers $1.20. Babe turns to Stan and says, "Go see what's keeping that driver, and tell him we're in a hurry." Stan gets out of the cab and exits toward the house.

Cut to interior of the room. Stan enters with his mind all made up to tell the driver to hurry. He says, "Hey, what's the idea?" Then seeing the driver with a piece of the puzzle in his hand he points out to him the position in which it should go, and before we know it they are both again absorbed in the puzzle.

Back to Babe in the taxi. By this time he is seeing blood. The meter jumps to $2.25. Babe springs to his feet and dashes out of the taxi.

Cut to interior of the room. Stan and the driver are still wrapped up in the puzzle. Babe enters and starts to bawl them out.

Cut to exterior and show a motor cop drive up. Seeing the cab parked in front of a fire plug he jumps off his motorcycle and exits toward the house.

Cut to the neighbor watching the cop with suspicion.

Cut to the interior; Babe is still bawling out the driver, telling him that he is twenty minutes late already, etc., when the cop enters and wants to know whose taxicab that is parked near a fire plug. The driver tries to explain, but the copy pays no attention to him and pulls out his book and starts to write a ticket.

Babe seeing the predicament tries to explain to the cop that it wasn't the driver's fault altogether. The cop continues to write out the ticket, telling them to tell it to the judge. While he is writing the ticket he looks over and sees Stan, who is about to make a false move with the puzzle. He calls Stan's attention to it and says, "Why don't you put that where it belongs?" and before we know it all four are absorbed in the puzzle.

Cut to the home of the bride. The organ is playing "Here comes the Bride" as the father leads her down the stairs. We shoot this over the shoulder of the minister. At the foot of the stairs the procession stops. The father looks at his watch and becomes very impatient.

Cut back to the room where we see Babe and Stan with the cop and the taxi driver all very much absorbed in the jig-saw puzzle, just looking at it. The door bell rings.

The butler opens the door and a tramp character almost falls into his arms. He is an emaciated character and almost starved to death. He gets over that he hasn't had a bite to eat in three days.

The butler goes over to Babe and tells him there is a starving man there, dying for the want of food. Babe very abruptly tells the butler, "Well, get him something to eat." The butler leads the tramp to a chair in the room and tells him to wait there while he gets something to eat.

As the butler goes to exit, we hear another ring at the door bell. The butler opens the door and we see a cross-eyed postman, who tells the butler he has a registered letter for Mr. Hardy. The butler takes the letter, and leaving the door open he hands it to Babe. Babe, who is still absorbed in the puzzle, takes it without taking his gaze from the puzzle. The butler exits toward the kitchen.

Cut to the postman, who enters the room, goes over to Babe and asks him if he will kindly sign for the registered letter, and hands the slip to Stan. Stan still engrossed in the puzzle takes no notice. The postman, getting no satisfaction, looks over Stan's shoulder to see what they are doing, and he too becomes interested in the puzzle.

By this time we notice that the tramp who was on the verge of collapse, has now sufficiently recuperated to be quite interested in the puzzle. He has moved from the chair and is now leaning over the table. By his side there is a smaller table, and as the butler enters he places a tray of chicken, etc., on this table and motions to the tramp, saying, "Here you are, my good man – eat this." The tramp, still watching the jig-saw puzzle, without turning pushes the tray aside and continues gazing at the puzzle.

Cut back to the home of the bride. Once more the wedding march plays and the procession proceeds down the steps. At the bottom the procession stops and the father again looks at his watch and nearly goes nuts. In a rage he grabs the telephone and starts to dial.

Cut back to Babe's room. They are still engrossed in the puzzle. The telephone starts to ring violently. They take no notice at first, until the ringing becomes so insistent that Babe turns to Stan and says, "See who that is."

Stan goes to the telephone, and looking into the receiver says, "I can't see anybody – it's dark in there." Babe says, "Well, answer it!" Stan speaking into the phone says "Hello."

Cut to Finlayson at the other end of the phone. In a rage he yells, "What's the idea of holding up this wedding?" Looking at his watch he says, "Do you realize you're forty minutes late? Where's Oliver?"

Stan, still with his eyes fixed on the jig-saw puzzle, calls to Babe and says, "Oh Ollie – it's for you." Babe says, "Can't you see I'm busy?" Stan calls back into the phone, "He's busy," and hangs up.

Cut back to Finlayson; he snaps the receiver back on the phone in a rage, turns to one of his flunkeys and tells him to get his hat and cane and order his car immediately.

Stan comes back to the jig-saw puzzle and starts to look at it. Babe without taking his eyes off the puzzle says, "Who was it?" Stan says, "It was your new father in law. He wants to know if you're going to get married." Babe asks abstractly "What did you tell him?" Stan says, "I told him you were busy." Babe says "good," then suddenly realizing his predicament he jumps up and says, "Good heavens, what am I doing here? Come on!" He pulls Stan and the driver away and starts to hustle them out of the room.

Cut to exterior where we see the taxicab has registered $4.60. Babe pushes Stan in and jumps in himself, and just as the driver gets all set Babe says to Stan, "Are you sure you have everything now? Where's the ring?" Stan feels in his vest pocket for the ring but takes out a piece of the puzzle. Without saying a word he exits from the cab and goes toward the house. Babe watching him suddenly realizes the situation, takes it big and rushes after Stan.

Stan enters the room and going straight to the puzzle places the piece right into position, and does a satisfied takem and starts to leave. Babe enters the room and in a rage bawls Stan out, saying "What do you think you're doing?" Stan replies, "It fitted perfect." Babe looks to see what Stan has done, picks up the piece, reverses it and says, "You would have it wrong – it goes like that." By this time the puzzle is almost completed, and they both gaze on it with satisfaction.

Cut to exterior. A swell limousine drives up right behind the taxi and Finlayson gets out and rushes into the house. The taxi driver sees him and starts to follow. The neighbor watches this suspiciously.

Finlayson enters the room, burning with rage. He bawls Babe out and sks him what's the idea of holding up the wedding, saying "If that's what you think of my daughter, the wedding is off!" Babe realizing that an apology is necessary, tries to explain and says, "Pardon me, Mr. Cucumber – I hardly know what to say, but you see we were so engrossed in this picture---" Jimmie says "Hang the picture!" and brings his fist down with a thud on the table, and we see the jig-saw puzzle slightly dislodged. Stan says, "Hey listen, you can't do that!" Jim still in a rage says, "What do you mean, I can't do that – I've been doing these things for years." He starts to place the puzzle back in position, and we see that the center piece is missing. Jimmie says, "There's a piece missing. Where is it?" They all start to look and before we know it everybody is searching around the room, pulling drawers out, searching in each other's pockets, Stan going through Babe's pockets, etc.

Cut to front of the house next door. The neighbor is in conversation with a plain clothes detective. She is telling him that there is strange goings on going on in the house next door – that people keep going in but they never seem to come out. The detective glances at the house and exits toward the taxi. He looks at the meter and we insert it, registering $36.50. He then exits into the house.

Cut to interior of the house where we see all the characters still busily searching for the lost piece. The detective enters and sees Stan going through Babe's pockets, giving him the idea that it is a holdup.

The detective says, "Wait a minute – what's going on here?" Everybody stops. Stan releases his hand from Babe's pocket and says, "Well, you see, we got her body together but we can't find her head." The detective takes this big and says, "What?" Babe a little apologetically brushes Stan aside and explains to the detective that they were just working a jig-saw puzzle and they have it completed all except the last piece, which happens to be the head. He shows the detective the puzzle.

Dick: "Can't you find it?"

Babe: "No sir."

Dick: "Who brought it here?"

Stan: "Please sir, I did."

Dick: "Was it complete when you brought it in?"

Stan: "Yes sir. It was all wrapped up."

Dick: "Then it must be in this room."

The detective turns to the cop and says, "Guard the doors." Finlayson steps up and says, "What does it matter?" The detective says, "What does it matter!" He looks at Finlayson mysteriously and says, "Oh, so it's you – Jimmie the Spider. When did you get out of the

big house?" Jimmie all indignant says, "What do you mean, sir? I'll
have you know my name is not Jimmie the Spider!" Stan butts in and
says, "No it's Peter the Cucumber, and he's a big oil maggot that eats
cheese." The detective says, "Nevertheless, nobody leaves this room
until we find the missing piece!"

The detective paces up and down mysteriously. Everybody is
waiting for something to happen.

Cut to Stan and Babe. Stan says, "What are you going to do about
the wedding?" Babe says, "Come on," and they cautiously start to
open the window to make an escape. The detective sees them and
yells "Hold on there!" He grabs for his gun which is in his hip pocket,
and in tugging to get it out the gun shoots several times, blowing out
the seat of his pants. The other characters, hearing this, start to
scramble for hiding places. Babe ducks under the table.

Finlayson stands up and says, "You can't do that! We've got to
get to my daughter's wedding!" The detective turns to Finlayson and
says"Sit down!" and pushes him violently into a rocking chair, which
completely overturns, knocking up against a stand lamp, which
knocks over a grandfather clock, which in turn knocks over against
an iron standard with a large fish bowl on it. The bowl starts to topple.
Stan sees it, grabs the table away to save the puzzle, and in doing so
lets the fish bowl clunk on Babe's head, who was hiding under the
table. Babe gets infuriated and pushes Stan up against the wall, which
knocks down a picture from the wall onto Stan's head.

Stan gets sore, and seeing the cross-eyed postman nearby he
thinks it is he who clunked him with the picture. He goes to kick him
in the fanny, but misses and hits the mail bag, and all the letters are
scattered over the place. The postman burns up, and looking around
to see who did it, catches sight of Stan. He picks up an object and
throws it in the direction of Stan but misses him and hits the
policeman by mistake. The policeman is trying to dodge it bumps into
the tramp, who is now eating a big piece of pie, and the pie is smeared
all over the tramp's face.

The policeman catches the taxi driver trying to make a getaway
through the kitchen door, grabs him by the collar and whirls him
around violently, causing him to lose his balance, and the driver grabs
at the bell cord, causing the bell to ring.

Cut to the tramp, who has just disengaged his face from the pie.
He looks very annoyed, and seeing the taxi driver he throws the pie in
his direction.

Cut to the door; the butler pokes his head in and says, "Did you ring, sir?" just in time to receive the pie in the face.

Stan picks up a small vase with the hopes of finding the missing piece in there. He discovers that he can't get his hand out and starts to pull on it. He braces himself by putting his foot on the fanny of Jimmie, who is under the table. Jim sprawls forward, and looking back infuriated starts to get up and bumps his head on the table. He comes from under the table and gives Stan a violent push.

Stan in trying to get the vase off his hand, swings it in the air and it breaks over Babe's head, who was behind him. By this time a general battle is in progress, with furniture, pictures, etc., being hurled around in wild confusion. Over this we hear the sound of the siren of a police car.

Cut to the police car with siren going as it arrives outside the house. The woman next door points to the house and tells the chief that's where the trouble is. The cops dash into the house.

The police enter the room and the detective tells them somebody has stolen the last piece of this jig-saw puzzle. The chief says, "Take them all to court – we'll find out who's got it." There is a general commotion of protest as the cops pounce on them and drag them out.

After the police have taken the various characters into the patrol wagon, cut back to the room and show it entirely wrecked and apparently empty of all characters. We hear some "Oh's" and a clatter at the fire place as Babe comes down the chimney and appears in the fire place, followed by bricks and soot. His clothes are in shreds, hair disheveled and grimy with soot. He crawls up into the room, glares at the jig-saw puzzle, which is still intact on the table, and looking around him he calls for Stan.

The top of the piano rises and Stan's head emerges from inside the piano, and as Stan climbs out of the piano we hear discordant musical sounds. Babe glares at Stan and says, "Jig saw puzzle! Bah!" and pushes him from him.

Stan looks over to the corner of the room and amongst the debris he rescues the missing piece, and smiling as if nothing had happened says, "Look, I found it." He goes to place it in position as Babe snatches the piece from his hand, and in doing so knocks it to the floor. Stan dives under the table, rescues the piece and hands it to Babe. Babe places it in position in the puzzle and strikes a contented attitude, as Stan suddenly rises under the table, uplifting it and throwing the puzzle all over the floor. Babe jerks Stan to his feet and looks at him helplessly. Fade out.

DIRTY WORK

Production history: Production L-16. Script written late July-early Aug. 1933. Filmed circa Aug. 7-19. Copyrighted Oct. 24, 1933, by MGM (LP 4206). Released Nov. 25. Two reels.

Produced by Hal Roach. Directed by Lloyd French. Assistant director, uncredited, Jack Roach. Photographed by Kenneth Peach. Edited by Bert Jordan. Sound by Warren B. Delaplain.

With Stan Laurel (Himself), Oliver Hardy (Himself), Lucien Littlefield (Professor Noodle), Sam Adams (Jessup, the butler), Jiggs the chimpanzee (Ollie rejuvenated).

Chimney sweeps Stan and Ollie are summoned to clean the flue of one Professor Noodle, who is working on a rejuvenation formula. The professor tells his butler, "With just a few drops of this solution, I could make you thirty years younger!" Happily, the scientist is too absorbed in his studies to notice the shambles that Laurel and Hardy are making of his home, unintentionally destroying the chimney and causing soot to spew all over the living room. When the professor finally succeeds in creating his magic elixir, he invites the boys to witness a demonstration, and runs off to find the butler. Stan and Ollie's curiosity gets the better of them, and they decide to try the solution on a fish. Unfortunately, Ollie accidentally falls into a large tank filled with water; so does the entire beaker of the precious potion. When Mr. Hardy emerges from the tank, he has regressed several stages backward but at least has proven Darwin's theory.

The tentative title for this film while it was in production was *Monkeydoodle*. Thank goodness, the Roach folks were prevented from using it because earlier in 1933, the title had been registered for an exceedingly strange cartoon made by animator Les Elton and starring his character "Simon the Monk."

If *Dirty Work* had been filmed as written, it would have expanded from two reels to three. The suggested gag where the boys use a vacuum cleaner to remove the soot in the living room, causing its bag to explode, was not used. The film substitutes a great scene in which Stan is shoveling the soot into a burlap sack that Ollie is holding at his waistline; Ollie unknowingly drops the bag, and Stan just as unwittingly begins shoveling the soot into his trousers.

The sequence in which the professor demonstrates his rejuvenation formula is greatly condensed in the film. We never see him plunge into the tank, nor do we hear his voice coming from some mysterious alternate plane of existence. In the movie, he runs off to find his butler, presumably to try an experiment on him. Left to their own devices, Stan and Ollie predictably spill the entire container of the precious solution into the tank when Stan causes his partner to fall into it, and a very rejuvenated Ollie emerges as a chimpanzee wearing a derby. Since he has been reacting to Stan's clumsiness all through the film with "I have nothing to say" – a statement which

The boys before they begin their day's work...

...and after, showing just how efficient they are.

appears four times in the script – it's surprising that the writers didn't think of this as a wrap-up line.

The script suggests a couple of different supporting actors. Richard Carle had played a genial but crazy professor who wanted Laurel and Hardy to go to a cemetery and dig up a body for his experiments in the 1928 silent *Habeas Corpus*. Frank Austin had played a very frightening butler in the 1930 short *The Laurel-Hardy Murder Case*. They might have played these roles very nicely, but it's hard to imagine *Dirty Work* without the bravura performance of Lucien Littlefield as Professor Noodle and the dry humor of Sam Adams as the butler, Jessup.

Littlefield (1895-1960) had grown up in San Antonio and Dallas, but by age 19 was in Hollywood working for the Famous Players-Lasky studio. He worked in almost 300

"Professor Noodle" was Lucien Littlefield in the film...

...but Richard Carle in the script.

"Jessup," the butler, was Sam Adams in the movie...

...but the script suggested Frank Austin.

The original "title lobby" card from 1933.

They intend to clean the chimney, but wind up destroying it.

movies, proving his versatility as an old settler in William S. Hart's *Tumbleweeds* (1925), a strange doctor in the 1927 horror-comedy *The Cat and the Canary*, and any number of pompous officials, such as W. C. Fields' supervisor in *Man on the Flying Trapeze* (1935). He'd made eight short comedies for Hal Roach in 1925, and would return to the L&H fold a couple of months later in 1933 to portray veterinarian "Horace Meddick" in the team's feature film *Sons of the Desert*. Thanks to a prominent noggin that went bald very early, Littlefield was frequently cast as characters much older than he really was; he turned 38 during the filming of *Dirty Work*.

Sam Adams (1870-1958) plays the butler who is given to odd pronouncements such as, "You'll know which is the closet – it has a door on it." A Toronto native, he performed in vaudeville in Canada and all over the United States as a singing comedian, playing a rustic character. He debuted on Broadway in 1915 and in the movies in 1932, as the Secretary of State of Klopstokia in Paramount's zany *Million Dollar Legs*. Through 1944, he appeared in 21 films, but returned to the Broadway stage in the '40s and sang in the chorus of many shows, including *On the Town*.

By this point, Laurel and Hardy had made several films as "blue-collar" handymen, and a few with otherworldly or frightening settings. *Dirty Work* is an enjoyable combination of both elements.

A 1933 British newspaper advertisement indicates that the film had a different title in the UK.

L-16 Laurel & Hardy

Fade in on the laboratory set in the professor's home. The professor (type like Richard Carle) is seated at a bench, mixing all kinds of ingredients. Alongside of him is standing a butler, type like Frank Austin. As the professor puts the ingredients into the glass jar, each one has a different effect. First the liquid bubbles, then as he puts a drop of something else in, it starts smoking. The professor, between each ingredient, is referring to papers and books. He turns to the butler and says, "It won't be long now." The butler shakes his head with a disgusted look and says, "It shouldn't be, you've been at it twenty years." The professor says, "True, my boy. But remember, Rome wasn't built in a day. If this test proves successful it will be the greatest scientific discovery of the age! Something the world has been waiting for – rejuvenation! Just think—with a few drops of this solution I could make you thirty years younger!"

On the wall in back of the professor we see a cuckoo clock. At this point the clock strikes three, with three cuckoos. The professor and butler take it. An old fashioned doorbell rings, and the butler exits to the front door, and as he opens it we discover Stan and Babe standing there. They are carrying chimney sweeps' outfits comprised of brushes, poles, shovels and some sacks. Babe speaks to the butler and says, "We've come to clean your chimney." The butler says, "This way."

Stan and Babe enter and he closes the door and ushers them into a sitting room. Stan and Babe start to work, covering the furniture. The butler goes in to the professor, who is still mixing ingredients. The professor says, "Who was it?," and the butler says, "The chimney sweeps, sir. They've come to clean the chimney." The professor says, "Good. While they're at it, have them clean my pipe," and hands him a big calabash pipe. The butler says, "Very good sir," and taking the pipe, he exits.

Cut back to Stan and Babe. They have the furniture all pretty well covered with gunny sacks, and laying on the floor in front of the fireplace is another gunny sack. Stan is now nailing some sackcloth up on the mantle shelf. As he is hammering the nail into the mantle, the corner drops off. Babe runs over and takes the hammer and nail from him and says, "Why don't you be careful?" Stan has his hand on the mantle shelf and Babe spitefully goes to hit Stan's fingers with the hammer. Stan is a little quicker than Babe, and Babe misses. This burns Babe up. Stan puts his hand back on the mantle again, and Babe takes another crack at it. Stan is again too quick, and Babe misses it again. It develops into trying to hit Stan's fingers, and they get interested in this game. Stan finally holds his hand in front of a vase, Babe quickly makes a pass at it, but Stan is again too quick and pulls his hand away, and Babe smashes the vase.

Babe, very annoyed, says, "Will you stop playing and let's get to work. Now this is the way to do it." He picks up the cloth and, placing a marble vase on one end of the shelf, he runs the sackcloth along and, picking up the marble clock, he puts that on the center. He continues to run the sackcloth to the other end of the shelf and places the other vase on that end. He then gives Stan a nod. In the center of the sackcloth, which is covering the whole fireplace, there is a hole which the extension poles go through. Babe now takes the head of the brush and, lifting up the sackcloth from the bottom, pushes the brush into the chimney and pushes the handle out through the hole. The cloth is now covering him. He says to Stan, "Now put on the extension." Stan takes the handle off the brush and starts to walk away with it to pick up a pole, and pulls the ornaments off the fireplace, the clock hitting Babe on the head.

Babe comes from under the sackcloth. Stan readjusts the clock and ornaments, and Babe says, "Now keep pushing it up while I go up on the roof and I'll tell you when it's in the clear." He exits.

Stan continues putting in extensions and putting the brush up the chimney.

Babe comes into the hallway and, seeing the butler, says, "How do I get on the roof?" The butler points and says, "There's a skylight in that closet at the top of the stairs." Babe starts up the stairs.

Back to Stan, still putting in more extensions.

Cut to the roof of the house. Babe comes through the skylight and makes his way over to the chimney very cautiously and looks down. As he does the brush pops up and hits him in the face, covering him with soot. Babe becomes a little enraged at this, and, grabbing the brush, he gives it a terrific yank.

Cut below and show Stan pulled up through the fireplace.

Back to Babe, pulling the pole up hand over hand. Finally Stan appears, all black. Babe gives him one of those defiant nods and calmly lets go of the brush, and Stan disappears. The pole starts down the chimney again. Babe is looking down, watching Stan, and the top of the brush hits him on the back of the neck, then disappears down the chimney.

Cut below. Stan lands in a cloud of soot, and we see that the bottom extension of the pole is broken in two.

Back to Babe. He says, "Now push it up slowly and be careful." Stan gets up and starts to push the brush up. Babe says, "Further." Stan tells him that that's as far as it will go, and Babe says, "Put on another extension." Stan says, "there's no more." Babe says, "Well, do something." Stan looks around to see what he can use for another extension. He sees hanging on the wall a gun rack, an old fashioned double barrel shotgun with long barrel. He gets an idea, takes this down, and the pole of the brush fits perfectly into the barrel of the gun. He starts to push it up. Babe hollers down, "A little more." Stan by this time has his hands down toward the trigger of the gun. Babe says, "One more push and we've got it." Stan gives it a last push and accidentally pulls the trigger, and there is a big explosion.

Cut to Babe. He takes it big as the head of the brush goes flying past his head and spins in the air. He looks up and watches it, and the head of the brush comes down, hitting him on the head and knocking onto the roof, and he does a big "Ohhh."

Back to Stan, hearing this. He runs up the stairs.

Cut to the roof. Babe is standing on the door of the skylight, holding his head. The door suddenly opens and Stan pops up, which throws Babe into the other side of the roof, and he slides off with a loud "Ohh," and there is a big glass crash. Stan goes to the other side and looks down, and we show that Babe has gone through a conservatory. Babe is lying flat in a manure bed in the center of the hothouse, with lilies all around him. He picks himself up, looks at Stan in a very resigned manner, and says, "Would you mind opening the front door and letting me in?" Stan starts to exit.

Cut to the professor, still mixing his formula.

Cut to the hallway and pick up Stan, just coming down the stairs. He opens the front door, and Babe is standing there, very dejected looking. Stan motions for Babe to come in. Babe does so, and Stan closes the door and then, in a very plaintive manner, says, "Did you hurt yourself?" Babe looks at him for a minute and says, "I have nothing to say," then motions for Stan to go back into the living room, and he exits up the stairs.

Stan goes back into the living room and starts to adjust the pole again.

Cut to the roof. Babe comes up through the trap door and picks up the head of the brush, which is laying near the head of the chimney. He looks down the chimney for the head of the pole. The pole comes into the picture and hits him square in the eye. He does another big "Ohhh." He then grabs the pole and starts to fasten on the head of the brush.

Cut to Stan below, looking up the chimney.

Back to Babe. He viciously pushes the pole back down the chimney.

Cut below, and the butt of the gun hits Stan on the head. We hear a cocoanut sound effect, and the second barrel explodes.

Cut to the roof, and the shot blows Babe's hat off. He picks it up and we see that it is riddled with holes. Babe now takes the brush again and viciously pushes it down the chimney.

Cut below and it again hits Stan on the head. Stan gets mad now, grabs the butt of the gun, and viciously shoves it up the chimney.

Cut to the roof again. The brush comes up, hits Babe under the chin, and knocks him on his fanny. Babe gets up quickly, grabs the brush like he was going to shove it down the chimney again, but at this point we cut to Stan, who has the gun in his hands, and he pulls the brush down the chimney with a mighty tug.

Cut to the roof, Babe hanging onto the end of the brush. The chimney gives way, and Babe disappears with a loud "Ohhh!"

Cut below. Stan is standing by the fireplace. The butler rushes in just as Babe lands with a cloud of soot, which goes all over the butler. As Babe is sitting there, several bricks keep dropping on his head. After he feels that the last one has dropped, he looks back up to see if there are any more, and another one drops, hitting him on the forehead. Stan gets interested in this, and he looks up the chimney. Babe pushes him out, and as he does, another brick comes down and hits Babe again. Babe now gets mad and picks up a brick to throw at Stan. Stan makes an effort to get out of the way, and in doing so he steps on the end of a shovel which is laying across a log on the fireplace. The shovel comes up and catches Babe under the chin. Babe just puts the prick down calmly. He then turns and sees the butler, who has bee watching this without a move. The butler looks at them both, shakes his head and says very dramatically, "Somewhere, an electric chair is waiting." He turns and exits. Stan and Babe look at each other, and Stan says, "What did he mean?" Babe says, "I still have nothing to say." He picks himself up, picks up one of the sacks, and holding it open, motions for Stan to shovel the soot into the sack. Stan starts doing so. The sack starts to get a little heavy, and Babe says, "Wait a minute." Holding the sack in his hands, he places his thumbs into the top of his pants so that he can brace the bag. He then tells Stan to go ahead. Stan starts shoveling, and we insert the shovel picking up a couple of bricks with the soot. He shovels them into the sack, and the weight of the bricks brings Babe's pants forward, making a gap. Stan gets another shovelful of soot and bricks, and accidentally puts it down Babe's pants instead of the sack. Babe drops the sack and gives a disgusted look. Stan, not knowing what it's all about, looks at Babe and says, "What happened?" Babe says, "I still have nothing to say."

Cut upstairs, and show the butler filling up the bathtub.

Cut to Stan and Babe, who now have the sack filled with soot, and are just finishing tying it up. The sack is packed full, and the corners on top of it look like two ears. Babe takes hold of the ears and tells Stan to help him get the sack on his back. He does so, and Babe gets it onto his shoulders. He gives it a last pull to get it into position, and in doing so, tears the top off. Stan is still holding the bottom of the sack. The soot falls all over Babe, ending with the sack laying over his head and giving the appearance of a monk. Babe just looks pleadingly at Stan again and says, "Well?" Stan says, "I have nothing to say."

Babe bursts into a rage now, and says, "Get that shovel and clean up this mess." Stan gets the shovel and Babe holds another sack. Stan shovels into the heap of soot, getting a shovelful of it, and as he goes to lift up the shovel, we hear a terrific rip, and we discover that Stan has cut out part of the carpet. Babe throws down the sack, picks up the shovel, and deliberately hits Stan on the head with it, making a big bong.

At this point, we see the butler, all cleaned up, coming downstairs.

Back to Stan and Babe. Stan is just recovering. He picks up the shovel, gets a shovelful of soot, and throws it on Babe. Babe takes the shovel, deliberately takes a shovelful, and goes to throw it on Stan, but it goes all over the butler, who just enters the room. The butler gives a helpless gesture and exits.

Babe says, "Get a broom and clean up this mess!" Stan exits to the hallway as the butler is just going up the stairs. Stan yells after him and says, "Have you got a broom?" The butler just turns and motions to the closet under the stairs. Stan goes to the closet, opens the door, brings out a broom, then looks back in, changes his mind, puts back the broom and pulls out a vacuum cleaner. He brings this into Babe, who is now picking up the brushes, etc. Stan plugs in the cord, comes back to the machine and turns the switch on, and the vacuum starts drawing in the soot. Stan has the cord stretched pretty tightly across the room. Babe turns with the armful of brushes and poles, trips over the cord, and does another brodie.

Cut to the professor. He has now finished his mixing and is very excited and nervous. He goes over to a crate, takes out a duck, places it in the tank, and as it starts to swim around, we lap dissolve the duck, making it disappear, with nothing left but the clear water. The professor now takes the small bottle or jar that he has been using to mix the formula in, and using an eye-dropper he puts one drop into the tank. The water starts seething like a bromo seltzer effect. As it clears away, by means of lap dissolve, we come back to the clear water and there is a young duckling paddling in the water. The professor takes the duckling out of the tank, places it on the floor, and does a dance around it, going nuts, shouting "Success!," etc.

Cut to the hallway. The butler is coming downstairs in a bathing suit.

Cut to Stan and Babe. Babe is still picking up the brushes, sacks, etc. and Stan is still vacuum cleaning. By this time he is near the door, and we see that the vacuum bag is just about ready to bust. As the butler enters, the bag does bust with a terrific explosion, covering the butler again from head to foot. Before he has anything to say, the professor comes running in, yelling, "I've got it! I've got it! Come and witness the greatest discovery the world has ever known!" He is so excited that he doesn't see any of the wreckage, or care about the butler's condition. The butler just gives him a wave, and starts up the stairs. Stan and Babe follow the professor into the laboratory, and are all eyes. The professor is still going nuts. Babe says, "What's it all about?"

The professor says, "I've made a wonderful discovery, and it's mine! All mine! Look! I'm going to make this duckling younger than it is now!" He picks up the duckling and places it in the tank. Stan and Babe look on with open mouths as the duckling disappears in the same manner as before. The professor says, "Now, watch!" He again puts a drop of the solution in the water and the tank foams, and when it clears away we see a duck egg. The professor picks it up out of the tank, and showing it to Stan, he says, "What do you think of that?" Stan, in a daze, says "I have nothing to say." Babe gives him a push and says to the professor, "I don't believe it." The professor says, "Watch!" He goes to a small tank, gets a barracuda and places that into the big tank as Stan and Babe watch the same performance. The fish turns out to be a little minnow, which we leave swimming in the tank.

The professor now is more elated than ever. Stan and Babe look at each other. Babe nods and says, "It's a fake." Stan says, "Show us another one." The professor says, "Very well, then. I'll get in there myself." Stan and Babe take it. The professor hands Babe the glass jar and the eye dropper and says, "Now, when I disappear, put in thirty drops of that solution, and you'll see for yourself. Don't forget—thirty drops, no more, no less, because the more drops you put in, the younger it will make me."

He dramatically walks up the little ladder which is fastened to the side of the tank, and standing on the top, he raises one arm toward Stan and Babe a la Sid Carten in "the Only Way," and says, "'Tis a far, far better thing I do now than I have ever done before." He suddenly realizes, takes off his glasses, hands them to Babe and says, "I won't need these when I come out." He steps into the tank and disappears.

Stan and Babe are a little scared now. A voice comes from out of the water, although we do not see the professor, and says, "All right, boys, put in the thirty drops." Babe is all nervous and trembling. He hands Stan the glass and the eye dropper and in a trembling voice says, "You do it."

Stan very nervously starts to climb up the ladder alongside the tank. He trips on the step, breaking the glass containing the solution. The voice comes out of the water and says, "What happened, boys?" Babe, in a trembling voice, say, "I'm sorry, but my friend broke the bottle and lost the solution." The professor groans and says, "Oh, for crying out loud." Stan starts to cry and says, "What are we going to do?" The professor's voice says, "Quick! As I give the directions, you fix some more solution. Get it right, because I've got to get out of here!" Babe says, "What do we do first?," and the professor says, "Get me a glass like the one you just broke."

Babe crosses to the bench where all the paraphernalia is, picks out a measuring glass and says, "Now what?" The professor says, "Three drops of fernaka paluta." Babe says, "Where is it?" and the voice says, "You'll find it next to the fernaka patan." Babe finds the bottle, and as he starts to put it in the glass, he says to Stan, "Go find out what's next." Stan goes to the tank and says, "What's next?" The voice says, "Three melograms of anti-macassa in the crystal form." Babe yells to Stan, "What was that?" and Stan replies, "Three telegrams of anti-macassa in the crystal form." The professor then says, "Now add a pinch of nanty cateva and spray it with hippy pippy cacuanna." Stan says, "I never heard of it." The professor says, "I know you haven't. That's my own idea."

Cut to Babe. He just finishes spraying into the glass with a spray gun and he says, "hippy pippy cacuanna."

VOICE: Have you got that?

BABE: Yes, sir.

VOICE: Good for you, sonny boy! Now take that blue bottle and pour in two half drops of that solution.

STAN: What is it?

VOICE: That's a concoction that's taken me years to put together.

Babe picks up the blue bottle containing a syrup-like liquid and says, "How much do we put in?" The professor says, "Two half drops and no more."

Babe looks at Stan, and says, "Now, how are we going to get two half drops?" Stan suggests that Babe pour the drops, and he will cut them in half. He picks up a large knife which is laying on the bench, and Babe very carefully tries to pour a drop into the glass. As a drop comes out, Stan cuts it in two, but the knife continues and comes down Babe's waist, cutting his suspenders, and his pants fall down. Babe takes it with a disgusted look, and in reaching down to pull up his pants, his head hits the bench with an awful bump. Babe pulls his pants up quickly, takes the knife from Stan, throws it aside, picks up a pair of surgical scissors and hands them to Stan. He then goes to pour another drop, and we go to insert of the drop and the scissors cutting it in half.

The voice comes from the tank and says, "Did you get that?"

BABE: Yes. What next?

VOICE: Just one more item. A quarter of a pinch of multi boni bevi.

BABE: Where is it?

VOICE: You'll find it in a green bottle on the top shelf near the tank.

Babe looks over toward the shelf and sees a green bottle with the label on it, "Multi Boni Bevi." Babe has difficulty in reaching it. He starts to climb up the shelves to get to the bottle, and grabs hold of the support of the shelves to steady himself. He reaches the bottle, but as he does the support breaks way, and he falls backwards out of the scene, throwing the bottle into the air. The bottle hits Stan on the head, knocking him cold, and Babe falls into the tank and disappears with a lot of "Ohhh's."

Babe is yelling to Stan, "Do something to help me." As he hears no answer from Stan, he keeps yelling, "Where are you? Why don't you answer," etc. While all this is going on, Stan comes out of it in a daze. He looks around the room and hears Babe shouting, "Stan! Stan!" Stan finally picks himself up and looking around says, "Where are you?" Babe says, "I'm in the tank!" Stan goes over and looks into it and, seeing nothing, he says, "What did you go in there for?"

> BABE: Don't ask me stupid questions at a time like this! Have you got that green bottle?
>
> STAN: You mean the one you threw at me?
>
> BABE: I didn't throw it at you.
>
> STAN: You did too!
>
> BABE: I did not!
>
> VOICE: Will you cut out this argument and get us out of here? This is most embarrassing!
>
> STAN: How much do you put in?
>
> VOICE: A quarter of a pinch.

Stan takes up a pinch of the powder, divides it into a quarter, and puts it into the glass jar. It has some effect on the liquid.

> BABE: Did you do that?
>
> STAN: Yes.
>
> VOICE: Now get the eye dropper and put thirty drops into the tank.
>
> BABE: And if you ever did anything right in your life, do it now.

Stan takes the eye dropper and the glass and cautiously starts up the steps. He stands on the top step and, dipping the dropper into the solution, he fills it. As he is doing this, the steps start sliding away from the tank , and Stan does a brodie into the tank, taking glass and dropper with him.

We get back and show the tank going wild. Water and foam spouting up. It finally settles down, and as it does, three monkeys climb out of the tank, representing Stan and Babe and the professor. The monk representing Babe finds Babe's derby laying on the floor, picks it up and puts it on. The one representing Stan is scratching his head, and the one representing the professor picks up the glasses and puts them on. We fade out on the funniest action the monks might happen to do.

THE LIVE GHOST

Production history: Production L-20. Script written late Oct.-early Nov. 1934. Filmed circa Thursday Nov. 8 through Wednesday Nov. 14. Released Dec. 8. Copyrighted Dec. 11, 1934, by MGM (LP 5220). Two reels.

Produced by Hal Roach. Directed by Charles Rogers. Assistant director, uncredited, Chet Brandenburg. Photographed by Art Lloyd, ASC. Edited by Louis McManus. Sound by James Greene.

With Stan Laurel (Himself), Oliver Hardy (Himself), Mae Busch (Maisie), Walter Long (Captain), Arthur Housman (Tipsy sailor), Leo Willis (Sailor who has bet with Stan), Charlie Hall (Sailor who has bet with Ollie), Art Rowlands (Sailor with eye patch), Jack "Tiny" Lipson (Burly sailor with mustache), Hubert Diltz (Sailor who does a 108 after being clunked), John Power ("Why, she's 'aunted!"), Charles Sullivan, Baldwin Cooke, Dick Gilbert, William Mann "Peter Potter" Moore, Bobby Callahan (Sailors), Harry Bernard (Bartender), Pete Gordon (Chinese waiter), Tony Campanaro (Organ grinder outside saloon), Josephine (Monkey).

Tough sea captain Walter Long is having a terrible time assembling a crew for his latest sailing expedition, because his craft has a reputation as a "ghost ship." Long happens across Stan and Ollie and convinces them to shanghai some sailors. Unfortunately, the boys' method of rendering the sailors unconscious works on them as well, and when they recover, sailing aboard Long's ship, they realize that the other crew members want to exact their revenge. The captain vows to protect Laurel and Hardy, and snarls that if anyone utters the word "ghost," he'll twist his head around so that "when he's walkin' north, he'll be lookin' south!" This insurance works fine until one drunken sailor falls into a tub of whitewash and stumbles aboard the ship, convincing the boys that it is indeed haunted. When they make the mistake of inadvertently telling Captain Long what they've seen, he carries out his highly unique method of punishment.

The Live Ghost is easily the best of the Laurel and Hardy horror-comedies; it boasts some impressive sets, colorful costumes, and lots of extras, giving it the polish worthy of a feature film.

The script is more violent and morbid than the movie, however, suggesting that the opening scene should be a barroom brawl – followed by a sequence in which Stan and Ollie attempt to commit suicide. Instead, the film's first scene is quite genial, with sailors happily quaffing beer in the saloon and all agreeing that Long's ship is haunted. The captain exits in frustration, to be met at the door by sailor Arthur Housman, who is coming inside for "a little teensy-weensy" even though he's obviously already had several teensy-weensies.

The scripted scene where Laurel and Hardy are at the end of a wharf and about to drown themselves was scrapped in favor of a bit where Long finds them angling on

The original 1934 one-sheet poster had artwork by New York-based illustrator Bela Rieger, who cleverly inserted his name on the boys' caps.

their day off from cleaning fish at a nearby market. "Just a little form of recreation," Ollie explains. The suicide routine was, ah, exhumed in 1939 and used in the team's feature film *The Flying Deuces*.

Although in the script the captain explains that he's sailing for Port Said – which is in Egypt, at the northern end of the Suez Canal – the movie depicts his arrival in a port that's clearly Oriental, with several Asians as extras.

After Stan and Ollie have been convinced to help shanghai a crew for Long, they don't employ "a big piece of pipe" for hitting the sailors on the head as per the script; rather, they use a discarded cast-iron skillet as their "clunker." The script proposes that Long give Ollie a five dollar bill for each sailor thus clunked, but in the film the boys work for much less, getting only one dollar per clunk. The script does not contain the great gag where the captain hurls each unconscious sailor into the ship's cargo hold under the deck; the camera holds on Long as he looks down, and there's a long, long pause before we finally hear the sailor hit the floor.

Arthur Housman's character is much more malevolent in the script than he ever was in any Laurel and Hardy movie. Hal Roach told Richard W. Bann, "Stan Laurel liked Housman. Whenever I saw the guy, he seemed to be feeling no pain. I was never sure if he was acting the part of a drunk to impress me so I would use him, or if he was really just drinking all day. I never knew the difference. Laurel told me he was drinking most of the time, and preferred gin. From experience, we found the trick was to get across that Housman was a rich guy, and a nice guy. Anything else and people would either feel sorry for him, or be angry with him."

Sadly, the continual drinking which had become Arthur Housman's onscreen stock-in-trade after 1930 began to take over his offscreen life as well. On August 14, 1939, he was jailed for 119 days for public intoxication. He died of pneumonia on April 7, 1942, only 52 years old.

In the script, Housman has a gun and vows to "catch up with the guys that got me on this ship," but in the movie he only wants to go ashore and catch up with a few more teensy-weensies. He isn't rich, but he's nice – except in the eyes of "dear old Maisie." That would be Mae Busch, who has a small but pivotal role as a, shall we say, working girl escorted by Long to his ship, just in time for her to see the whitewashed Housman, her long-absent husband.

The most notable absence from the script is Captain Long's stated method of punishment, to be meted out to any crew member who says the word "ghost" to him. Having seen Housman stumbling around the deck covered in whitewash, Laurel and

Sea captain Walter Long persuades the boys to shanghai a crew for him.

Hardy are certain that they've encountered just such a wraith. The movie's final shots show Long doing some fancy twisting, putting Stan and Ollie's faces now in the same direction as their backsides. Hal Roach was not nearly as fond of these freak endings as was Stan Laurel (he finally vetoed one for *Block-Heads* in which the boys' heads were to be seen as hunting trophies mounted on a wall). It might be that Stan had the movie's ending in mind all along but didn't include it in the script, so as not to arouse the displeasure of The Boss before the gag could be filmed.

The film boasted some very impressive sets, including the deck of Captain Long's "ghost ship."

Tipsy and ghostly Arthur Housman rejoins his wife, "Dear old Maisie," as Long, Laurel and Hardy look on.

LAUREL AND HARDY
'The Live Ghost'
Comedy
21 Mins.
Capitol, N. Y.
: Roach-Metro
Very comical short, meaty both
on ideas and laughs. Belongs on
the best shows.
Stan Laurel and Oliver Hardy
this time figure in a shanghai
frameup. Skipper of a ship hires
them to assist him in getting a
crew together. Means by which
Laurel and Hardy shanghai the
hangers-on in an ocean front bar
start the laughs. They continue on
board, after both comedians have
also gotten shanghaied.
Direction is excellent. *Char.*

Variety usually panned Laurel and Hardy's films, but *The Live Ghost* earned a rare favorable review.

L-20 Laurel & Hardy

Fade in on interior of a typical waterfront bar room. A bunch of tough seamen are drinking over the bar. One picks up his beer and throws it in another's face. A brawl ensues, wherein one seaman kicks the other in the face, knocking him across the floor and against a table, which crashes. This is to get over the toughness of the joint and the jovial spirit of the characters. The character has crashed against the table picks up a large pitcher and hurls it across at the first seaman. He ducks and the pitcher hits the door just as it opens, and a hard-boiled captain enters.

On his entrance, the place becomes a bit quieter, as the sailors are instinctively a little afraid of this captain, even though they're ashore. The captain bawls out, "Everybody have a drink on me!" As he gets them grouped around the bar, he says, "Listen you mugs, I've got to sail tonight and I'm short a crew. Whaddya say?" There is a general murmuring of discontent, then one burly sailor speaks up. "You don't get me on that stinkin' tub of yours! I ain't superstitious, but if there's any ghosts in the world, you've got 'em all workin' for ya!" Again there is a loud mumbling of agreement to this, and the captain shouts above the noise. "All right, all right! When you run out of money to buy beer, come and see me. I'll be waiting for you!" He exits.

Cut to Stan and Babe on a set at the end of a wharf. Stan is wearing a long overcoat and muffler around his neck. He is in the act of tying a big rock to the center of a length of rope. He then takes one end of the rope and ties a slip knot around Babe's neck. Babe takes it and says, "Not so tight! Do you want to kill me?" Stan finishes tying the knot, picks up the rock and swings it back and forth to throw it in the water, counting "One – two – " Babe stops him.

BABE: Wait a minute! How can I be sure you're coming in with me?

STAN: Do I have to commit suicide too?

BABE: Of course you do! Wasn't that the agreement? I'd never rest in my watery grave if I knew you were running around without me to look after you!

STAN: (Takes a look at the water) Well then, couldn't we go someplace where it's not so deep?

Babe gives him a dirty look, quickly ties the other end of the rope around Stan's neck and says, "Now, come on." Babe picks up the rock and starts swinging it back and forth, counting "One—two—." This time

Stan stops him. Babe sets the rock down and Stan reaches out to shake hands.

STAN: Goodbye, Ollie.

BABE: Goodbye, Stan – Whaddya mean, goodbye? We're not
        going to separate, are we?

STAN: Well, after we're drowned, we can't be sure we're going to
        the same place, and – I don't know where you're going.

BABE: Pick up that rock!

Stan picks it up and starts counting again, "One– two–"

BABE: Wait. We'll throw it in together. Close your eyes. It's just
        as well you don't look on this ghastly deed.

Both close their eyes very tight, and both reach down, but they pick up the wrong rock. They swing it back and forth, counting "One–two–three–" and let it go. Babe lets out a big "Ohh-hoh" and Stan starts to cry. As the rock reaches the water, a big splash comes up, drenching them and also the captain, who has just entered the scene. As Stan and Babe stand there a moment, waiting to drown, the captain takes in the situation. He finally snaps them out of it.

CAPTAIN: Hey! What's the racket?

They open their eyes, and become embarrassed as they see him.

BABE: Well you see, admiral, my friend and I have nothing to live
        for. The future looked so black, we decided to take a trip
        into the great beyond.

CAPTAIN: How would you like to take a trip with me?

STAN: Where are you going?

CAPTAIN: I'm sailing for Port Said tonight, and I'm short a crew.

STAN: I'm sorry, but we don't like the water.

CAPTAIN: (Pointing off) My drunken crew is in that saloon over
        there. For every man you bring aboard, I'll pay you five
        dollars.

BABE: How are we going to get them aboard?

CAPTAIN: Use your own judgment!

He exits. Babe turns to Stan.

BABE: It means five dollars a head, but we might have to do some
        fighting.

STAN: Then I'd better take off this coat.

Stan starts to take off the coat, revealing a life preserver, which he has forgotten, around his waist. Babe does a slow burn, gives Stan a violent shove, and says, "Come on!"

Wipe dissolve to a set up where we see an alley at the corner of the saloon, with the front of the saloon in evidence. Babe and Stan are

standing in the alley; Babe has a big piece of pipe in his hand. They
creep up and look in through the window, where we see the drunken
sailors. Babe says, "Now go inside and do what I told you." They give
each other the nod. Babe hides in the alley, and Stan goes into the
saloon.

We go through a series of gags in which Stan tricks the seamen
into chasing him, and as they pass the alley, Babe conks the tough
guys on the head with the pipe. The captain, who is standing nearby,
gives Babe a five dollar bill for each one, grabs the sailors as they are
clunked, and leads them to the ship, where he dumps them into the
hatchway. Finally Babe, considering that Stan is pretty well played
out, decides to go in himself. He enters the saloon, tries to pull one of
the same gags that Stan has pulled, but fails and the guy punches him
on the nose and chases him as far as the door. Babe keeps on running,
and as he passes the alley Stan clunks him by mistake. Realizing what
he has done, Stan bends over to help Babe. The captain comes
forward, gives Stan a conk on the head, takes the money out of Babe's
pocket, and starts to drag them off toward the boat.

Wipe to the hold of the ship, where we see the shanghaied crew
with Stan and Babe gradually coming out of their coma. Housman gets
up, looks at the porthole, discovers that they are at sea, and says,
"We've been double crossed!" Realizing that Stan and Babe have been
the cause of this, all the sailors start toward them menacingly as the
captain enters. He tells them that he will stand for no rough stuff on
this boat, that if they have any grievances to settle, wait until they get
into the next port, when they're ashore they can do as they like, but
on this boat he is the captain, and they'll behave or be put in irons.

The Housman character gives him the laugh and says, "Listen,
you double-crossed me, but there ain't a boat from here to Timbuktu
that can hold this bird if he wants to get away." The captain says, "Oh,
no?" and clips him on the chin, adding, "That'll hold you for a while."

Dissolve to the ship docking at Port Said, where it is very foggy.
We hear the clang of bells and the moaning of foghorns. Cut to the
sleeping quarters of the crew, where we see the hammocks and bunks.
The captain enters and tells the crew they can take six hours shore
leave, but to be back on time or they'll get what's coming to them.
Housman takes this with a growl, as the captain turns to him and
says, "That goes for all but you. You're going to stay right here. I'll not
stand for you going on a drunken brawl and forgetting to come back."
He turns to the gang and says, "And you leave these two mugs alone,"
indicating Stan and Babe. The captain and the crew exit, and as Stan

and Babe hesitate, Housman says to them, "Well, why don't you go? I think the boys want to give you a nice little party." He gives them a grin, shows them a gun under a pillow and says, "It won't be long now. I've been double crossed, but I'll catch up with the guys that got me on this ship."

Stan and Babe become very nervous and exit. Show them come to a set up on deck where the captain is standing. They look off and see the crew waiting on the dock for them to come off. They become very nervous and ask the captain if it would be all right if they remained on the ship, as they are very tired. He tells them it will be okay with him and says, "As long as you're going to be here, I'll go ashore myself for an hour. Keep an eye on that drunk below." He exits, and Stan and Babe realize they are alone on the boat with Housman.

Cut to Housman in the bunk room, hurriedly getting dressed and mumbling, "I've been double crossed." He loks out to see that no one is coming, then concocts a dummy, puts it in his bunk, covers it with a blanket and says, "Now you wait here until I get back." He exits.

Back to Stan and Babe. Remembering that Housman has a gun under his pillow, they go to a port hole and look into the bunk room, where they see the dummy in bed. Thinking it is Housman asleep, Babe whispers, "If we can only get that gun before he wakes up." They sneak toward the bunkroom entrance.

In the bunkroom, they go through a short "noisy burglar" routine, trying to get the gun. Finally Stan reaches under the pillow and drags the gun out, and as Babe goes to take it from him, the gun explodes with a terrific report. For a minute they are dumbfounded, and suddenly realize they must have killed Housman. Stan becomes all excited, puts his hand on the body, and realizes it is stiff. Babe suggests the best thing they can do now is to bury the body at sea before anybody gets wind of what happened.

Cut to Housman, very drunk, coming along the dock. He stumbles and falls right into a big trough of white mortar. He struggles in this until he is completely covered, finally gets out and staggers off in the direction of the boat.

Cut to Stan and Babe in the hold. They look around and find a big sack and Babe says, "Now put some coal in it." Stan says, "Does he have to take his own coal with him where he's going?" Babe says, disgustedly, "Does he have to – that's to weigh it down! Come on!" They start shoveling some coal into the bag. Housman, all white, staggers into the bunkroom, throws the dummy under the bunk and takes its place in bed, covering up and passing out. Stan and Babe enter, get Housman into the sack, and after assuring themselves that there is no one in sight, they take the body up and dump it overboard. There is the sound of a foghorn, which scares the life out of them, and they dash back into the bunkroom and hurriedly start to get into their nightshirts.

Cut to a saloon in Port Said, where we see the ship's crew assembled, drinking. They are in a huddle. They see the captain taking a drink at the other end of the bar and decide that now would be a good time to go back to the ship, get Stan and Babe, and give them the works. They start to exit.

Cut to Housman coming up over the side of the boat, still all white, muttering, "I've been double crossed."

Cut to Stan and Babe. Stan pokes his head out from under the sheets, and as he reaches up to close the port hole, he sees Housman coming onto the boat. He takes it big and tells Babe that he has seen a ghost coming over the side of the ship. Babe scoffs at this, and tells Stan it is all in his mind, that he has heard so much about ghosts since he's been on this ship that he'll be believing it soon. With that he gets out of bed and goes looking for the ghost to reassure Stan. The moment Babe leaves the scene, Housman comes into the room. Stan sees him, lets out a cry, and tears out of the bunkroom. Stay with Housman and he gets back into the bunk, covering up. Babe returns to the room, sees Housman covered up in bed, thinks it is Stan and starts bawling him out, saying "You saw a ghost! Childish! Even if you did see a ghost, what is there to be scared of?" He is climbing into the bunk as he says this. Seeing that Housman is taking up most of the bed, he pushes him over and says, "And don't take up all the room! The idea – being afraid of a ghost." In settling down, he pulls the covers part way off of Housman. As Babe gets well covered up, with his back to Housman, he sees Stan's face peering through the porthole. He suddenly realizes somebody else is lying beside him, slowly starts to look in the direction of Housman, and through the corner of his eye he sees Housman rise to a sitting position, at the same time saying, "So you're the guy who double-crossed me! Where's my gun?" Babe lets out a yell, jumps out of bed and rushes toward the door, followed by Housman. Stan, from the porthole, sees this and rushes off.

Cut to the deck. The crew is coming up the side of the boat to get Stan and Babe when they suddenly see the ghost, take it big, and all dive into the water.

TIT FOR TAT

Production history: Production L-21. Script written early December 1934. Filmed Monday December 10 through Thursday December 20, 1934. Released January 5, 1935. Copyrighted January 29, 1935, by MGM (LP 5304). Two reels.

Produced by Hal Roach. Directed by Charles Rogers. Photographed by Art Lloyd, ASC. Edited by Bert Jordan. Sound by William Randall.

With Stan Laurel (Himself), Oliver Hardy (Himself), Mae Busch (Mrs. Hall), Charlie Hall (Mr. Hall), James C. Morton (Policeman), Bobby Dunn (Friendly shoplifter), Baldwin Cooke (Customer), Jack Hill, Viola Richard (Passersby).

Stan and Ollie are proudly opening their new electrical supply store. Their next-door neighbors are Mr. and Mrs. Hall, who run a grocery. Soon, all of them remember their previous skirmish when Ollie's gout had necessitated a trip to a mountain retreat. Old grievances flare up and cause a new reciprocal battle, Mr. Hall abusing or destroying a significant amount of electrical equipment, while Stan and Ollie use various foodstuffs to adorn their neighbor.

Even though it is a sequel to an earlier L&H movie, *Tit for Tat* works perfectly on its own. It establishes the personalities of its characters and their relationship to each other, it provides a motivation for the story line, its plot comes to a believable conclusion, and every element that is introduced has a purpose. Along with that, it has inventive visual comedy, some clever dialogue, and a running gag that not only provides punctuation throughout the film, but ends with its own satisfying fulfillment.

The script has none of these qualities. Hal Roach's decree of "fifty percent of the script will not play" was almost always, to use another Hal Roach pet phrase, "one hundred percent right." There were exceptions, though. *Helpmates* had such a good script that the film deviated from it only in one very brief dialogue exchange. On the other hand, *Tit for Tat* had such a sorry script that, aside from the most basic idea of the story, everything worthwhile in it was created on the set.

The script runs four pages, but nobody seems to have consulted it. As Stan recalled in a letter of May 18, 1959 to his friend Marie Hatfield: "Glad you enjoyed *Tit for Tat*, we had a lot of fun on that film, we were behind on our schedule, so had to start shooting without a script & had to figure out the gags & routines as we went along. It was lucky it turned out as well as it did."

In the written outline, the battle begins when Stan's electric fan sprays Charlie Hall with the trash he has just finished cleaning up from the front of his store. To be fair, there is a mention in the script of Stan and Ollie's previous skirmish with Charlie and Mae, but it's just a suggestion. The film, however, has a lengthy scene where Mae sings

Mr. Hall finds a creative new use for a curling iron.

"The Old Spinning Wheel," prompting Stan to punctuate it with "pum pum" as he did in *Them Thar Hills*. Once the memory of their prior encounter has returned, Ollie makes every effort to now be friends: "Let's help each other! You send people to our store, and we'll send people to your store." Hall's sullen, outright rejection of this has a purpose – we're immediately on Laurel and Hardy's side in the battle that follows.

The film provides a further reason for the back-and-forth destruction when, through a Laurel-caused mishap, Ollie is propelled onto the Halls' second-story window ledge. Mae sees his predicament and helps him inside to the Halls' upstairs bedroom. Mr. Hardy walks downstairs with Mae, both of them giggling; Charlie wonders why Ollie's being so gallant to his wife. Ollie then assures Mae, "I've never been in a position like *that* before!," kisses her hand, gives a haughty look to Mr. Hall, and struts out. This is a mighty daring line for a movie made after the initiation of the Production Code, but there's no mistaking its intention, as it makes Charlie think that Ollie has "had a clandestine meeting" with his wife.

The individual gags proposed by the script seem unnecessarily violent. In the film, the ever-mounting insults emphasize injury to one's dignity. This is punctuated by another running gag in which Stan and Ollie keep stealing marshmallows from a bin right by the exit of Mr. Hall's store; the boys display the confections defiantly to Charlie before eating them and taking their leave. Charlie exacts his revenge by dusting the marshmallows with alum powder, which subsequently causes the boys' lips to pucker uncontrollably.

Finally, the movie provides a much better wrap-up than the script, which only

Charlie Hall won't be in clover, but his cash soon will be.

suggests a weak gag involving cocoanuts. Policeman James C. Morton prompts all of the parties to explain the reason for the hubbub, and when Charlie accuses Ollie of that clandestine meeting, Mae chimes in with, "Oh, what nonsense!" The parties apologize and shake hands all around – although Charlie boots Stan in the rear when he tries to kiss Mae's hand. One senses that now all will be fine in Stan and Ollie's world – or would be, if the friendly little man who has been systematically shoplifting from their electrical store hadn't hired a moving van to take away everything that was left.

With its excellent structure, brisk pace, plausible motivation, creative visual humor, well-placed running gags, witty dialogue and satisfying resolution, *Tit for Tat* is a model of comedy construction. (It proves the inaccuracy of Hal Roach's frequent statement that "in story, Laurel wasn't worth a nickel," especially when one compares it to something like *Bonnie Scotland*, a Roach pet project, which doesn't resolve any of its story threads.) Its excellence was noted by the Academy of Motion Picture Arts and Sciences, which nominated it for the "Best Short Subject – Comedy" award for 1935. It placed second to the MGM Robert Benchley short *How to Sleep*, a fine film; nevertheless, Laurel and Hardy proved with *Tit for Tat* that they could still make truly great two-reelers. Unfortunately, their own popularity was about to remove them from this format.

LAUREL and HARDY
'Tit for Tat'
Comedy
20 Mins.
Projection Room, N. Y.
Metro

Newest L.&H. short, and perhaps the last, since they split recently, is another topnotch two-reeler with a sufficiency of laughs and novel situation accompaniment. Has Mae Busch and Charley Hall in support and was directed by Charles Rogers.

Stan and Oliver are in the electric business this time and Hall and his wife (Miss Busch) have a grocery store next door. Fight starts. Hall cleans up the electric store and Laurel and Hardy clean up the grocery.

Nothing much new about this situation but it's handled for speed and some effective laughs. One bit neatly worked up is a man walking in and out of the electric store and walking out with increasingly large bundles. The fat boy and his thin partner are too busy fighting with their neighbors to bother with him and for a tag finish the crook comes up in a truck to clean out what little is left.   Kauf.

Bobby Dunn's improvised gag as a genial shoplifter attracted special attention in a *Variety* review published on March 27, 1935.

Kids outside the Casino Cinema in Amite City, Louisiana in October 1935 are likely about to enjoy *Tit for Tat* more than George Raft in *Stolen Harmony*.

TIT FOR TAT

Fade in on a section of a street, showing two stores, next to each other. One is an electrical store, run by Babe & Stan. The other is a grocery, run by Charlie Hall & Mae Busch.

At the electrical store we discover Babe placing a ladder up to an electric sign, which is out over the sidewalk. The base of the ladder rests on a sidewalk elevator. Babe is placing new globes in the sign.

Stan is busy washing the exterior of the store windows with a rubber cleaner. He proceeds to dry the windows with an electric fan.

We pan over to the grocery, where Hall is busy sweeping up a pile of dirt and sawdust from in front of his store, and he sweeps it right over in front of the electrical store. Stan unconsciously puts the fan down by the side of the dirt and it blows the rubbish back on to Hall's side, smothering Hall with it. Hall just gives him a dirty look and exits.

Cut to Babe on top of the ladder. He is busy replacing electric globes in the sign. He tells Stan to go down in the cellar and get some more globes. Stan steps on the elevator, pushes the button, and the elevator starts down. This causes the ladder to lower and throws Babe and the ladder right through the plate glass window of the grocery store. Hall and Mae come running out to see what happened. They bawl Babe out, and Babe apologizes and promises to pay for the damages.

Babe turns to Stan, who has just entered, and bawls him out for lowering the elevator.

Mae tells Hall that he better lower the awning, in order to protect the provisions displayed outside. Stan offers to help Hall, and in doing so Stan lowers the awning so that the water that has been lodged in it falls all over Babe. Hall gives a wild laugh and exits into his store.

(A retrospect shot may be used here, showing that Babe and Stan seem to recall Hall's voice, and then remember having had trouble with him on their trailer trip.)

Babe now turns to Stan and tells him to go down the back way into the cellar for the globes. Once more placing the ladder on the elevator, Babe starts to climb up as Stan leaves for the cellar.

We cut to Hall, in front of his store, taking the lid off a case of marshmallows.

We show Stan in the cellar putting a box of electric globes on the elevator and pushing the elevator button.

Cut back to Babe on the ladder. The elevator starts up, causing the ladder to overbalance, and Babe falls into the awning. He crashes right on through the awning and falls on top of Hall. Hall's head emerges through the tear in the awning. He is covered with marshmallows, including one in each of his eyes.

Stan, who has come up on the elevator, walks over to see what happened. Seeing Hall, Stan proceeds to take the marshmallows out of his eyes, but they stick and stretch out like elastics. Hall starts to bawl Babe out, but just then a woman customer comes over and asks if there is anyone working in the electrical store. Babe and Stan leave to wait on the customer, and Hall and Mae are burned up.

Hall looks around in his store for something to retaliate with, and picks up some limburger cheese and exists toward the electrical store.

Babe & Stan have entered their store with the customer and are proceeding to demonstrate an electric range to her. Unobserved by Babe and Stan or the customer, Hall comes in and throws the limburger cheese into the oven of the range, and exits. Babe and Stan continue with the demonstration until the odor nearly knocks them all over. The woman exits in disgust. Babe finally opens the oven door and the melted cheese runs out.

Babe & Stan, realizing that they have been done out of a sale, leave to go over to the grocery. When they close their door, Stan hangs a sign on the knob, reading, "WILL BE BACK SOON".

In the grocery, Hall is now busy with a customer, trying to sell him a can of molasses. Hall has the lid of the can open. As Hall turns to get another can of a different brand, Stan takes the opened can of molasses and dumps the molasses into the cash register on the money—unnoticed by Hall or Mae. Stan and Babe exit from the grocery.

The customer pays Hall for the molasses, and when Hall goes to ring up the money and give the customer change, he gets his fingers all messed up with the molasses. Realizing that Stan & Babe have done this, Hall and Mae exit toward Stan & Babe's store.

Hall and Mae enter the electrical store and look around for something to get revenge with. Hall sees an electric curling iron, plugs the connection in the wall, and deliberately snaps the iron on to Babe's nose. Babe gives a big yell and takes the iron off, and we see the imprint of the curling iron on his nose.

Stan looks at Babe's nose, and realizing what has been done, he takes the curling iron in one hand, presses on Hall's throat with the other hand, causing Hall's tongue to pop out, and then snaps the curling iron on Hall's tongue. Hall takes it big and runs around. Stan finally takes the iron off Hall's tongue, gives Babe a nod of satisfaction, then hands the curling iron to Babe, with the hot end toward Babe. Babe takes hold of the hot iron and lets out a wild yell.

Mae sees Hall still suffering with his burnt tongue and says to him, "You're not going to let him get away with that, are you?" Hall tries to bawl the boys out, but speaks very thickly and indistinctly because of his burnt tongue.

Mae then takes an electric globe, puts it down in the seat of Stan's pants, and gives him a swift kick. We hear a loud report, and glass drops down on the floor from Stan's pants. Mae and Hall exit.

We cut to the sidewalk in front of the store, where we see a cop standing. As Mae and Hall cross from the electric store to the grocery, the cop watches them, as he stands on the other side of the door.

We cut inside the grocery and see Hall fixing a basket of eggs up over the door, so that they will fall on Stan & Babe when they enter the door.

We go back to the electrical store, where Babe is finishing helping Stan get the glass out of his fanny. Stan looks around for something to retaliate with. He picks up a large electric globe and gets over that he intends it for Mae. They exit.

Stan and Babe enter to the front of the grocery, but go in through the broken window instead of the door. Hall shows his disappointment that they have escaped his egg 'trap.'

Stan and Babe walk over toward Mae and walk around in back of her. Stan is holding the light globe behind him, getting the impression over to the audience that he probably intends to put it in the seat of Mae's pants if he can. As Mae moves around, Stan follows, with Babe just behind him. Hall also comes over and joins them to see what they are up to. Finally they get near a seat of some kind. Stan quickly slips the globe down on the seat and Babe pushes Mae on to it. We hear the loud pop of the glass, and Mae yells. Stan gives Babe a nod of satisfaction.

Mae, infurated, gets up, grabs Babe's derby and places it in a meat slicer, and we see it quickly cut into slices.

Babe & Stan start to look for something else to do to Mae, but she starts to scream loudly, so Stan takes a piece of sticky wrapping tape and places it right across her mouth. We insert the tape, showing a printed slogan on it, "ALWAYS OPEN." Babe & Stan exit toward their store.

Hall and Mae now look around their store for some other means of getting even. Hall picks up a large can of pepper and exits toward the electrical store.

Mae and Hall enter the electrical store, and Hall pours the pepper on the counter and then reaches for an electric fan, but Stan beats him to it by quickly grabbing an electric drying blower and blowing the pepper all over Mae and Hall. They both choke and sneeze. Finally Hall throws his head down with a big sneeze. Stan picks up the electric clippers and runs them right down the center of Hall's head, leaving a bare streak across his head. Hall turns to a mirror to get a look at himself, then picks up some electrical device and crashes it right through the mirror. Hall and Mae exit in a rage.

We follow Hall and Mae over to the grocery. Hall, in his rage, forgets all about the egg gag he placed over the door for Stan & Babe, and when he enters the door the contraption works and Hall gets the eggs all over him. Possibly the last egg hits Mae.

We follow this up with a series of retaliation gags, alternating the feud between the electrical store and the grocery. Each time they leave their store, Stan hangs the sign on the door knob. We also show the cop go from door to door.

Finally Hall and Mae rush into their store and lock the door. Babe & Stan enter in front of the broken window, and Hall and Mae start throwing eggs at them. Babe & Stan return the 'fire' with electric globes.

We show Babe & Stan go into their store and fill a washing machine with electric globes, and then push it out on the sidewalk. They use the washing machine as a shield and throw the electric globes from behind it.

During this battle, we cut to various characters getting hit by the eggs.

Babe & Stan both try to hide behind the electric washer and at the same time reach in for globes to throw at Mae and Hall. Babe tells Stan to run and get more ammunition. Stan runs in and returns with more boxes of globes. When he is setting the globes down, his arm presses on the switch on the washing machine and starts it turning. This churns up all the globes in the machine, and they pop off like a Maxim gun.

Stan leaves again for more globes. When he returns, Babe is covered with broken glass. Babe turns to bawl Stan out, and as he does so the washing machine starts rolling down the street, unobserved by Babe. Babe starts to get well pelted with eggs, and finally realizes that his protection, the washing machine is gone. He gets excited and tells Stan to get some more fortification.

Stan runs into the electric store and brings out the electric bath cabinet. Babe and Stan both try to get inside it for protection, but Babe's head gets stuck outside through the hole in the top. He gets socked with plenty of eggs. Finally a couple of cocoanuts bounce against his head, and we fade out.

EPILOGUE

After *Tit for Tat*, Laurel and Hardy starred in only two more short subjects before embarking upon a "features only" policy. Stan and Babe both regretted the move, but by 1935 Roach's distributor, MGM, was making its own short subjects and no longer needed an independent producer for them. Along with this, many exhibitors were omitting short subjects from their programs in favor of double features – a top quality "A" picture supported by a lesser quality, but feature-length, "B" movie. In order to stay in business, Roach had to convert to longer films.

Because the L&H feature films cost anywhere from $200,000 to $700,000 to make – much more than the $35,000 average cost of a short – their scripts were more detailed. This doesn't mean that there weren't radical deviations from them during the filming. *Sons of the Desert* had a lengthy finale involving a séance after the boys were presumed drowned in a shipwreck. *Way Out West* suggested a climactic battle with a tribe of Indians. *Block-Heads* proposed a scene in which Stan and Ollie sing and dance to a song dating back to the World War.

A host of new writers worked on these scripts, as Hal Roach felt that they should be crafted by fresh talent. *Our Relations* had on its writing staff Richard Connell, author of the famous story *The Most Dangerous Game*. Felix Adler, who would later write many Columbia shorts, joined the crew for *Way Out West*, while silent-screen comedy great Harry Langdon was on board for *Block-Heads* and the next three L&H features, finishing up with *Saps at Sea*, which was the team's last film for Hal Roach.

Laurel and Hardy signed with 20th Century-Fox in 1941, and Stan was dismayed to discover that he would not be allowed to contribute to the scripts. *Great Guns* and *A-Haunting We Will Go*, the first two Fox features, were written by Lou Breslow, who displayed talent as a writer-director later on with the charming *You Never Can Tell*, but was lost when attempting to write for Stan and Babe; his scripts give them the same snappy dialogue that he wrote for Milton Berle in *Whispering Ghosts*. The final four Fox films had scripts credited to W. Scott Darling, and it is a blessing indeed that director Malcolm St. Clair allowed the team to make significant changes on the set, so dreadful are those screenplays.

During this same 1941-45 era, Laurel and Hardy worked in two MGM features, and although Stan was able to get Charlie Rogers on the writing staff of *Air Raid Wardens* it didn't help much. Four credited writers were joined by two uncredited assistants on that film; the other MGM release, *Nothing But Trouble*, had four credited writers with help from five who were not credited, including Buster Keaton. Their combined efforts resulted in a script that was even worse than Breslow or Darling could have written on his own. At no point did the producers of these films consider having Stan Laurel write a screenplay; the team still had enough marquee value to guarantee a certain amount of profit no matter how bad the movie might be, so the goal was to make the films as quickly and cheaply as possible. (*Jitterbugs* had some decent production values because it was a showcase for young singer-comedienne Vivian Blaine.)

Stan wrote the scripts for the team's three live-appearance tours of the UK – *The Driver's License Sketch, On the Spot* (or *A Spot of Trouble*) and *Birds of a Feather*. These were very funny, and the team earned excellent reviews, playing to packed houses. But in 1950 there was one more film, to be made in France – *Atoll K*. The original screenplay for this, assembled by four writers, was atrocious (Ollie disappeared for most of the story), and Stan made an emergency call to his friend, comedy veteran Monty Collins. Together they added a lot of material which made for a much better film than the first script would have engendered, but other factors, such as the language barrier and Stan's health problems, prevented it from being a total success.

In his retirement years, Laurel found it impossible to stop thinking up gags and situations for Stan and Ollie – not that he wanted to. He delighted in writing down these bits of comedy business as they occurred to him. After Stan died in February 1965, his friend and biographer John McCabe found among his effects hundreds of notes with these ideas jotted on them; McCabe included many of them in his 1974 book, *The Comedy World of Stan Laurel*. Stan was always most proud of his ability as a gag man, and his talent in this arena was undimmed until he passed on.

The scripts for the Laurel and Hardy movies, particularly those they made in their prime years with Hal Roach, demonstrate the inventiveness of the gag men as well as the expectation that better material would be created on the set. They are fascinating documents that reveal the initial ideas for films which are still entertaining the world many decades after they were made. We are fortunate that some of them survive today.

Acknowledgements: My thanks go to Dave Lord Heath, whose astonishing and greatly informative website *Another Nice Mess* (www.lordheath.com) is a tremendous resource for anyone interested in learning about the films made by Hal Roach and his stars. His site provided some of the frame captures used here. Candid photos from *One Good Turn* were located and posted online by Tracy Tolzmann, Richard W. Bann and the late Bill Diehl. Jorge Finkielman worked his remarkable restoration magic on many of the photographs. Dean McKeown, Jack Taylor, Jessica Rosner, Ed Watz and Peter Mikkelsen supplied some of the illustrations. My longtime friend and mentor Jordan R. Young provided the scripts for the first seven entries. Douglas Hart of Backlot Books and John McLaughlin of The Book Sail graciously allowed me access to their collections of scripts. Special thanks to David Koenig, who suggested the idea for this book and contributed his skill in design and layout. Continued gratitude to Hal Roach, Stan Laurel, Oliver Hardy and the many gag men, supporting players and technicians who made the films which we love so much, and which we celebrate here.